nsk

Wladivostok

D1243436

Guide to the Soviet Navy

Guide to the Soviet Navy

SIEGFRIED BREYER

Translated by Lieutenant Commander M. W. Henley, DSC.,
Royal Navy (Retired)

United States Naval Institute
Annapolis, Maryland

1970

Frontispiece: A *Kashin*-class guided-missile destroyer conducts air-defense exercises in the Pacific.

Copyright © 1970
by the
United States Naval Institute
Annapolis, Maryland

Second Printing, January 1971
This book is an updated and expanded translation of
Die Seerüstung der Sowjetunion. Copyright © 1964 by
J. F. Lehmanns Verlag, Munich.

Library of Congress Catalogue Card No. 70–97170
ISBN 0–87021–237–0

Printed in the United States of America

Publisher's Preface

The Tsarist Navy was an inventive one: both the world's first armored cruiser and its first minelayer were Russian warships. Though in 1904 and 1905 it showed lassitude and ineptitude in Russia's disastrous war with Japan, only ten years later it battled the Germans with vigor and effectiveness in the Baltic and Black seas, and some of its ships fought fiercely even after the mutinies of 1917.

The Soviet Navy, which had been completely rebuilt in secrecy during the 1930s, entered World War II with a great deal of strength: for example, it had more submarines than any other navy in the world. However, it was a strength in numbers only, not in skill or in doctrine, and those numbers soon evaporated under the assaults of German dive bombers and minelayers.

Russian officers and men were not lacking in bravery, but they showed little skill in submarine or antisubmarine warfare, in minelaying or in mine countermeasures. It seemed that their admirals neither understood naval war, nor appreciated the extent to which activities at sea could influence events ashore. Nevertheless, the men of the Red Navy were not completely inept, and they demonstrated that the spirit of innovation had not been destroyed by the totalitarian demand for conformity of mind and spirit. When it appeared necessary to launch an attack upon the Germans from the sea, the Soviet naval commander in the Sea of Azov was not deterred by the fact that he had no amphibious craft: he simply gathered up all the fishing boats he could lay his hands on and used them as assault craft. In 1955, that man, S. G. Gorshkov, was chosen to head the Soviet Navy.

Experience in our country suggests that even the most able man can be retained too long in the same high position, be it civilian or naval. Yet, Admiral Gorshkov is still commander-in-chief of the Soviet Navy, and the fact that most of the interesting ships described in this book have been produced under his leadership indicates that his long period in that office has not stultified creativity and that he has served his country well. Indeed, it might be that years hence, when we look back upon this time, we will consider him the most important naval officer of the era.

Just as other navies do, that of the Soviet Union has one purpose for peace and another for war. Likewise, its fleet deployments in peace are not the same as they would be in war. In peace, Soviet ships can, and do, voyage to the South Atlantic, the Indian Ocean, the Mediterranean, the Caribbean, in short, wherever the Soviet Union wishes to emphasize its presence. There are those who believe the Soviet Navy is essentially a political navy, intended to win its battles without combat. That is a belief worth serious consideration. Be that as it may, in war, ships on such distant stations as the South Atlantic or the Indian Ocean would be isolated from their bases by the U.S. and NATO fleets, and probably would be sunk before many weeks had passed.

It appears likely that the wartime missions of the Soviet surface fleet would be carried out in the waters most important to the Soviet Union. These are the routes to the open seas, and they are not distant waters. In order for the Pacific Fleet to operate in the Pacific, the Japanese islands would have to be surely placed in Soviet hands. For the Black Sea Fleet to fight in the Mediterranean, first the Turkish Straits and then the Greek islands in the Aegean Sea would have to be taken. To fight in the North Sea and Atlantic, the Baltic Fleet would have to open the Danish Straits to unhampered passage by Soviet ships. Although Murmansk provides the Northern Fleet with an opening to the wide oceans, it would be important for the Soviets to seize at least the ports in northern Norway in order to deny them to the forces of NATO and make them available to their own shipping. That these are the main tasks of the Soviet Navy is suggested by its many modest-sized amphibious and escort ships, its clouds of large, fast patrol craft armed with surface-to-surface missiles or torpedoes, and by the fact that it has not much seaborne aviation and no transoceanic amphibious capability. Only if those tasks were successfully accomplished would the Soviet Navy have need of a fleet that more closely resembled that of the United States.

The Soviet submarine force, still the world's largest, is devoted partly to so-called "strategic warfare," with about 50 of its roughly 380 ships armed with ballistic missiles. In the event of war, most of the remaining submarines, those armed with torpedoes or guided missiles, would probably be deployed in search of the elusive ballistic-missile submarines of the United States, Great Britain, and France, and of the aircraft carriers of the United States and its allies which, though few in number, appear to concern the Soviet Union greatly. Submarines that were not detailed to any of those tasks would have the mission to which the main efforts of German and U.S. submarines were directed in World War II, namely, the destruction of enemy shipping.

Up to now, the most interesting and, perhaps, the most important of the ships built by the Soviet Union in the Gorshkov era are the *Moskva*-class antisubmarine cruisers. In an attempt to equate them with some class in their own navy, Americans have called them helicopter carriers or LPHs (helicopter-bearing amphibious assault ships), and, sometimes in the general press, aircraft carriers. When the first *Moskva*-class ship showed herself in the Mediterranean in 1968, her activities indicated that she was an antisubmarine ship, rather than an amphibious ship, and the shape of her hull, quite different from that of an American LPH of the *Iwo Jima* class, confirmed what her activities suggested. She has, of course, some ability to conduct amphibious warfare, but that asset is, apparently, not as important as her antisubmarine and antiair missions, for both of which she is well armed. Plainly, the *Moskva* and her sister set the pattern for the cruisers of the future. If Soviet officers succeed in combining VTOL combat aircraft with their *Moskva*-class cruisers—and the Soviet Union appears to be more interested and further advanced than is the United States in that type of aircraft—they will have brought the cycle of cruiser development back to its starting point. As did the cruisers of the past, these ships will serve all purposes, will be able to conduct wartime missions independently and, just as the classic cruiser feared no ship inferior to a battleship, will have no cause to fear any ship inferior to an attack aircraft carrier.

The *Moskva* class is not the only innovation of Admiral Gorshkov's fleet to be described in this book. There are the guided-missile cruisers of the *Kynda* and *Kresta* classes. Curiously, the interesting and powerful *Kynda*s and *Kresta*s are dependent on an outside source to locate their targets and provide guidance for their weapons. Such a source could be a satellite, an airplane (shore-based if fixed-wing, ship-based if rotary wing), a surface ship, or a submarine. Ships so largely dependent for their value on an independent unit which might have been destroyed, injured, or misled by the enemy, or rendered useless by any one of the normal failings to which men and their creations are subject, are themselves not totally reliable instruments of war, except when their weapons are aimed at targets ashore, such as cities and air bases. However, if these ships come within visual range of a naval target, they shed this weakness and under those conditions, except for submarines, there is hardly a ship in the Western world that could engage them with much chance of victory.

There are many indications that the men of the Soviet Navy not only have the ability to be as inventive as were their forebears in the Tsarist Navy, but also that they can catch on to, and make use of, the ship developments and seagoing techniques of the U.S. Navy and its allies. By way of illustrating that this is so, the following accomplishments are cited: some of the large new Soviet surface warships have gas turbines; nuclear power has been applied successfully to the submarine fleet; surface-to-surface missiles have been installed in large, fast patrol boats; a force of small ships for underway replenishment, repairs, and support has been created; a fleet of trawler-like intelligence ships is at work on the high seas; the techniques that have been developed for at-sea replenishment of both surface ships and submarines have made it possible for their ships to range, in peacetime, as far and wide as American ships do.

It is curious that while the Soviet Navy has been growing and adopting new concepts in many areas, its interest in mine warfare seems to have declined. Unlike their predecessors, the large new ships show no mine tracks on the weather decks. As for mine-countermeasures, though the Soviet Navy possesses hundreds of minesweepers, few have been built in recent years. And fewer yet are built of wood. It may be that, in time,

some with fiberglass or ferrocement hulls will show up, but now almost all their minesweepers, including those of the latest design, are of steel construction, a characteristic that cannot help their survival when they enter a field of magnetic mines. One does not know, of course, whether this defect is evidence of a failure on the part of the designers of the Soviet Navy, or of a low appraisal on their part of U.S. and NATO minelaying capabilities.

Be that as it may, Siegfried Breyer has described in detail this many-faceted war fleet. The United States Naval Institute became interested in this book of his when it was published in the German language by J. F. Lehmanns Verlag of Munich, Germany, in 1964. Since that time, many significant things have happened in the Soviet Navy. Consequently, in recent months, while Lieutenant Commander Henley was translating the book, Herr Breyer was bringing it up to date. The Naval Institute owes many thanks to Professor Robert W. Daly, of the history faculty at the U.S. Naval Academy, for some of the information on the locations of the Soviet naval colleges, for information on Soviet naval visits to foreign ports, and for much help throughout this work.

The transliteration of Russian names in this book follows the system of the Library of Congress. Hence, some words differ from the usage found in such well-known sources as *Weyer's Warships of the World* and *Jane's Fighting Ships.*

Opposite: The Kildin-*class guided-missile destroyer*
Bedovyi *works through heavy seas in the Atlantic.*

Table of Contents

Preface

When the German edition of this book was published in 1964, the Soviet Navy was engaged in a comprehensive reorganization designed to implement a concept in maritime strategy completely new to the Soviet Union. At that time, there seemed to be no chance of a conversion from the old and conventional to the modern being achieved at the rate Moscow desired. It was not the material aspects of the change that appeared to present the most formidable obstacle, but the need for the Soviets to break free from their age-old continental outlook and comprehend fully the importance of sea power. Today, only six years later, the transition seems to have been made.

During the Second World War, the Soviet Union saw how Allied maritime supremacy affected the conduct of the war on its own continent and, for the first time, began to appreciate the advantage to be derived from mastery of the high seas. Recognizing that its aim of disputing that mastery with the world's greatest sea power could not be attained with a fleet organized, as the Soviet fleet used to be, for the support of land forces, the Soviet Union has produced the means to take offensive action at sea. However, in order to avoid becoming closely engaged and so risk losing the ability to attack again, its current naval policy is to challenge the maritime supremacy of the enemy with a form of "hit and run" cruiser warfare.

Obviously, this type of offense cannot provide the Soviet Union with mastery of the seas, but it can seriously endanger the supremacy of the Western Alliance.

The aim of the present-day Red Fleet is to reduce the offensive power of the Western Allies by forcing them to commit far greater forces to the defense of the sea lanes than the Soviet Union commits to their attack. Furthermore, the Russians have not neglected other aspects of sea power, for their rapidly growing merchant and fishing fleets are providing them with experience in the economic advantages of mercantile traffic.

Since there can no longer be any doubt that the Soviet Union has learned to think and act as a maritime power, its importance in that respect cannot be measured by the same yardstick that was valid up to the immediate postwar years. The purpose of this book, then, is to examine the military equipment and capabilities of the world's second greatest sea power. Russian sea power is today, and will be even more in the future, a factor in international politics that cannot be assessed too highly.

Red China, now ideologically opposed to the Soviet Union, and North Korea have not been included among the satellite states dealt with in Chapter 10.

I am indebted to the translator, Lieutenant Commander M. W. Henley, Royal Navy (Retired), for his painstaking work, and to the United States Naval Institute for making this English-language version possible. My thanks are due also to all those friends and organizations who, by word and deed, have contributed to the success of this book.

Siegfried Breyer

Hanau, West Germany
January 1970

Guide to the Soviet Navy

CHAPTER 1

Organization of the Soviet Navy

Immediately after the Bolshevik Revolution, a Revolutionary Naval Committee was set up to administer the Navy. Some three months later, on 22 February 1918, the Council of People's Commissars formed from a Higher Naval Collegium, which had been set up the previous December to direct naval activities, the People's Commissariat for Naval Affairs. At first, this new body took the name of its parent organization, the Higher Naval Collegium, but it later became known as the Council of People's Commissars for Naval Affairs. From the end of 1918 onwards, there was naval representation on the Revolutionary War Council. A Commander-in-Chief, subordinate to the Commander-in-Chief of the U.S.S.R., was appointed to the operational command of the fleets and forces on the rivers and lakes and, at the same time, a Navy General Staff was formed.

At the beginning of 1918, the Navy consisted of the Baltic Fleet and the Black Sea Fleet, but on 18 June 1918 the latter was scuttled near Novorossisk to prevent it from falling into German hands. As time went on, flotillas, some of them short-lived, came into being on certain inland waters and rivers: Lake Peipus, Lake Ladoga, the Sea of Azov, the Caspian and Aral seas, and the Eastern Dvina, the Western Dvina, the Amu-Darya, the Amur, the Don, and the Volga-Kama rivers. Lastly, there were the Siberian and Tsaritsyn (Volgograd) flotillas. The Pacific Fleet was formed in 1932, and the Northern Fleet the following year.

On 30 December 1937, the People's Commissariat for the Navy was set up, and its first Commissar was P. A. Smirnov, who served until April 1939, when he was succeeded by N. G. Kuznetsov. In February 1946, the

3

services were integrated under a People's Commissariat for the Armed Forces, which, on 15 March, became the Ministry for the Armed Forces of the U.S.S.R. The division of that Ministry into a War Ministry and a Navy Ministry, which took place in February 1950, lasted only three years. When the Ministry for the Defense of the U.S.S.R. was established in 1953, the first to serve as Minister of Defense was the political Marshal N. A. Bulganin, who was succeeded in 1955 by the hero of World War II, Marshal G. K. Zhukov. In 1957 Marshal R. Y. Malinovskii became Minister of Defense and served until his death in 1967, when the post was given to Marshal A. A. Grechko.

The Defense Minister is the commander-in-chief of the armed forces, to whom the commanders-in-chief of the rocket/air, land, and maritime forces are subordinate. An integrated headquarters—a sort of general staff of the armed forces—ensures co-ordination between the services. Close contact is maintained between the Defense Minister and the Military Section of the Central Committee of the Communist Party, not only upwards to that Committee, but downwards through the Political Directorate of the Armed Forces.

Admiral of the Fleet S. G. Gorshkov is at present Commander-in-Chief of the Navy. He has a First Dep-

Admiral of the Fleet of the USSR Sergei G. Gorshkov.

uty, whose duties, if the post of commander-in-chief is related to that of a Secretary of the Navy, are similar to those of an Undersecretary of the Navy. Also immediately subordinate to the C-in-C, are the Naval War Council and the Higher Political Directorate of the Navy. The former is a high-level consultative body that has no powers of decision; while the latter, which is responsible on the one hand to the commander-in-chief for morale and disciplinary matters, and on the other, to the Military Section of the Central Committee for political "alignment" within the Navy, is a distinguishing feature of Communist organization. There are political directorates, in appropriate size, but always with the identical structure, in all units down to the smallest. Operations, training, and security are the responsibility of the Chief of Naval Staff.

There are now four fleets—the Baltic Fleet, the Northern Fleet, the Black Sea Fleet, and the Pacific Fleet —each of which has a commander-in-chief, and comprises not only the seagoing units, but the shore-based naval infantry, naval air forces, support bases, and dockyards and their associated facilities in its area. Land-based naval forces include coast defense units—artillery and air defense—together with operational troops, such as naval infantry and engineer units.

Guided-missile cruisers of the Pacific Fleet anchor in line at Vladivostok.

Besides the fleets, there are flotillas on the large rivers and inland waters: the Danube Flotilla based on Ismail; the Amur Flotilla based on Khabarovsk; the Azov Flotilla based on Kerch; and the Caspian Flotilla based on Astrakhan and Baku. These flotillas are under the operational control of the commander of the local land forces but, since the Caspian Sea may be the main training center for the Soviet fleet, particularly for submarine training, it is possible that the flotilla based there is directly subordinate to the Chief Training Directorate.

The Baltic (Red Banner) Fleet is the strongest of the Soviet fleets. It is usually commanded by a vice admiral, whose headquarters are on the Naval Base at Baltiisk (Pillau), and who has under his command all the seagoing forces, attached naval air force units, coast defense forces, ports, support bases, aids to navigation, and a hydrographic section.

Present fleet strength is about 140,000 men. Most of the seagoing forces are divided into two groups: a Southern Group based on Baltiisk, and a Northern Group based on Tallinn (Revel). Each group includes two or three cruisers, ten destroyers, one squadron of submarines, three squadrons of minesweepers, three of fast patrol boats, and three of submarine chasers.

Naval aviation units presently stationed in the Baltic area have available approximately 220 aircraft, including helicopters. The commander of the Baltic Fleet Naval Air Force has his headquarters in Kaliningrad (Königsberg). The Logistic Command is in Leningrad and is composed of freighters and tankers for replenishment purposes. In early 1969, the Baltic Fleet, including units assigned to training duties, consisted of:

  5 cruisers
  3 guided-missile cruisers
  9 guided-missile destroyers
 16 destroyers
 30 frigates
 64 submarines
  6 guided-missile submarines
 63 guided-missile patrol boats
135 fast patrol boats
100 submarine chasers
120 minesweepers
 73 landing ships
300 (approximately) auxiliaries.

Ships not allocated to a battle group are based at one or other of seven ports between Baltiisk and Leningrad. Most of the vessels in that category are minesweepers and fast patrol boats, but some of them are escort vessels. The amphibious group is based on Leningrad.

This concentration of naval force makes the Soviet Union the strongest military power in the Baltic and implies aggressive intentions. The same can be said of the land forces stationed around the Baltic. The geographical boundaries of the Estonian Military District include the present-day Estonian, Latvian, and Lith-

Sailors of the Baltic Fleet run to their Osa-class missile boats during Operation Sever, a 1968 naval exercise.

uanian Soviet Republics and the part of East Prussia that is under Soviet "administration"—the so-called Kaliningrad Ost-blast. The Leningrad Military District is bounded by a line that runs from Narva, to the west of Leningrad, through Kronstadt, to Viborg to the northeast. Both districts are among the six western border districts of the U.S.S.R. whose armed forces are in such a high state of preparedness as regards manpower, weapons, and logistic support, that they could become operational at a moment's notice.

The staff of the Baltic Military Area is located in Riga and, in the event of mobilization, would become the staff of the Baltic Army Group. Fifteen army divisions with armored units, equipped entirely with modern tanks and armored vehicles, are now stationed in the area, and six tactical air divisions are attached. Besides the Ministry of Defense, the Committee for State Security (KGB) and the Ministry of the Interior (MVD) both have troops stationed in the Baltic area.

The KGB has about 80,000 elite troops organized in divisions and regiments, with their staff in Riga. The offshore patrol sections are divided into groups, and each section has six or seven border patrol boats.

The MVD has about 15,000 operational troops, organized, trained, and armed along military lines.

There are units of paramilitary organizations for support of the armed forces. Elements of these organizations, which include the DOSAAF (see page 15) and the local Civil Defense organizations (MPVO), are attached to all military commands and, in time of war, they would perform military duties.

There is also the civil air transport organization, which is subordinate to the air commands for the northern districts and which, with its aircraft and crews, would take over transport support duties in wartime.

The strength of the forces stationed in the Soviet coastal area of the Baltic, including the occupied and "administered" territories of East Prussia, is estimated at:

Army	approximately 200,000 men
Navy	approximately 140,000 men
KGB	approximately 80,000 men
MVD	approximately 15,000 men
Total	approximately 500,000 men

Northern Fleet components, in mid-1967, were estimated to be:

    4 cruisers
    6 guided-missile cruisers or destroyers
   25 destroyers
   80 frigates, submarine chasers, and so forth
  130 or more submarines
  100 minesweepers
  100 fast patrol boats
  120 (approximately) aircraft of the naval air forces.

Black Sea Fleet components in mid-1967 were:

  5 cruisers
  8 guided-missile cruisers or destroyers
15 destroyers
80 frigates, submarine chasers, and so forth
60 submarines
 . . landing craft, special-purpose ships, auxiliaries
120 aircraft and helicopters of the naval air forces.

No details of the shore-based organizations and units are available.

The Pacific Fleet (at one time, called the Far East Fleet) is divided into the southern group and the northern group, and those groups have recently been designated the 5th and 7th fleets, respectively. The 5th Fleet is based on Vladivostok, and the 7th Fleet is based on Petropavlovsk and Sovetskaia Gavan. Over-all strength of the Pacific Fleet is approximately:

  4 cruisers
  4 guided-missile cruisers or destroyers
30 destroyers
80 frigates, submarine chasers, and so forth
140 submarines, 20 of which are atomic-powered
120 minesweepers
130 fast patrol boats
160 or more naval aircraft.

A submarine of the Northern Fleet returns to base.

Seagoing forces in the Far East are estimated at 60,000 men, the shore-based units also at 60,000 men, and the naval air forces, about 12,000 men.

Some reports give the strength of army and air force units in the Far East as:

21 infantry divisions
6 mechanized divisions
2 armored divisions
1 airborne division.

Altogether, the armed forces in the area comprise nearly 500,000 men, or 20 per cent of the total of manpower in the Soviet armed forces. As early as 1956, the air force had available more than 1,000 fighters, 1,000 light and medium bombers, 250 heavy bombers, 500 transports, and 300 reconnaissance and communication types—in all, about 3,000 aircraft.

Nothing definite is known about the strength and disposition of units stationed on rivers and inland bodies of water.

A Mediterranean squadron, consisting of from 8 to 12 W-class submarines, 4 *Riga*-class frigates, and a number of depot and supply ships, was based on Saseno, Albania, until the summer of 1961, when the base was given up and the ships were withdrawn from the Mediterranean.

Since then, however, Soviet warships have become a familiar sight in the Mediterranean, as constantly increasing numbers of them pass through the Bosporus and make extended stays there. These vessels must be considered a threat to the U.S. Sixth Fleet, which has been stationed in the Mediterranean since the end of World War II.

According to well-informed sources, some permanent task groups have now been formed, each consisting of one or two cruisers (cruisers are believed to be the flagships), eight to ten destroyers and/or frigates, a submarine section, and a replenishment group of four tenders and supply ships. Three such groups are thought to be serving in northern waters, two in the Baltic, two in the Far East, and one in the Black Sea. Icebreakers have probably been assigned to the groups in northern waters.

Another innovation is the formation of amphibious groups which, besides landing craft, comprise minesweepers, smaller vessels, and destroyers, these last obviously being intended for escort and support duties. The amphibious group in the Baltic is based on Leningrad, and has a strength of approximately 8,000 men.

At the present time, the total strength of the Soviet Navy is estimated at 600,000 men, 200,000 of whom are thought to serve afloat, 100,000 with naval air forces, 50,000 with naval infantry forces, and 250,000 with coast defense and other shore-based activities.

Opposite: Units of the Black Sea Fleet, including the helicopter carrier Moskva, *anchor at Sevastopol.*

Organization of the Soviet Navy

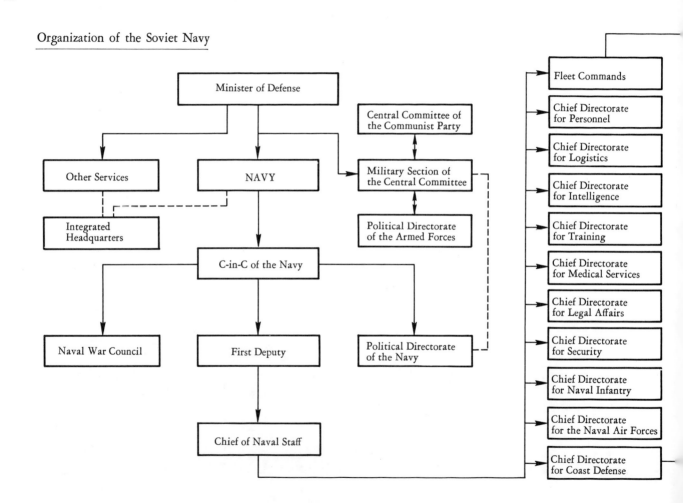

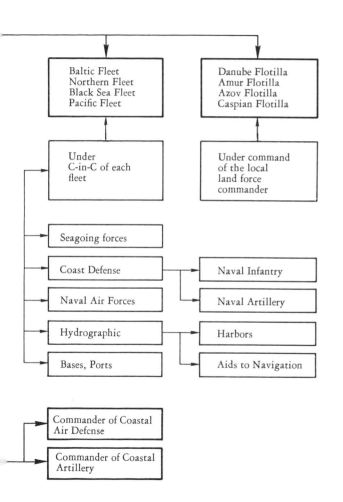

Command of the Soviet Navy as of 1 January 1969

Commander: Admiral of the Fleet of the USSR S. G. Gorshkov
Political Direction: Admiral V. M. Grishanov
Chief, War Soviet* of the Navy: Admiral of the Fleet V. A. Kasatonov

Baltic Fleet
　　Commander: Vice Admiral V. V. Mikhailin
　　Chief of Staff: Vice Admiral F. I. Savel'ev
　　Political Director: Vice Admiral IA. G. Pochupailo

Northern Fleet
　　Commander: Admiral of the Fleet S. M. Lobov
　　Chief of Staff: Rear Admiral N. M. Baranov
　　Political Director: Vice Admiral F. IA. Sisov

Black Sea Fleet
　　Commander: Vice Admiral V. S. Sysoev
　　Chief of Staff: Vice Admiral L. V. Mizin
　　Political Director: Rear Admiral I. S. Rudnev

Pacific Fleet
　　Commander: Admiral N. N. Amel'ko
　　Chief of Staff: Vice Admiral G. M. Egorov
　　Political Director: Admiral M. N. Zakharov

* This organization was established in 1958.

CHAPTER 2

Training and Personnel

General

On 1 September 1939, the Soviet Union enacted a law making military service obligatory. Until 1955, the length of compulsory service in the Navy was five years; it is now three years for all branches except the Naval Air Forces, where it is only two years. The draft age has been reduced from 19 to 18. Approximately one-third of the 600,000 men who now serve in the Navy are long-service volunteers, and the remainder are conscripts.

Pre-Service Training

Most naval ratings have had the benefit of pre-service training, either in the All-Union Voluntary Organization for the Furthering of the Army, Air Force, and Navy (DOSAAF) or in the Young Communist League (Komsomol). The main task of DOSAAF, which is supported by the Defense Ministry, is to prepare for and ensure co-operation between the Navy, the civil authorities, and the population in time of war. The section of DOSAAF that assists the Navy trains young men in seamanship, radio operation, and communications, before they enter the military service. Most of the men chosen to be petty officers are members of DOSAAF. When men who belong to DOSAAF have completed their compulsory service, they are required to attend regular training periods, which goes some way to solving the problem of training reserves. The Defense Ministry supports DOSAAF on such a large scale that the Navy has to assign to it instructors and even small escort vessels.

Other sources of pre-service training are the naval preparatory schools, most of whose students are sons of officers and petty officers.

15

Basic Training and Specialization

Since most recruits have had some training when they join, the basic course that follows their call-up is relatively short, generally not lasting more than a few weeks.

In the Soviet Navy, as in all navies, there is a whole series of specializations for enlisted men and petty officers and, after their basic training, recruits are sent to school for up to two years of thorough and comprehensive training in a career specialty.

Service Conditions

During the first two years of a man's service, he is given leave only in exceptional circumstances. Pay is very low. Food is plentiful and nourishing, but it lacks variety. One hundred grams of vodka are issued to junior enlisted men twice a year—on 1 May to celebrate socialist Labor Day, and on 7 November to celebrate the anniversary of the Bolshevik Revolution.

Rates

Soviet Navy	U.S. Navy
Matros	Seaman Recruit/Apprentice
Starshii Matros	Seaman
Starshina 2-ĭ Stat'i	Petty Officer Second Class
Starshina 1-ĭ Stat'i	Petty Officer First Class
Glavnyĭ Starshina	Chief Petty Officer
Michman	Warrant Officer

Officer Training

In theory, every Soviet citizen has the opportunity to become an officer. In practice, however, only the sons of privileged families—Party and government officials or officers—are accepted, and then only if they have attended one of the four Nakhimov schools where their preparation for a career as an officer emphasizes ideological subjects. Nakhimov schools are comparable to the former cadet schools, inasmuch as students enter when they are seven years old and follow a complete secondary-school program. Discipline in these schools is distinctly military.

An officer candidate who has no naval or military service enters a formal college between the ages of 17 and 21 years: promising service men can enter up to the age of 23. Entrance examinations lay the same stress on physical and mental qualities as do similar examinations in Western countries. After completing a short course of basic training, candidates are sent to a naval officers' college, where they undergo an intensive course of instruction that lasts four years.

As of 1969, the naval colleges were:

Higher Naval College of the Order of Lenin, Red Banner, Order of Ushakov named for M. V. Frunze, Leningrad.

Higher Naval College of Submarine Navigation named for the Leningrad Komsomol, Leningrad.

Sailors of the Black Sea Fleet run to their combat stations.

Higher Naval College of Radio-Electronics named for A. S. Popov, Leningrad-Petrodvorets.
Higher Naval Engineer Order of Lenin College named for F. E. Dzerzhinski, Leningrad.
Leningrad Higher Naval Engineer College, Pushkin.
Sevastopol Higher Naval Engineer College, Sevastopol.

Black Sea Higher Naval College named for N. S. Nakhimov, Sevastopol.
Pacific Higher Naval College named for S. O. Makarov, Vladivostok.
Caspian Higher Naval College named for S. M. Kirov, Baku.
Final Higher Naval College of the Order of Lenin, Red Banner, Order of Ushakov named for M. V. Frunze, Kaliningrad.
Kiev Higher Naval Political College, Kiev.

A few officers are obtained by transfer, upon graduation, from other service colleges—the twenty military aviation colleges, for example.

Officers for the fleet train and possibly the line are obtainable from the colleges run by the Ministry for the Merchant Marine. These are:

Leningrad Higher Engineer Sea School named for S. O. Makarov.
Odessa Institute of Engineers of the Sea Fleet.
Rostov Nautical School named for G. IA. Sedov.
Odessa Higher Nautical School.
Vladivostok Higher Nautical School.

In August 1968, a Higher Nautical School named for Mikhail Lomonosov was inaugurated. *Red Star* has not disclosed its location but, since Lomonosov is scientifically associated with the Arctic, this Merchant Marine college may be in the burgeoning area of Murmansk.

Calisthenics on board a cruiser.

Along with the thorough training in a military specialty that all naval candidates are given, goes a course in ideology. Whole classes of students are sent, for varying periods, to training ships or shore-based training units to gain experience of operational conditions and to be given practical instruction.

Transfers from one specialty to another are not permitted: once a candidate has chosen his specialty, he must remain in it. When he has passed the final examination for commissioned rank, he is promoted to junior lieutenant and appointed to six months' service afloat or in a shore-based or naval air force unit, as appropriate.

After that, he goes immediately to another school for more specialized training. Such schools known at present are: gunnery schools in Murmansk, Tuapse, Riga, and Sevastopol; torpedo schools in Zhdanov (Mariupol), Kronstadt, and Lepaia; radar school (with radar arsenal) in Arkhangelsk; logistics school in Leningrad; and a Naval Infantry school in Viborg. The hydrographic school in Moscow has many field subsidiaries.

Most of these schools have seagoing training squadrons attached. The hydrographic school has three old submarines and five motor vessels of 1,200 tons, the latter being formed into a "survey brigade" under command of the head of the hydrographic school, a rear admiral. The logistics school, which is part of the logistics command in Leningrad, has two 2,000-ton freighters, some amphibious vehicles, heavy trucks, loading gantries, floating cranes, and railway equipment.

In all, the Soviet Navy has some 37 colleges and schools, capable of training 10,000 men per year, including the 1,500 newly promoted junior lieutenants who leave the officers' schools every twelve months.

Senior officers are required to attend a naval war college: line officers go to the Voroshilov Academy, engineers to the Krylov Academy, and political officers to the Lenin Academy. Prominent among the subjects taught at these institutions, are national economy, Leninism, and international politics. Since 1950, the emphasis placed on "oceanic thinking" has been increasing.

Officer Ranks

Line officer ranks are the same as those of the merchant marine and the Northern Seaway Administration. Coast Defense, Naval Air Forces, staff, and medical officers have army ranks, the last-mentioned having the words *Meditsinskaia sluzhba* following their rank, a practice that corresponds to the use of the words "Medical Corps" in the title of a medical officer in the U.S. Navy. Engineer officers have naval ranks preceded by the word *inzhener*—for example, *inzhener leitenant*.

Soviet Navy	U.S. Navy
Kursant	Midshipman
Mladshii Leitenant	Ensign
Leitenant	Lieutenant (j.g.)
Starshii Leitenant	(None)
Kapitan-Leitenant	Lieutenant
Kapitan-3-go ranga	Lieutenant Commander
Kapitan-2-go ranga	Commander
Kapitan-1-go ranga	Captain
Kontr-Admiral	Rear Admiral
Vitse-Admiral	Vice Admiral
Admiral	Admiral
Admiral Flota Sovetskogo Soiuza	Admiral of the Fleet

Opposite: A Kresta-*class guided-missile cruiser, one of the most distinctive of Soviet warship designs.*

CHAPTER 3

Warship Construction

Every navy that builds its own warships eventually develops in them what might be called a "national look," and arrival at that stage denotes that a certain degree of independence from foreign technical influence has been reached. Japan and some smaller sea powers began to acquire this look in about 1910. The Russian Navy, on the other hand, did not acquire that sign of independence until after the Second World War.

That the Tsarist Navy went abroad for assistance is illustrated by the fact that the large battleships of the *Gangut* class, launched between 1911 and 1915, and of the *Imperatriza Maria* class, launched soon afterwards, were built according to the ideas of Vittorio Cuniberti, and their prototype was the first Italian dreadnought, the *Dante Alighieri.* At that time, the Russian Navy was not independent even in the construction of small warships, for at the turn of the century, the German shipyards Schichau and Vulcan-Stettin delivered plans and built the propulsion machinery for some 50 torpedo boats. Furthermore, shortly before the outbreak of the First World War, Germany was building for Russia two light cruisers, which were approaching completion, and the heavy components and machinery for five destroyers and a battle cruiser. At that time, the destroyer *Novik,* which was also built from German plans, attracted considerable attention because her machinery was supplied complete by the Vulcan shipyard in Stettin. Naturally, the outward appearance of all these ships reflected these foreign influences.

In the years following the Bolshevik Revolution, any

21

ships that were worth repairing and returning to service required modernization. So far as the outside world could see, the modernization was done in quite a simple way: for example, the forecastles of battleships and cruisers were raised by merely adding an extra deck, about half the normal deckhead height above the original forecastle, with a curved stem and a sharp step or break at the after end, giving them an appearance similar to that of contemporary Swedish armored coast-defense ships. The object was to improve their seakeeping qualities. Enormous cranes fitted at funnel height on the Russian battleships and cruisers were original and, on the former, were supposedly for launching motor torpedo boats carried on board.

The first new surface ships to be completed under the Soviet regime and to become known abroad were the large, *Leningrad*-class destroyers, built between 1933 and 1940. Although French technicians were involved in their construction, their silhouettes marked them as of independent design. They were the first Russian-built warships to adopt the "unit" type of machinery layout, which accounts for the distance between their funnels. This layout provides for two separate and self-contained power units—each engine has boilers and auxiliary machinery adjacent to it—and is a form of dispersion intended to reduce the danger of battle damage putting both sets of machinery out of action and, thus, completely immobilizing the ship. Many navies have used this layout for many years and, since it was incorporated in the *Leningrad*-class destroyers, it has been the normal arrangement in Soviet ships.

Links between the Italian and Russian navies had been forged in Tsarist times, and in about 1935 there began a period of Russian dependence upon Italian ship design. The operational areas of the Italian Navy lay in confined waters, as did those of the Russian Navy, and the choice of Italian designs indicates how little Russian construction was, at that time, directed towards operations on the high seas. So strong was the influence of that factor that the overriding requirement for Russian warships was high speed, and the small distances involved made it possible to sacrifice fuel capacity in order to attain it. Furthermore, in the 1930s, Italian machinery had reached a very high state of efficiency and shipbuilding costs in Italy were lower than anywhere else in Europe.

Shortly after an Italian cruiser, the *Zara,* with quadrupod foremast, whose legs disappeared almost entirely into the bridge and director, had made her appearance, the *Kirov* and the *Molotov* (now the *Slava*), the first Soviet-built cruisers, were laid down, and they had the same type of foremast. A third ship of the class, the *Maxim Gorki,* had a control tower similar to the one that had been introduced by the Italians on the *Raimondo Montecuccoli* in 1934. The *Chapaev* class, laid down between 1939 and 1940, had the same type of control towers but they were larger, and those that appeared on the *Sverdlov* class, laid down some ten years later, were larger still. Both the *Chapaev* and the *Sverdlov* followed Italian style in other respects also: their funnels were not raked, but vertical like those of Italian light and heavy cruisers, and their funnel cowls were also in the Italian style.

Another noticeable feature of Soviet cruisers built in the years between the appearance of the *Kirov*s and that of the *Sverdlov*s is that, as in cruisers of other navies, the forecastle deck extends well aft, presumably to improve seaworthiness by providing a higher freeboard.

The *Gnevnyi*-class destroyers, which followed the larger *Leningrad* class, also had a feature first seen in the Italian Navy—a single funnel. This innovation indicated a departure from the "unit" machinery layout, but it proved to be temporary. The big destroyer *Tashkent,* launched in 1937, was built in Italy, and Soviet constructors may well have been influenced by her hull form and by the arrangement of her main armament in pairs. Italian *Leone*-class destroyers of 1923–24 were among the first to have twin gun mounts.

An experimental destroyer, the *Opytnyi,* the only one of her class and the first to be built without direct assistance from abroad, appeared in 1941. She represented an attempt to produce a destroyer of rather less than average size and of especially light construction. Presumably because of the requirement for very high

speed, only one gun was mounted on her forecastle so as not to restrict the lift of her bow. As on some Japanese and American destroyers the fore funnel was the thinner of her two, a reversal of common practice. This may have meant that she had only one boiler room forward and two aft, a layout that would also meet the requirement of minimum weight forward. Although the *Opytnyi* certainly reached and reportedly exceeded the required maximum speed (during trials she is supposed to have attained a speed of 41.6 knots) she was not a successful design, for her lightly built hull was not equal to the stresses and vibration effects of high speeds. Outwardly, she was a forerunner of the *Sil'nyi* class and was used to try out, among other things, the latter's machinery arrangement.

There is structural similarity between all the destroyers built between the time of the *Sil'nyi* class and that of the *Skoryi* class, and their severely raked, very broad, squat funnels have become the hallmark of Russian destroyers.

All Japanese destroyers built since 1926 have a triangular fairing situated where the flare of the bow meets the straight side of the midship section of the hull, and Russian destroyers from the *Gnevnyi* to the *Otlichnyi* class displayed the same feature, as did some Italian heavy cruisers.

The Russian destroyers followed Italian practice in their stowage arrangements for the bow anchors. Up to and including the *Nastoichivyi,* the only ship of the *Tallinn* class,* which appeared in 1954, cruisers and destroyers had anchor stowage at forecastle level, which, even at high speeds, kept the anchor clear of the bow and thus prevented it from being a source of resistance or of spray: it also enhanced seakeeping qualities by helping to keep the fore part of the ship dry. Ships using this method of anchor stowage should, of course, have exceptional sheer, a feature that Soviet ships of that period displayed only in modified form, if at all.

Bows and sterns are designed to meet the requirements of climate and geography in the areas where Soviet warships are likely to operate. In order to maintain speed and maneuverability in icy conditions, a massive stem is necessary, and some Soviet cruisers and destroyers have V-shaped girders welded to their stems.

Soviet naval constructors adopted the transom stern for all cruisers, except the *Sverdlov* class. Incorporation of this feature is a departure from Italian practice, and the reason for it is convenience for minelaying. However, the extent to which Soviet naval constructors did depend upon Italian construction was demonstrated when the battleship laid down in 1938–39 was captured at Nikolaevsk by the Germans and her hull was inspected: she had exactly the same system of underwater protection as did the *Vittorio Veneto* class.[1]

* "Tallinn" is a NATO designation and is applied herein to both the class and the ship.

The era of close association with Italian shipbuilding practice, which embraced all types of warship, ended with the *Sverdlov*-class cruisers and the *Skoryi*-class destroyers built in the years immediately following World War II. Although the development that took place from then on might be described as "new Russian," it was still subject to foreign influence.

In the meantime, another line of development had followed German practice which, for a while, was in favor. On the basis of the Russo-German Agreement of 1939, the Soviets demanded, among other things, not only the heavy cruisers *Prinz Eugen, Seydlitz,* and *Lützow,* then under construction, but also the plans of the *Bismarck* class, the 15-inch twin turret, fire-control equipment, and so forth.[2] However, Germany delivered only the uncompleted hull of cruiser "L" (ex-*Lützow*). Delivery took place on 15 April 1940, in compliance with a purchasing agreement signed in February 1940, and at the same time, 70 German engineers and technicians were sent to Leningrad to help the Soviets with her completion.[3] The German Naval High Command also agreed that, in order to allow the Soviets to gain experience for the essential trials of cruiser "L," a Soviet Naval Commission should attend the contractors' sea trials of a German heavy cruiser.[4]

In addition, the Soviets were given samples of fire-control and range-finder equipment. Obviously, Soviet constructors made a thorough study of the shipbuilding methods used both in cruiser "L" and in the German ships that fell into their hands in 1945, and adopted them for their own use. Thus, they became aware of the well-advanced method of electric welding. In good photographs of Soviet ships, welded seams are clearly visible. The treatment and mating of the plates are not always of the best, but this is probably due less to a lack of technical efficiency than to the Communist practice of setting goals to be achieved by workers. The Soviets also became aware of the form of construction developed by the *Reichsmarine,* in which the hull is stiffened by rather widely spaced transverse frames and closely spaced longitudinals.[5] Cruisers from the *Sverdlov* class onwards and destroyers from the *Skoryi* class onwards have this type of construction.

German weapons and other equipment also found favor with the Soviet Navy. Thus, the *Chapaev* and *Sverdlov* cruisers and destroyers from the *Tallinn* onwards were equipped with antiaircraft or dual-purpose twin mounts similar to the German C/38 turret, and later classes of cruisers and destroyers were fitted with quintuple torpedo tubes. Another case in point is the stabilized, hemispherical antiaircraft director fitted to cruisers and to the destroyer *Tallinn.* Almost exactly the same director, but without a radar antenna, was to be found on German battleships and heavy cruisers, where they were known in seamen's slang as *Wackeltöpfe* (wobbling pots). These directors, having been delivered

by Germany under the terms of the Russo-German agreements of 1939, had, in fact, been fitted to Soviet ships before the end of the war (see note, page 67).

Thus, it is not surprising that, at first sight, the appearance of the *Kola*-class frigates is similar to that of the German fleet torpedo boats of 1939, but closer inspection reveals certain differences of construction. Very prominent is the sharp angle, or "knuckle," low down on the forepart of the hull, whose main purpose may be to enlarge the living spaces. If this is correct, the advantage of a drier weather deck, which a high "knuckle" would offer, has been deliberately foregone (see page 110).[6]

So far as can be judged from outward appearances, the lines of the new types of Soviet warships that have become known since about 1955 indicate a "new Russian" trend. The first type to show this trend was the *Tallinn* which, because of her high freeboard and the unusually high mounting of her director control tower, was at first assumed to be a type of scouting cruiser. In fact, her silhouette is, in many respects, reminiscent of the German reconnaissance cruisers of 1939, but she turned out to be a destroyer. She was the first large Soviet warship to have a flush deck, and that feature, which provides the advantages of better seaworthiness and a greater number of protected internal compartments, has been retained on most subsequent types.

It appears that the stability of the *Tallinn* was not

very satisfactory and that deficiency might explain why the class is represented by only a single ship. Her superstructure presents an appearance that is most unusual for a destroyer and results, apparently, from the arrangement of the main machinery. The considerable distance between the funnels indicates that the engine rooms are between the boiler rooms, and such an unusual arrangement must greatly influence the layout of the upperworks, which are, in fact, a series of islands not connected with one another.

Soviet ship types that have become known to the West since 1955 have a most pronounced sheer which, in some cases, extends well aft and clearly indicates how much effort has been directed towards obtaining high speeds in heavy seas. For all practical purposes, the freeboard of the forepart of a ship determines the speed at which she can steam into a seaway. Other factors—for example, the shape of the stern and the flare of forward transverse frames above the waterline—improve seaworthiness by ensuring a rapid lift of the bow and a corresponding damping of the downward pitch,[7] but they do not have much effect on speed. The latest classes of destroyers and frigates have an extreme sheer, making the trend towards obtaining optimum speed in heavy seas unmistakable. Technically, the design is interesting, as the sheer starts by making quite a sharp bend from the horizontal deck, then rising in a straight line; in some cases, it has a second bend at the forecastle, instead of the more usual smooth curve. This design may be simpler and, therefore, quicker to build, and its only disadvantage is that it results in somewhat ungraceful lines.

Riga-class frigates also have a solid bulwark around their bows. In this connection, severely raked stems are very prominent on the newer ships, especially on the *Kynda* and *Kresta* classes of guided-missile cruisers, the *Kotlin, Kildin, Krupnyi,* and *Kashin* classes of destroyers, and the *Sasha* class of minesweepers.

All cruisers up to and including the *Chapaev* class, destroyers previous to the *Skoryi* and most smaller types, were built with transom sterns. On the other hand, the *Skoryi*-class destroyers, the *Tallinn,* and the latest class of escorts have sterns of a very distinctive shape. The upper part is square and flat, the lower part is cut away, counter-fashion, the cut-away being greater outboard than on the center line, so that if the three edges were joined, the result would be a flat triangle. Except that it did not have the square upper part, a comparable type of stern was to be found on German destroyers built between 1938 and the end of World War II. Adoption of this type of stern was dictated by the requirement for minelaying, and two openings in the square upper part, each a short distance inboard, contain minelaying ramps. Prior to the *Otlichnyi* class, the edges of destroyers' upper decks were rounded off aft to facilitate the laying of mines, but this is not so on the newer ships, which have only the openings described above.

Later classes of ships have considerably fewer scuttles in their sides than did their earlier counterparts, and older cruisers and destroyers have recently had many of theirs blanked off. The advantages of this innovation are that hull strength is increased, the ship would be safer if battle or other damage should cause her to settle in the water, and it is easier to darken ship and close down. Closing down is a protective measure against NBC (nuclear-biological-chemical) weapons—if, indeed, there is such a thing as protection against them. Naturally, the change brings some disadvantages: for example, less efficient ventilation of living spaces and the constant necessity for artificial illumination, both of which have a bad effect on habitability. The disadvantages have obviously been accepted in the interest of greater ship safety.

Almost all recently built ships have low, squat funnels, usually topped with raked cowls. The very latest ships, however, have funnels that, from broadside on, look decidedly narrow but are, in fact, quite broad, as each one contains two uptakes—*Kynda*s, *Krupnyi*s, and *Petya*s, are examples. Funnels are always raked, those on destroyers and frigates the most sharply. The U- or ring-shaped excrescences on some funnels apparently accommodate boiler-room intakes, which are thus protected from spray—*Kotlin*-class destroyers, *Kronstadt*-class submarine chasers, *Tovda*-class depot ships, and T-301-, T-43-, and *Sasha*-class minesweepers. On the *Krupnyi*s

the excrescences have been replaced by intakes on either side of the base of the funnels. The slits in the funnels of this class and of the *Kynda* and *Kashin* classes are unusual, and are probably intended for the intake of cooling air.

The development of radar is mainly responsible for the very interesting, progressive modification of the masts of Soviet warships from destroyers downwards. In the days when there were no large radar sets, most destroyers and lesser vessels had simple pole masts carrying aerials and signal halyards. As in other navies, when navigation and early-warning radars were introduced into the Soviet ships, supporting legs were fitted to the masts to give them added stiffness and to reduce vibration. Bigger and heavier equipment followed, and the tripod mast had to be braced both horizontally and diagonally, at first, rather widely but, as time went on, more closely, and finally the lattice mast made its appearance. For example, when the *Skoryi*-class destroyers were designed, only small navigation and range-finding radars were available, and a simple pole mast forward and a smaller one aft were sufficient: apparently, the mainmast carried only an IFF aerial. Later on, as the *Skoryi*s received larger and heavier radar sets, bigger and bigger platforms extending aft from the masts, were built to carry them. The platforms themselves required extra support, while the masts were still further stiffened by additional cross bracing in order to avoid affecting the radar performance. Then, when the mainmast received equipment that was more sensitive and had to be kept clear of funnel gases, it was moved forward. A significant step was taken when the *Tallinn* became the first Soviet ship to be fitted with a large all-round search radar. In order to leave the foremast free for navigation and gunnery radars, the search radar was mounted on the mainmast, which had to be strengthened and raised and, on the *Kotlin*s and modernized *Skoryi*s, it is as high as the foremast.

Radars finally became so big and heavy that the arrangement of overhanging platforms supported from below had to be changed. The result was the "blunted" lattice tripod, which first appeared on the later *Riga*s. Between 1958 and 1959 it became a quadrupod, common in present-day warship construction in many countries, but with a trapezoidal layout of the legs. It is interesting to note that, while the foremast on the *Kildin*s and *Krupnyi*s has grown higher, the mainmast (tripod) has not changed (see page 101).

The foremast of the *Tallinn* also was greatly affected by the development of radar. At first, it was a simple, slightly raked, pole mast firmly attached to the platform surrounding the base of the director tower, which itself had at this time only a relatively small radar antenna. When that antenna was replaced by a larger one that projected to a much greater extent, the arrangement of the mast had to be completely altered to enable the director and its antenna to rotate. The rake was increased, which meant that the mast could no longer be braced by the original attachment to the director tower, and two supporting legs had to be added. At the same time, the radar that had been mounted at the masthead was replaced by one of higher performance but requiring a shorter wave guide. (At certain frequencies, a long wave guide complicates operation.) This may well be the reason why an overhanging radar room was built on to the back of the bridge and a similar room was built high up on the mainmast of the *Sverdlov*-class cruisers. When compared with earlier cruisers, both the *Sverdlov*s and the rebuilt *Kirov*s show how radar has influenced mast arrangements.

Kotlin-class destroyers also had to have their masts modified when large antennas with projecting feedhorns were fitted to their directors. So as to enable the antennas to rotate, the forward legs of the mast had to be bent, and the upper third of the mast had to be made narrower and more strongly braced.

As far as outward appearances are concerned, the upperworks of *Kynda*-class guided-missile cruisers mark the beginning of a new period for the Soviet Navy. Just as had happened earlier in the U.S. Navy, electronic development played a major part in dictating the shape of the superstructure, and the *Kynda*s now have an "electronic" look similar to that of contemporary NATO types. From this standpoint, it can be presumed that, outwardly at least, they represent the first direct equivalent to corresponding Western types. Of course, it must be remembered that, since no details of Soviet radar performance are available, it is impossible to make a real comparison with Western development, which is based on a great deal of experience. The two high, tower-like masts, which are, in fact, encased, quadrupod masts similar to those of the British County class, are novelties in Soviet ship construction. Each one is topped by an all-round search antenna of the type first seen on the *Krupnyi*s. Halfway up each mast, there is a sizable platform that extends forward on the foremast and aft on the mainmast. On each platform is a large antenna, apparently part of the missile-guidance system.

Also new on Soviet warships are the main-deck bulwarks on either side of the bridge structure of the *Kotlin* and *Krupnyi* destroyers, the *Riga*-class frigates, and the latest escort vessels. A solid bulwark on the weather deck, abreast the bridge, helps to keep the deck dry. All American flush-deck destroyers since the *Fletcher* class, which were launched in 1942, have incorporated this feature, and its presence on Soviet vessels might be said to reflect American influence. This protective measure has enabled the Soviet constructors to devise a unique boat stowage: the bulwarks on the *Kotlin*s are about five feet high and extend to the sides of the ship. Thus, the boats are well protected not only from seas breaking over the bow but also from those breaking over the sides.

This is a neat arrangement, but it must make it difficult to launch the boats in a heavy sea.

Worth brief mention, is the Soviet method of lowering boats into the water and hoisting them out. Cruisers use derricks or cranes, but whereas, on small ships davits are used, even for heavy boats, on the *Kotlin*s a boom is mounted on each of the tripod mast's after legs. The heel is supported by a hinge piece fixed to the lower part of the leg, and the blocks for the topping lift are attached to an extension of a horizontal cross brace that joins the two after legs at about funnel height. The extension is braced from below by a diagonal support onto the leg. This device has made it possible to dispense with the weight of king posts, such as had to be used on the *Tallinn*.

At first, Soviet submarine construction tended to follow British and Italian designs. The new construction that began in 1928 was designed by the Italian shipyard Cantieri Riuniti dell'Adriatico and resulted in the *Dekabrist*, or D, class, for which the *Fratelli Bandiera*, built by the same yard at about the same time, may well have been the prototype. A parallel development was the L class, for which the Soviet constructors used the British *L-55* as prototype. This boat was built during World War I and sunk during Allied operations off Kronstadt in 1919. She was salvaged in 1928, repaired, and put into service with the Red Navy. Both classes were oceangoing and were intended for occasional minelaying.

The L class was more successful than the D class, and improved versions of it continued to be built until well into World War II.[8]

The two classes had the same gun arrangement—a trainable mounting on a platform either forward of the conning tower or built into the tower itself. In spite of the fact that this layout was used for a short time on Italian submarines, it was typically British and, in adopting it, the Russians were quite clearly influenced by the *L-55.* However, the height of the mounting differed: in the D-class submarines, it was level with the top of the conning tower, whereas in the L class, it was at half the height of the tower.

The next oceangoing class, apparently the first "all-Russian" postwar type, was the P class, which proved unsatisfactory in operational service and the ships of that class spent most of their time as transports. In that class also, the Russians adopted the British style of gun mounting but, abaft the conning tower, they built a second platform on which they mounted a low-angle gun, and this addition made the entire superstructure about a quarter the length of the surfaced boat. With the exception of the S-class boats, all Soviet submarines had the long, flat conning towers obviously favored by the Russians: on the S class, the tower was tall and narrow, similar to that of the German Type IA built at about the same time. On some boats of this class, the Russians dispensed with the protected gun installation

and, in line with general practice at that time, mounted the gun on the forward casing.

Designed for limited oceangoing use, the SC class appeared in 1930, and a number of improved versions were built between that time and the end of the Second World War.

Similar numbers of a smaller coastal type, the M class, were built between 1933 and 1955 and, like the SC class, were improved many times. The conning tower was the same in both classes, and the overriding factor in designing its shape seems to have been streamlining: in the SC class, the platform for the antiaircraft gun was built into the conning tower. It is interesting to note that the M-class boats, whose construction was begun as far back as 1934, were built from sections that had been prefabricated inland and carried, partly by road on special transporters and partly via the canal system on barges, to the shipyards for assembling. The plan to mass-produce this class in the event of war, was not carried out because the necessary material was diverted to other war uses.[9]

The last prewar submarine was the K class which, outwardly, closely resembled the P class. Here again, the gun was mounted on an enclosed platform built into the conning tower.

Although each of the several new classes that appeared after 1945 probably incorporated more of the technical improvements of the German Type XXI than its predecessor did, the first postwar class, the W, could not have been identical to the XXI, since its development was complete by the beginning of 1944. W-class boats were about the same size as the German XXI and there were other external similarities, but it is both technically and chronologically impossible for them to have been identical, as it has frequently been suggested. Not until the Z class could the Russians have taken full advantage of their knowledge of the Type XXI boats, but even they had certain structural details that were in accordance with older Russian ideas. At first, both the W and the Z class had guns, weapons whose tactical value in a submarine began to be questioned in the middle of World War II. This question seems to have been answered in the Soviet Union much later than elsewhere: the newer W and Z boats were not fitted with guns, and many of the earlier boats that were so fitted have had them removed.

Being triple-screw boats, the smaller Q-class submarines cannot be included in the same line of development. The control tower is also quite different from those on other Soviet submarines: from its after end, the snorkel mast rises half again as high as the tower and is enclosed in its own tower-like plating.

As far as propulsion machinery is concerned, the Russians are obviously reluctant to break new ground. For instance, it is reported that cruisers up to the *Sverdlov* class and destroyers, at least up to the *Skoryis*, were not equipped with high-pressure, super-heated boilers, such as the American and German navies had developed years earlier for many types of ship. The boilers of Soviet warships are thought to operate at a pressure of 440 pounds per square inch, whereas 1,000 pounds per square inch was common in German ships, and up to 1,600 pounds per square inch was used in some cases. Just as the Germans had done, the Soviets seem to have had difficulty in operating the complicated and, therefore, very easily mishandled machinery that they found in the German cruisers, destroyers, and other vessels that fell into their hands. In fact, it has been reported that some of the boilers of the cruiser *Admiral Makarov* (ex-German *Nürnberg*) were damaged beyond repair by inexpert handling and that the ship was finally left with only her cruising diesels.* Mishandling could explain why, in the early postwar years, ex-German destroyers and torpedo boats apparently had to make frequent visits for repairs to the Neptun Shipyard at Rostock.

Diesel propulsion plays an important part in the Soviet Navy, as it does in most other navies, a feature that dates not just from the time when it acquired German ships as reparations, but from as long ago as the 1930s. At that time, the *Kirov*-class cruisers were fitted with diesel engines for cruising, and escort vessels, minesweepers, and minor craft had diesel main propul-

---

* Although the former *Nürnberg* has been broken up, her cruising diesels are still in use in a tanker.

sion. There has been no significant development of this form of propulsion since 1945, but small ships are still being fitted with it and, recently, it has been fitted in large support ships also.*

However, there is no sign of a change-over to diesel propulsion in the large, fast ships, or of any effort being made to bring one about, even though, considering the state of the art in Germany, the German technicians "under contract" could well have given valuable guidance. Simpler but more reliable turbine machinery is obviously preferred, because the problems of diesel propulsion for large, fast warships have not yet been satisfactorily solved. Lately, more attention has been paid to gas-turbine propulsion units, and the newest escort vessels, other than fast patrol boats, and guided-missile destroyers have been fitted with them as well as with conventional machinery.

There seems to be no doubt, however, that Soviet interest is centered on nuclear propulsion for submarines. Next to nothing is known of the present state of Soviet development in this area, but the details that are known about the icebreaker *Lenin,* the first Soviet ship to have nuclear propulsion, provide an interesting glimpse of present-day Soviet shipbuilding practice.[10]

* The first surface warships to be fitted with diesel propulsion were two Russian gunboats employed on the Caspian Sea, the *Kars* and the *Ardagan.* They were built between 1908 and 1909, had a displacement of 620 tons, a speed of 14 knots, and were armed with two 4.7-inch and two 3.9-inch guns.

Unquestionably, the *Lenin* is employed in research and for making experiments with reactors, as well as for icebreaking. In her, reactors of almost any weight and size can be tested and can provide all the information needed to improve nuclear power for submarines. This slow, systematic process of development shows an apparent self-imposed caution which may have the following psychological explanation: in those fields of scientific research and development where the Russians lag behind other nations, they allow little or nothing of their own efforts to become known because, to do so, would prevent them from maintaining that they are "the greatest." It is only in areas where they are ahead of other nations—their launching of the Sputnik in 1957, for instance—that they flood the rest of the world with technical details and propaganda, and this is done for the purpose of arousing respect and, maybe, even fear. They have not succeeded in taking the lead in the construction of warships, especially nuclear submarines, and it is questionable whether the American advantage can now be overtaken.

The *Lenin* was built in sections, some weighing as much as 75 metric tons (one metric ton equals approximately 1.1 U.S. tons) and is of all-welded construction. The lines of her steel hull are characteristic of an icebreaker: her forward plates are 2 inches thick, midships plates about 1¼ (waterline, almost 1½), and aft, almost 1¾ inches. Eleven transverse bulkheads extend to

The nuclear-powered icebreaker Lenin *in the Barents Sea.*

the upper deck and divide the hull into 12 watertight sections. Her longitudinal bulkheads are close to the outer skin in order to keep flooding and consequent list to a minimum. Her superstructure was prefabricated in three sections, each weighing 300 tons, and placed in position after the hull had been launched. Living quarters, lounges, smoking and music rooms, officers' messes, and so forth, which by Russian standards are quite comfortable, are forward. Near that area, there is a laboratory that is well equipped for a variety of research activities. The reactor ventilators are atop the mainmast. The boilers are amidships and are connected, both fore and aft, to turbo-generators with a power output that amounts to 30,000 kilowatts. Turbo-electric propulsion was chosen because of its reliability in and suitability to ice conditions.

There are three pressurized-water reactors, one of which is always in reserve, and the output of each exceeds that of the first nuclear power station built in the Soviet Union. The heat generated in the reactors is transferred by the primary circulating water to the boilers where the secondary steam is produced. This, in turn, is led to the turbines and converted to electricity, which drives motors coupled directly to the propellers. Ordinary water is used as the moderator and as the heat-transferring agent in the reactors. Radioactive water and waste is collected in special containers and dumped on uninhabited Arctic islands.

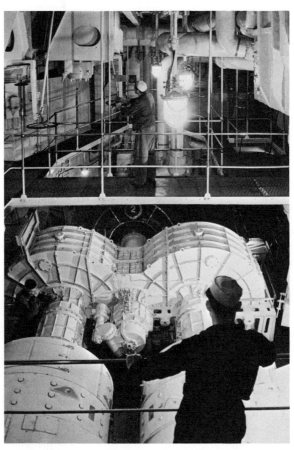

The turbo-generator spaces in the Lenin.

Because the ship is employed in areas where assistance could be provided only with the greatest difficulty, if at all, the expenditure on safety measures was considerable. Among other things, two entirely separate reactor-control positions have been provided, and adjustment and surveillance of the installation is completely automatic. The total weight of the shielding arrangements is more than 3,000 metric tons.

The power plant provides 19,600 shaft horsepower on the center shaft, and 11,500 shaft horsepower on each of the two outboard shafts. Thus, the ratio between displacement and power available is 1:2.75, 50 per cent greater than that of any other icebreaker. In open water, the *Lenin* has a maximum speed of 18 knots, and she can make two knots through ice more than 11 feet thick. Her heeling tanks have a capacity of about 4,000 tons. It has been said that her endurance without refueling the reactor is "several years."* This may well be an exaggeration, but endurance must be considerable, and it must be many times greater than that of any similar-sized ship with turbo-electric propulsion, which would have a full-power endurance of about 16 days. On the other hand, the very size of the *Lenin* has been found to have its drawbacks: for example, the ice floes she breaks off

are often so large that a smaller icebreaker must be used to break them up.

Protective arrangements in Soviet warships, particularly the armor of cruisers, can only be deduced from a few visible characteristics, or from the fact that such are not visible. The little that can be seen from outboard of the *Sverdlov* class, for instance, is waterline armor, the thickest section of which extends from the forward edge of the bridge to the after edge of the after 5.9-inch gunhouse. This belt of armor continues to the bow and stern, but is not as thick there as it is amidships: it probably extends some 6½ feet above the deep-load waterline. Obviously, it is thickest where it is abreast of important areas, such as the engine and boiler rooms and some of the magazines. On the basis of more detailed knowledge of similar ships of other navies, the armor plate is estimated to be somewhere between three and four inches thick amidships, and between one and two inches, at the most, fore and aft. The upper-deck armor may be from one to two inches thick, and the armored deck, two to three inches. The latter probably lies on the upper edge of the armored belt, but it is not known whether it is sloped towards the sides.

Since the uncompleted German heavy cruiser "L" (ex-*Lützow*) was handed over to Russia in 1940, and her sister ship the *Seydlitz* and the armored ship *Lützow* (ex-*Deutschland*) fell into Russian hands in 1945, it is fair to assume that Soviet constructors made use of the

---

* During 100 days of intensive operation, the *Lenin* is reputed to have consumed 200 grams of uranium. It would require 27,500 metric tons (1 metric ton is equal to approximately 1.1 U.S. tons) of oil to produce the same amount of power.

German practice of extensively subdividing the hull into watertight sections. The bulges and sloped side armor of the German ships do not seem to have been adopted.[11]

Motor torpedo boats are very important to the Soviet Navy because of their usefulness in restricted waters. Early representatives of this type came on the scene in 1930, and their hull and torpedo-launching arrangements resembled those on the 55-foot coastal motor boat developed in Great Britain by the John I. Thornycroft Company during the First World War. (The explanation for this resemblance might well be that the Russians salvaged one or more of the motor torpedo boats lost by the Royal Navy during the British attack on the Bolshevik fleet at Kronstadt in August 1919, and used them as prototypes.) The G-5 class, probably the first motor torpedo boats to be developed under the Soviet regime, were not built as displacement boats, but as single-step planing boats, i.e., the hull was V-shaped forward and U-shaped aft. Technically, displacement and planing boats differ as follows:

A displacement boat has a hull form that creates minimum resistance at all speeds. The water is divided by the stem and flows past either side of the hull. At high speeds, a small proportion of the water passes beneath the hull and causes the bow to lift slightly. Nevertheless, displacement does not vary, because the effect of the lifting of the bow is offset by a proportionate settling of the stern.

A planing boat, on the other hand, has a hull form that creates high resistance and, as speed increases, resistance increases until it exceeds the weight of the fore part of the boat and, thereby, forces the latter farther and farther out of the water. The water which then flows under the flat bottom supports the boat and causes it to skim along the surface of the water, rather than to pass through it. When planing commences, the displacement—not the actual weight of the boat—is reduced, as is the area of the hull that gets wet, so that skin friction, which normally increases with speed, is neither reduced nor significantly increased.

In the case of a displacement boat, the resistance curve steepens with every extra knot: consequently, to achieve speeds above a certain limit, much more powerful and disproportionately larger engines are required than is the case with a planing boat. The after keel in a planing boat is raised a little above the forward keel, which ends about halfway along the hull. When the boat is planing, the "step" so formed is above the surface, and the lift of the air cushion thus created serves to increase not only the total planing effect but also the stability.

A planing boat, with her one or more "steps," has, of course, certain disadvantages. For instance, interruption of the most important fore and aft component, the keel, causes a reduction of fore and aft stiffness. This drawback makes planing boats much less seaworthy than displacement boats and limits their use outside coastal waters. However, to attain the same speeds, the latter require more powerful engines than do planing boats.[12]

Dimensions of the G-5 Class

Length over-all — 62.6 feet
Length waterline — 56.6 feet
Beam —10.9 feet
Freeboard — 5.7 feet
Draft forward — 1.6 feet
Draft amidships — 2.1 feet
Draft aft — 4.1 feet
Design displacement — 14.85 metric tons

The G-5s had two motors, each developing a cruising power of 720 horsepower at 1,770 revolutions per minute, and a maximum speed of nearly 50 knots. Their armament consisted of two 21-inch torpedoes carried tail-first and launched astern, an extra-heavy 12.7-mm. machine gun and, reportedly, up to 16 depth charges as an alternative to the torpedoes. By and large, these boats appear to have been rugged and satisfactory, and were obviously used as models for types built since World War II. The latter, however, have two torpedo tubes on the upper deck on either side of the bridge.

During World War II, special types of motor gunboat were built in response to a particular operational requirement. They were equipped with tank turrets and took part in land fighting. At first, the 45-mm. turret from the T-26 tank was used, then the 3-inch turret from the T-34/76 and, after the end of the war, the 3.3-inch turret from the T-34/85. This arrangement was intended to be temporary, but apparently it proved very successful and, according to reports, is being incorporated in boats built chiefly for commando operations and the support of amphibious landings.

From time immemorial, shipbuilders have been seeking a way to increase the speed of ships and boats. Because hull resistance absorbs a large part of the energy produced, larger power units provide only a partial solution to this problem. However, if the hull can be lifted clear of the water, resistance can be reduced. Hydrofoils produce lift as soon as the boat is moving—in the same way as the wings of an aircraft lift it off the ground—and the hull is raised clear of the surface. Since hydrofoils offer very little resistance, speed is considerably increased and, because they create little wash, they have the important advantage of enabling boats fitted with them to travel along canals at high speeds.

Hydrofoils have been fitted to fast patrol boats of the P-8 type for trials, and in 1965 it became known that hydrofoil boats were being developed in the Baltic and Black seas. It is believed that the plan is to mass-produce this new class (NATO designation *Pchela*) for service as coastal patrol boats and submarine chasers. It can be expected that there will be more Soviet developments along this line.

Opposite: Sailors on board an SO-1 submarine chaser prepare to load antisubmarine-rocket launchers.

CHAPTER 4

Weapons and Equipment

It is quite apparent that there has been extensive standardization of weapons and equipment on board Soviet warships, and that weapon maintenance and the production of spare parts has been simplified. From the relatively small number of different marks of weapons, it may be assumed that each is produced in large numbers and that many are kept in reserve in armament depots. The fact that many of the weapons are not only outwardly similar to those used by the army, but are of the same caliber and have almost identical performance, indicates that they are adaptations of army weapons. From the technical and training point of view, this is unquestionably an advantage. Soviet army weapons are renowned for simplicity and ruggedness, and it may well be that Soviet naval weapons have the same attributes.

Guns

No heavy naval gun has been made in Russia since the Bolshevik Revolution: the Soviet Navy's heaviest gun (12-inch, 52 caliber, manufactured in 1910) dates from Tsarist times, and was mounted in the old *Gangut*-class battleships. The battleship that was laid down in 1938 or 1939 was to have had 16-inch guns, which the Soviets attempted, first, to get from an American armament concern, then, when they did not succeed, they turned to Germany for both guns and turrets. However, that plan, too, fell through when Germany attacked the Soviet Union in 1941.

The 7.1-inch, 57-caliber gun, with a maximum elevation of 40 degrees, delivered in 1933 and mounted in single turrets on the old cruiser *Krasnii Kavkaz,* is the

39

heaviest naval gun developed by Soviet armament constructors. *Kirov*-class cruisers, laid down between 1934 and 1939, were equipped with the same gun mounted in triple turrets. Apparently, however, it did not meet the required rate of fire, because the *Chapaev*-class cruisers, which were much larger than the *Kirov*s and were laid down between 1938 and 1939, were fitted with a smaller gun—5.9-inch, 50-caliber. This 5.9-inch gun was evidently intended to serve also as secondary armament for battleships. It probably did not become operational until after the war, when it was first seen by Western observers, and it is fairly certain that it is not yet fully automatic, as are the newer guns of the same or even larger caliber on British and American ships—for example, the 5.9-inch guns of the British *Tiger* class, and the 8-inch of the U.S. *Des Moines* class. The only characteristics of the Soviet 5.9-inch gun that are not in doubt are that it has a higher rate of fire than the 7.1-inch gun and, thanks to its maximum elevation of about 50 degrees, has some capability as an antiaircraft weapon. It was mounted on the *Sverdlov*-class cruisers, which succeeded the *Chapaev*s, both classes having triple mountings with individually laid guns, but because it is ill-suited to the continuous engagement of air targets, it can no longer be regarded as modern.

Also dating from Tsarist times is the 5.1-inch gun. The old, 55-caliber model, introduced into service in 1913, was taken over by the Soviets. During the 1930s,

A Sverdlov-*class cruiser exercises her 5.9-inch main battery.*

they developed for destroyers a 5.1-inch, 50-caliber gun, which appeared, first, in single mounts, later, in twin open mounts (*Tashkent* class) and, finally, in twin fully-enclosed gunhouses (from the *Otlichnyi* class to the *Skoryi* class). Since it was entirely hand-operated, its rate of fire was low, and its capability against air targets was limited. In the twin mounts, the barrels are not separately laid: they are connected by a solid coupling, which accounts for the small distance between them.

Outstanding among postwar developments is the 3.9-inch, 60-caliber gun that appeared in stabilized twin gunhouses on the *Chapaev* and *Sverdlov* cruisers. Stabilization of the gunhouses allows them to be tilted 25 degrees about their fore and aft axes. It is generally agreed that this gun is a fully automatic, multi-purpose weapon that can be used against both surface and air targets, but was probably designed primarily for use against the latter, and a high rate of fire can therefore be assumed. The trunk of the gunhouse in which it is mounted extends at least one deck down and encloses the ammunition supply shaft. The presence of this feature can be deduced from the absence of shipside scuttles abreast the position where the trunk is assumed to be, and the cupolas at the forward starboard corner of the gunhouse suggest the presence of a spotting radar. In outline, the turret resembles the 3.9-inch, C-38, antiaircraft gunhouse of the former German Navy, from which it was probably copied (see page 25). The gunhouses of *Tallinn* and *Kotlin* destroyers are very similar, but their multi-purpose guns are 5.1-inch and may well be an adaptation of the army's 5.1-inch M-1955 antiaircraft gun, which has an automatic fuze setter, an automatic rammer, an effective range of about 17,000 yards, and a rate of fire up to 15 rounds per minute. When performance requirements made the old 5.1-inch naval gun obsolete, a naval version of the M-1955 was developed for use on destroyers, and it is probably fully automatic.

Newer *Kola* and *Riga* frigates, *Purga* tenders, and *Don* depot ships have another mark of 3.9-inch gun in a single mount with a narrow shield. This gun has a high maximum elevation, but it is hand-operated; it may be a version of the 3.9-inch, land-based, M-1939 antiaircraft gun, which has a maximum range of about 11,000 yards and a rate of fire of from 15 to 20 rounds per minute.

A 3.3-inch gun has been seen mounted behind the shield of the older 3-inch 50-caliber, antiaircraft gun on *Kronstadt*-class submarine chasers; it has been seen on East Germany's *Krake, Habicht I,* and *Habicht II* minesweepers, also. It is probably closely related to the well-proved series of 3.3-inch, antiaircraft and antitank guns used by the land forces. The latter have an effective range of up to 11,000 yards, a rate of fire of from 15 to 20 rounds per minute, and a muzzle velocity of about 2,700 feet per second. The 3.3-inch, 51.5-caliber, SIS/S53 gun and the turret from the T-34/85 tank have been fitted on later motor gunboats: earlier boats of the same type have the 3-inch gun from the T-34/76 tank. *Otlichnyi*- and *Skoryi*-class destroyers have 3.3-inch antiaircraft guns in almost circular enclosed twin mounts with flat sloping fronts. The mounts project from the after deckhouse in somewhat the same way as did the antiaircraft gunhouses on the British battleships *Queen Elizabeth* and *Valiant* and battle cruiser *Renown* during World War II.

In 1962 it became known that the *Kynda*-class guided-missile cruisers had been fitted with a new type of 3-inch gun mounted in twin gunhouses, about 16 feet long, more than 9 feet tall, and nearly 13 feet wide. The barrels are mounted close together and may be rigidly connected: long slots permit high-angle fire. The limits of elevation may be from 10 to 85 degrees, a range that would permit the engagement of fast patrol boats at short range, as well as antiaircraft fire. These weapons are certainly fully automatic and, as of now, they are known to be fitted on *Kynda* guided-missile cruisers, *Kashin* guided-missile destroyers, and *Petya* and *Mirka* frigates.

Another postwar development worthy of note is the quadruple 47-mm. antiaircraft mount on the *Tallinn-* and *Kotlin*-class destroyers. The guns are mounted in pairs one above the other, as are the guns on the later 57-mm. mount. The two mounts can be distinguished by the relative positions of each pair of barrels when at zero elevation. On the 47-mm. mount, the muzzles are vertically above one another, whereas on the 57-mm. the lower pair projects beyond the upper. The 57-mm. version is being used primarily on the *Kildin-* and *Krupnyi*-class guided-missile destroyers, although certain auxiliary vessels, such as the *Lama*-class, are also fitted with it. The same guns, but in twin mounts, are carried on smaller vessels—minesweepers, landing vessels, and other auxiliaries. So far, the gun has been seen in a single mount only on rebuilt *Skoryi*-class destroyers and on *Sasha*-class minesweepers, in the latter case without a gun shield.

Another new 57-mm. antiaircraft weapon* came to light in 1964. It is twin-mounted and has appeared, so far, on the *Moskva*-class helicopter carriers, *Kresta*-class guided-missile cruisers, *Poti*-class submarine chasers, and *Ugra*-class depot ships. Projections on top of the gunhouse indicate that fire-control equipment is built in.

Among light antiaircraft guns, the 37-mm. has pride of place. An obsolescent model is mounted singly and has a crew of six: this model, also used by the army,**[14] was fitted on cruisers, destroyers, escorts, submarine chasers, and minesweepers built before and during the Second World War. Many of the ships built in the years immediately following the war have a 37-mm., semi-enclosed, twin mount—a development that seems to be purely naval. Both the single and the twin mounts are

---

* In the land forces, this caliber is represented by (a) antiaircraft: 57-mm. M-1950 field AA, 57-mm. S 60 L/73 on the SU-57-2 AA tank; (b) antitank: 57-mm. M-1943 L/73. The S 60 L/73 AA gun is a development of the German 55-mm. L/70.7 (Type 58) built during World War II. The latter was intended for shipboard use also, especially in destroyers, but never went into production.[13]

** Illustrations in the U.S. Army's *Handbook on the Soviet Army* (published in 1958) show that this gun is the 37-mm. M-1939 antiaircraft weapon that has been the standard Soviet light antiaircraft gun for a long time. Its characteristics are: muzzle velocity, 880 m. per sec.; barrel length, 259 mm.; operational weight, 2,100 kg.; rate of fire, 160-180 rounds per min.; max. height, 6,000 meters; max. range, 8,000 meters. Photographs leave no doubt about its similarity to the shipboard weapon.

hand-operated and are not, therefore, suitable for use against fast aircraft.

A new antiaircraft weapon that appears to have been developed for small fighting ships was first seen on the *Osa*-class missile patrol boats. Its barrels project from a domed gunhouse on a conical base, and it has been suggested that the 30-mm. ammunition, which it is now known to use, is belted, but this has not been confirmed. Besides the *Osa* class, *Shershen*-class patrol boats, and *Iurka*- and *Vanya*-class minesweepers are the only vessels on which this mount has been seen. The 25-mm. antiaircraft gun—possibly identical to the 23-mm. aircraft cannon—is another new development. Its effective altitude is estimated at 6,500 feet, and it also is found in a semi-enclosed, twin mount but, instead of being side by side, the barrels are one above the other, thus saving deck space. These weapons are fitted on fast patrol boats, submarine chasers, landing craft, minesweepers, tenders, and other types. For a while, this mark of gun was mounted in twin gunhouses of different shapes on the newer submarines (W and Z class). The twin 25-mm. antiaircraft gun with barrels mounted one above the other has only a shield and is somewhat older. Up to now, it has been seen on the *Kronstadt*-class submarine chasers, T-43 minesweepers, and coastal patrol boats.

A twin 25-mm. antiaircraft mount on a coastal patrol boat.

Soviet Naval Guns

Gun	Year Entered Service	Rate of Fire (Rounds per Minute)	Range (Miles)	Maximum Altitude (Feet)	Weight (Pounds)	Muzzle Velocity (Feet per Second)	Maximum Elevation (Degrees)
7.1″/57	1933	6	22.3	—	115	3,018	40
5.9″/50	1938	10	17.1	—	110	3,002	50
5.1″/50	1936	10	15.5	—	60	2,870	—
5.1″/60	1953	—	—	—	—	—	70
3.9″/60	1947	20	11.0	40,000	35	2,953	80
3.9″/50	1947	15	10.0	36,000	30	2,789	80
3.3″/51.5	—	—	—	—	—	—	—
3.3″/55	1943	18	8.6	30,000	21	2,707	75
3.0″/62	1961	—	—	—	—	—	85
57 mm.	1958/59	70	—	—	—	—	85
47 mm.	1953	—	—	—	—	—	85
37 mm./60	1944	150	5.0	18,500	1.5	2,900	85
30 mm.	1960/61	—	—	—	—	—	80
25 mm.	1950/51	—	1.25	—	—	—	85

Gun	Operation	Mounting	Ship types so armed
7.1″/57	semi-automatic	triple	*Kirov*-class cruisers
5.9″/50	semi-automatic	triple	*Chapaev*- and *Sverdlov*-class cruisers
5.1″/50	semi-automatic	twin and single	old destroyers and auxiliaries
5.1″/60	fully automatic	twin	new destroyers
3.9″/60	fully automatic	twin, stabilized	*Chapaev*- and *Sverdlov*-class cruisers
3.9″/50	semi-automatic	single	frigates and auxiliaries
3.3″/51.5	semi-automatic	single	motor gunboats
3.3″/55	semi-automatic	twin and single	submarine chasers and destroyers
3.0″/62	fully automatic	twin	guided-missile cruisers and destroyers and new frigates
57 mm.	fully automatic	quad, twin, and single	helicopter carriers and new cruisers and destroyers
47 mm.	fully automatic	quad	newer destroyers
37 mm./60	semi-automatic	single	small ships
30 mm.	fully automatic	twin	minesweepers and patrol boats
25 mm.	semi-automatic	twin	small ships and patrol boats

Soviet Naval Guns and Fire-Control Directors

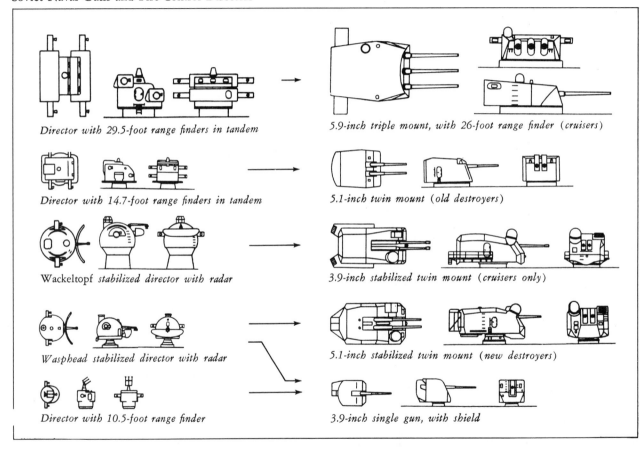

Director with 29.5-foot range finders in tandem

5.9-inch triple mount, with 26-foot range finder (cruisers)

Director with 14.7-foot range finders in tandem

5.1-inch twin mount (old destroyers)

Wackeltopf stabilized director with radar

3.9-inch stabilized twin mount (cruisers only)

Wasphead stabilized director with radar

5.1-inch stabilized twin mount (new destroyers)

Director with 10.5-foot range finder

3.9-inch single gun, with shield

Soviet Naval Guns and Fire-Control Directors

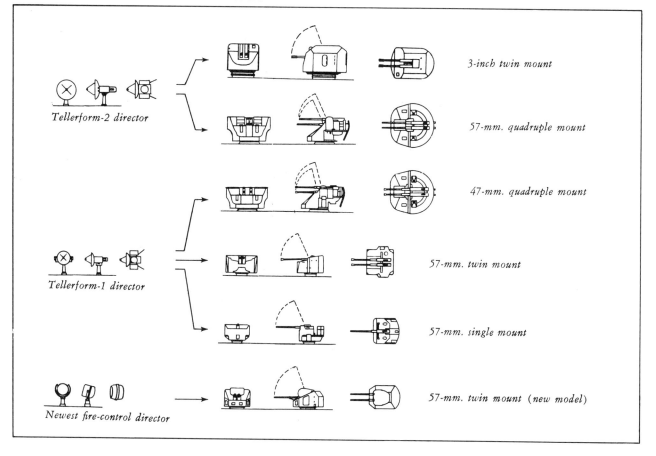

Tellerform-2 director

3-inch twin mount

57-mm. quadruple mount

47-mm. quadruple mount

Tellerform-1 director

57-mm. twin mount

57-mm. single mount

Newest fire-control director

57-mm. twin mount (new model)

Torpedoes

Very little is known about Soviet torpedoes. A 21-inch torpedo is in general use against surface targets: the 18-inch one used before the war by torpedo boats and escort vessels is no longer operational. The Naval Air Forces use a light torpedo—almost a ton—which may correspond to an 18-inch weapon. Surface ships fire torpedoes from single, twin, triple, quadruple, and quintuple tubes. Undoubtedly, the Soviets have made use of the latest German types, including pattern runners and homing torpedoes, that fell into their hands both during and after World War II, and have developed them further, especially for submarines.[15] They have developed antisubmarine torpedoes fired by surface vessels from trainable tubes, and it is now believed that they can fire antisubmarine or "normal" torpedoes from conventional tubes, as required.

A recent development is a special antisubmarine torpedo with a diameter of 15.7 inches, which is fired from relatively short (16½ feet) trainable tubes, mounted either singly or in groups of as many as five together. Submarine chasers of the SO-I class have had their after, 25-mm. antiaircraft mountings removed in order to allow these tubes to be fitted.

A 21-inch torpedo being eased through the forward hatch of an F-class submarine.

A coastal patrol boat launches a torpedo during a Navy Day demonstration at Sevastopol.

Mines

For many years, the Russian Navy has attached great importance to mines, because the shallow waters in which it is likely to operate are particularly well suited to that form of warfare.

Almost all types of ship are fitted with minelaying equipment. Rails, along which mines can be transported to ramps at the stern, are let into the deck: cruisers have twin sets of rails on either side of the upper deck with points, turntables, and cross-connecting tracks. Many submarines can carry mines in place of their torpedo outfit, and eject them through the tubes.

No details of the mines presently in use are available, but preference is probably given to those with non-contact firing—magnetic and acoustic—systems. There is a rumor that the Soviet Navy has developed nuclear mines, which could be laid, undetected by ordinary merchant ships, in important enemy harbors long before the outbreak of hostilities and, possibly, could be exploded by a long-running clockwork device.

Antisubmarine Weapons

Only since they were impressed by American nuclear submarines—especially the Polaris boats—have the Soviets pushed with any vigor for the development of special weapons for antisubmarine warfare.

Up to 1960, the primary weapon was the depth charge launched from single-barreled throwers mounted either rigidly to the deck or on trolleys that could be pushed along the minelaying rails, or from simple launchers. These fittings were, and in some cases still are, to be found near the stern on all types of ship. The old, cylindrical-shaped depth charges that are dropped over the stern by means of simple ramps and whose rate of sinking is slow, are still in use. Depth charges shaped to increase sink rates have not been seen.

Special depth-charge mortars appeared in 1955 and served as a stopgap pending the perfection of new weapons. They were fitted first on the *Kotlin* destroyers, then on the *Riga*-class frigates and T-43 minesweepers. Their barrels are quite short but have a large bore, and the fact that above each one there is a fixed container resembling a gas cylinder indicates the possibility that the depth charges are fired by compressed air, rather than by an explosive charge. Mortars appear to be loaded in much the same manner as are British Limbo and Squid mortars—that is, they are trained inboard about their fore and aft axes. Charges are brought to the mortar by means of small trolleys running along the

An SO-1 submarine chaser drops depth charges.

minelaying rails which, on the *Kotlin*s, at least, curve around the mortar.

A suspicion that the Soviets had an antisubmarine rocket launcher was confirmed only a short time ago, and since the equipment was first seen on the *Tallinn,* it is assumed that its trials were conducted on board her. Since about 1960, there have been two trainable mountings, each carrying 16 barrels in two layers one above the other, on the after end of her upper deck. Their diameter was estimated at not more than 10 inches and their range at almost 2,000 yards.[16] A five-barreled thrower, presumably for small vessels, appeared soon afterwards, and was followed by a version with twelve barrels mounted in a semicircle. A six-barreled launcher, thought to have the longest range of any antisubmarine rocket yet developed, has also been seen. A further development is the way in which this multiple launcher is arranged on the newer classes of ship. In contrast to the *Tallinn,* these ships have their launchers mounted so that they can fire forwards without the ship having to alter course. For example, the *Krupnyi*s have a 16-barreled launcher on either side of the bridge. This antisubmarine rocket launcher is probably now standard equipment on Soviet warships.

Special tubes for antisubmarine torpedoes were thought to have been fitted first to newer classes (see page 48). Meanwhile, however, one of the two conventional mountings on some *Skoryi*s and *Kotlin*s has been

A twelve-barreled antisubmarine-rocket launcher.

removed and the remaining tubes have been adjusted to launch both antiship and antisubmarine torpedoes. The space saved by this modification is available for the necessary preparation (see page 93).

Missile Armament on Submarines

The spoils that the two victorious powers of World War II acquired from Peenemünde provided the initial impetus for the use of submarines as missile launchers. Whereas the Americans based their early experiments on the V-1 rocket, it appears that, from the outset, the Russians concentrated on deploying V-2 ballistic missiles on their submarines. The technical basis for Russia's determination to acquire that ability was very probably the Lafferentz Project, full details of which fell into Russian hands. Started in Germany in the late years of the war, the project aimed at launching A-4 (V-2) rockets from U-boats in the following manner:

A Type XXI submarine, which could remain submerged for long periods, was to tow a V-2 rocket enclosed in a submersible container. When the firing site was reached, the container would be brought to a vertical position and ballasted by adjustment to its trim tanks until it just broke the surface. A party of men from the submarine would then take to a rubber dinghy and pull for the container: there, they would open the nose cap of the rocket, fill the latter with fuel from tanks in the container, and make the preparations necessary for firing. That done, the party would return to the submarine, and the missile would be fired by means of a connecting cable, whereupon the empty container would be sunk. Each submarine was to be capable of towing three containers.

Preliminary trials were carried out in the Baltic Sea towards the end of May 1944, but the military situation at the beginning of 1945 forced their discontinuance. Had this weapon become operational, the commanders would have faced difficulties:

1. The submarine had to surface in order to allow the missile to be prepared for firing.

2. The planned preparation time was between 20 and 30 minutes and, from the moment the container was brought to the vertical, the submarine was for all practical purposes, incapable of maneuvering: in the event of a surprise attack, she could only slip the container and dive. Under such circumstances, the container would be destroyed by a suitable automatic mechanism to prevent it from falling into enemy hands.

3. In order to fire as far inland as possible, the submarine had to launch her rockets from close to the enemy coast and, even without increased surveillance, a wide area of coastal waters would have been dangerous territory for submarines.

The sighting made some years ago of Soviet submarines towing large containers would indicate that the Soviets carried on this German concept by "navalizing" the T-1, surface-to-surface missile, which was developed from the German A-4. Obviously, however, that system was abandoned and the liquid-fueled T-1 was replaced by the Golem series of weapons, all of which had water- and pressure-tight skins and could be towed ready

A W-class/Twin Cylinder guided-missile submarine at Sevastopol.

for use. They needed only to be brought to the vertical, which was done by flooding internal trim tanks, and fired, probably while the submarine remained submerged.

Of course, towing either rockets or containers creates some major problems. The speed and freedom of maneuver of the towing submarine are reduced signifi-cantly and, should she be detected, she would have difficulty evading pursuers. Care must be taken to avoid mishaps that might cause the rocket or container to float to the surface and appear on a radar screen. Last, but by no means least, there is the danger of tows parting and a valuable missile being lost.

All of the foregoing information concerning early developments is based on supposition. It can, however, be said with almost complete certainty, that Soviet submarines no longer carry liquid-fueled rockets, whose volatile and highly explosive contents are a source of constant danger and most unsuitable for submarine use. Undoubtedly, the Soviets have turned to the development of solid-fueled rockets and, when first they entered that field they had to be content with modest performance.

Although there had been newspaper reports about Soviet missile submarines and there was no doubt that they existed, until the beginning of 1962 the outside world had not seen any, and had no documentary evidence to prove their existence. It fell to the Soviet military newspaper *Krasnaia Zvezda* to lift the veil of secrecy by publishing, on 23 February 1962, a picture of a modified W-class submarine with a missile launcher. With unusual candor, the caption over the picture noted that the missiles could be launched only when the submarine was surfaced. Since then, several classes of missile submarines have become known, and two lines of development that have probably proceeded in parallel, can be discerned.

The first line of development concerned arming Soviet submarines with types of missiles that had been carried for some years by surface vessels. This line might be compared with the development which the United States abandoned in 1959 in favor of the Fleet Ballistic Missile program. The American missiles were intended for use against land targets and had ranges up to 1,000 miles, whereas the Soviet versions have significantly shorter ranges, rationalized, perhaps, by calling them anti-ship weapons. Thus, the mission of submarines armed with these weapons would be chiefly tactical, and the implication is that conventional submarines armed with torpedoes can no longer approach fast task forces. However, missiles can be launched at a presumably safe distance. Nevertheless, there is a serious disadvantage that should not be overlooked: in order to launch an aerodynamic missile, a submarine must surface, and thus expose herself to detection by enemy radar.

The fact that no parent vessel with large detection and guidance radars has been seen indicates that these submarine-launched, surface-to-surface rockets are radio-guided. In any case, the weight of such radars and the space they take up make them unsuitable for submarine use. The submarines probably operate in groups and are deployed so that they can act as "relay stations" for the transmission of guidance signals to the missiles. Recently, a W-class submarine equipped with a large radar antenna was sighted, and it is fair to assume that she serves as a relay station. Her NATO designation is W class/Canvas Bag, and the missile concerned is probably the Shaddock, with which the *Kynda*-class missile cruisers are armed.

A midships view of a W-class/Twin Cylinder submarine, showing one of her two containers for Shaddock missiles.

Two different versions of modified W-class submarines armed with Shaddock missiles were the first to appear, and were followed by the J class and finally the E class. There have been three different installations for the missiles: first, they were housed in containers on the superstructure (W class/Twin Cylinder); then, in an extended conning tower (W class/Long Bin); and, lastly, in containers that were built into the upper part of the hull (J and E classes).

Efforts to reduce resistance and cavitation, which would, respectively, cut down speed and aid detection by the enemy probably account for the different installations. Abaft the conning tower of the modified W class/Twin Cylinder, there is a ramp on which are mounted two cylindrical launching tubes: the ramp can be elevated to about 25 or 30 degrees, but apparently it cannot be trained. Both launchers project outboard and have a sort of deflector plate on either side, probably to protect them against both head and beam seas. The chances are that only a few of these experimental conversions, first seen in 1958 or 1959, were made and that they have not been superseded.

A midships view of a W-class/Long Bin guided-missile submarine, showing the unusual configuration of her conning tower.

In the second W-class version—Long Bin—it is clear that attempts have been made to resolve resistance and cavitation problems and, at the same time, to double the outfit of missiles and, thus, increase the operational effectiveness of the submarines. It can be seen that an additional section, about 21 feet long, has been inserted into the hull and on it there is a new, streamlined conning tower, in which four forward-firing launchers with an elevation of about 14 degrees have been built. Greater elevation can probably be achieved by lowering the after ends of the launchers. The conning tower extends outboard of the hull, apparently to make room for the launchers to be mounted in pairs. The layout is similar to that on the *Osa* class of guided-missile patrol boats, and allows the rear launchers to fire over the forward ones. This version of W-class submarines originated in 1961 or 1962.

The third type of installation is found on the conventionally powered J-class submarines, which have a very high freeboard. These vessels have reverted to the concept of firing missiles from twin launchers with a common ramp built almost completely into the hull. There is one pair of launchers forward of the conning tower and another pair aft of it, and when the side plates are folded, the launchers can be elevated to some 25 or 30 degrees. The J class was probably an experimental version that proved successful, since a similar layout is now found on the large, E-class, nuclear submarines.

Not only do these submarines have to surface in order to launch their missiles, but they have another considerable disadvantage in that their missiles are carried in containers outside the pressure hull, and even though the containers themselves are pressure-tight, missile maintenance must be carried out on the surface. What this means in terms of vulnerability to detection in wartime requires no comment.

The second line of missile-submarine development emphasized ballistic missiles. At first, several conventional Z-class submarines were modified, followed by the G and H classes. They all have two or three launching tubes built into the sail, with one missile stowed in each tube. Launch is vertical and is similar to the Polaris system.

Presumably, the first missile especially intended for submarine use was the Comet-2 that became operational in 1958. It is a single-stage, liquid-fueled rocket, 49 feet long, 13 inches in diameter, and has a launch weight of 18 metric tons. With a maximum range of 500 miles, it has a programmed guidance system. Being liquid-fueled, this model may well have proved too dangerous for use on submarines, as has been suggested. The Sark (formerly Snark), which was operational by 1962, was probably the first really practical ballistic missile. A further development is named Serb, and there is little doubt that both can be armed with nuclear warheads. The Sawfly is the third generation of this missile.

Missile Armament on Surface Ships

Surface-to-surface missiles were obviously based on the German V-1, which is actually a small unmanned aircraft. Not long after the end of the war, the Soviets developed for their land forces the similar J series of missiles, from which a naval version, the Strela (SS-N-1), which became operational in 1957 or 1958, appears to have been derived. This missile, whose massive, 110-foot launchers take up a great deal of deck space is carried by *Kildin*- and *Krupnyi*-class destroyers. Its elevation cannot exceed 30 degrees, and it must be brought to zero elevation for loading. With its wings folded, it is pushed horizontally out of the magazine on to a loading ramp situated beneath a housing which resembles an upturned bathtub and which opens upwards and sideways. It is thought that this is where final preparations for warm-up and launching take place—an important consideration when operations in the Arctic are involved.

Running almost parallel in development was a weapon system for minor war vessels. This is the Styx (SS-N-2) and it has, so far, been fitted to the *Komar* and *Osa* classes of patrol boats, on which the forward-firing launchers are mounted with a fixed elevation of about 20 degrees.

As development proceeded, the Strela was succeeded by the Shaddock (SS-N-3), a considerably improved version of the surface-to-surface Shaddock missile used by the land forces. As of now, the naval Shaddock is

Guideline surface-to-air missiles on the Dzerzhinski.

carried by *Kynda* and *Kresta* guided-missile cruisers, and by a number of submarines. The missiles are stowed in cylindrical containers that look something like overgrown torpedo tubes, and quadruple mountings have been observed. On submarines, the launchers are fixed, but on the *Kynda*-class cruisers they can be trained through more than 250 degrees and elevated up to 30 degrees. There are magazines both forward and aft for the stowage of reload missiles. Installation on *Kresta*-class cruisers is similar.

Having given priority to the development of surface-to-surface missiles, the Soviets soon realized that they had left a gap in the antiaircraft defense of their warships and that, in order to close it, they needed a special weapon system. It is remarkable that, although several well-proved, land-based systems were available, it was a long time before any warship was equipped with one of them. This surprising shortcoming may have resulted from the difficulties of guiding a missile from a moving platform, such as a ship. Apparently, these problems were not overcome until 1961 or 1962, when the first trials of ship-launched, surface-to-air missiles were carried out. The ship involved was the cruiser *Dzerzhinski,* and the missile was the Guideline, which had been in service on land since about 1957. This shipboard installation was probably intended only for trials, since the size of the Guideline system makes it unsuitable for destroyers, and further development led to the Goa

A Goa surface-to-air missile on its shipboard launcher.

system. Here is another missile first developed for use on land, then adapted for use at sea. Both the Goa and the Guideline launchers are mounted on top of the magazine and are loaded in a vertical position, as are those on the U.S. Navy's guided-missile frigates.

Presumably, minor war vessels, particularly river craft, are fitted with launchers for free-flight rockets (successors to the well-known Katushas).

Naval Missiles

Strela (*SS-N-1*) has been operational since about 1957 or 1958. It is not rocket-powered, but is driven by a gas turbine. Shortly after launch, a booster rocket is automatically jettisoned. The Strela is a small unmanned aircraft rather than a rocket, and it carries a high-explosive, or possibly even a nuclear, warhead. Its speed is transonic and its range is not very great. It seems to have an infrared homing head but, since such a head cannot provide sufficient guidance against continually moving ship targets, the missile is probably tracked by radar and given course corrections by command radio. Because its cruise altitude is fairly low, the range of this system is limited by the curvature of the earth. If it goes below the horizon, relay stations, such as helicopters, ships in suitable positions, or surfaced submarines, have to be used to transmit guidance signals. When the missile gets within a certain distance of its target, the infrared homing head takes over and controls the final stages of the flight.

Styx (*SS-N-2*) is similar to the Strela. It does not have swept-back wings, but it, too, is powered by a gas turbine and has a booster rocket that is jettisoned. Its guidance system is, presumably, the same as that of the Strela but, because it has a lower radar horizon range, when it is launched from a missile patrol boat, its range must be significantly lower, and the use of a nuclear warhead is, therefore, probably out of the question.

Shaddock (*SS-N-3*) is a "navalized" version of the land-based tactical missile of the same name, which has been exhibited repeatedly at demonstrations of military power in Moscow's Red Square. It has three stabilizing fins, one situated centrally. Two boosters beneath the missile body are jettisoned as soon as the cruise motor takes over. This missile is believed to have command mid-course guidance and a homing head.

Sark (*SS-N-4*) formerly Snark, is a solid-fuel, ballistic missile with a separable, probably nuclear, warhead. It is known that, to begin with, this weapon could not be launched from beneath the surface, but it may well be that the problem of doing so has now been solved. Guidance is by an inertial navigation system. An unusual feature is that the seven 31-inch-long nozzles project from the base of the rocket.

Serb (*SS-N-5*) was first seen in 1965. It is capable of submerged launch and, while its external dimensions are considerably less than those of the Sark, its range is much greater.

Sawfly (*SS-N-6*) was first seen in November 1967. Its external dimensions indicate that it is larger than the Serb and smaller than the Sark. It has a nuclear warhead, but its range and launching capabilities are unknown.

Guideline (*SA-N-1*) is, as of now, the foremost area defense weapon of the Warsaw Pact powers. It is a two-stage rocket, the first stage probably being a booster that is jettisoned at "all-burnt." A beam-riding guidance

Sailors guide a Styx missile onto its launching rails aboard a patrol boat.

system is known to be used, very likely in conjunction with an infrared homing head.

Goa (*SA-N-2*), like the Shaddock, was introduced by the land forces, then adapted for use at sea. It is a beam-rider with two-stage, solid-fuel rocket propulsion. The first stage is for launching and is automatically jettisoned when burnt out. It appears to be the intention to make this weapon standard equipment on all Soviet warships big enough to carry it.

Kennel, Kipper, Kangaroo, and Kitchen are, basically, small unmanned aircraft with explosive warheads. They are carried beneath the fuselage of long-range bombers and, when the target has been sighted, they are released at a great altitude.

Soviet Naval Missiles

Type	In Service Since	Length (Feet)	Diameter (Feet)	Span (Feet)	Weight (Tons)	Speed (Mach)	Range (Miles)	Power Plant	Guidance System	Warhead
Surface-to-Surface Guided Missiles										
Strela (SS-N-1)	1957/58	29.5	4.9	11.4	6.0	1.2	62–112	ram jet and booster	radio and homing	high-explosive or nuclear
Styx (SS-N-2)	1959/60	21.3	2.9	6.8	1.2	0.8	12–18	ram jet and booster	radio and homing	high-explosive
Shaddock (SS-N-3)	1960/61	32.8	3.2	9.5	13.0(?)	2.5	216–248	fuel booster motors and 1 turbo-jet for cruising	radio and homing	high-explosive or nuclear
Surface (Underwater)-to-Surface Ballistic Missiles										
Sark (SS-N-4)	1959	49.2	5.9	?	18–20	5.0	372 (max.)	solid-fuel motors	inertial	nuclear 1 megaton
Serb (SS-N-5)	1963/64	35.1	4.9	?	15	7.0	1,242 (max.)	solid-fuel motors	inertial	nuclear 1 megaton
Sawfly (SS-N-6)	1967	42.6	6.0	?	?	?	1,500?	?	?	nuclear 1 megaton

Type	In Service Since	Length (Feet)	Diam- eter (Feet)	Span (Feet)	Weight (Tons)	Speed (Mach)	Range (Miles)	Power Plant	Guidance System	Warhead
Surface-to-Air Guided Missiles										
Guideline (SA-N-1)	1958/59	34.4	1.6	9.8	2.5	2.1	25	solid-fuel motors	radar (beam rider) and homing	high-explosive
Goa (SA-N-2)	1961/62	20.3	0.9	4.5	0.4– 0.6	2.0– 2.5	9–12	solid-fuel motors	radar (beam rider) and homing	high-explosive
Air-to-Surface Guided Missiles										
Kennel	?	26.2	?	?	?	?	56	?	?	?
Kipper	?	31.1	?	?	?	?	112	?	?	?
Kangaroo	?	49.2	?	?	?	?	372	?	?	?
Kitchen	?	?	?	?	?	?	496	?	?	?

Soviet Naval Missiles

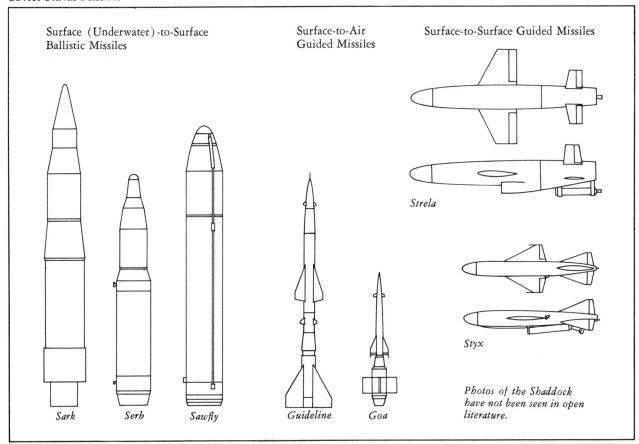

Surface (Underwater)-to-Surface
Ballistic Missiles

Surface-to-Air
Guided Missiles

Surface-to-Surface Guided Missiles

Strela

Styx

Sark

Serb

Sawfly

Guideline

Goa

*Photos of the Shaddock
have not been seen in open
literature.*

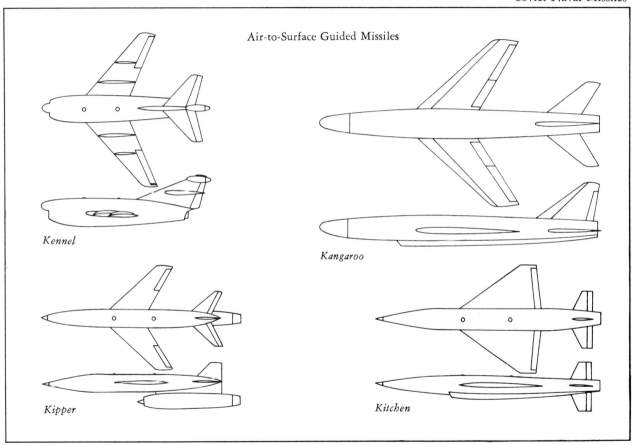

Air-to-Surface Guided Missiles

Kennel

Kangaroo

Kipper

Kitchen

Soviet Shipboard Missile Launchers and Missile Guidance Antennas

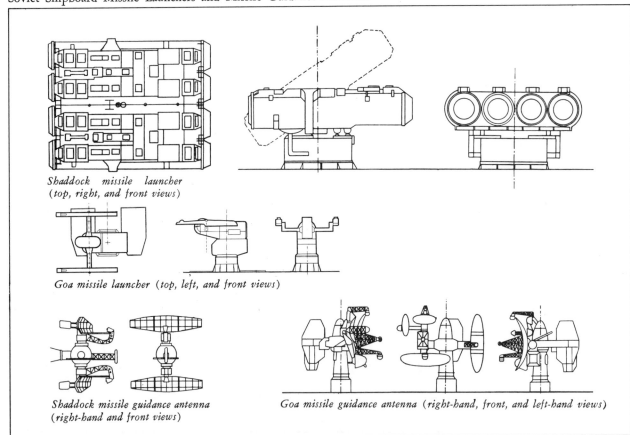

Shaddock missile launcher
(top, right, and front views)

Goa missile launcher (top, left, and front views)

Shaddock missile guidance antenna
(right-hand and front views)

Goa missile guidance antenna (right-hand, front, and left-hand views)

Naval Aviation Weapons

The Naval Air Forces have recently been partially rearmed. Bombs, torpedoes, and conventional aircraft cannon and machine guns have been replaced by air-to-air and air-to-surface missiles.

A series of the latter has been developed especially for use by the Naval Air Forces. Badger-B-type bombers carry two Kennel missiles under their wings, and Badger-Cs are fitted to carry a Kipper missile beneath the fuselage.

Some bombers of the Bear-B type carry one Kangaroo air-to-surface missile, and the Blinder type, carrying the Kitchen missile with a range of 500 miles, is reported to have entered service with the Naval Air Forces.

Antisubmarine helicopters are generally armed with small free-flight rockets.

Fire-Control Equipment and Radar

Soviet warships are equipped with numerous optical range finders and fire-control devices. All cruisers and destroyers up to and including the *Skoryi* class have rotatable director towers, on which two or three range finders, whose base lengths run between 13 and 30 feet, are mounted in tandem. This tandem mounting is typically Russian and had appeared earlier on the rebuilt battleships of the *Gangut* class and on the cruiser *Krasnii Kavkaz*. There are no less than eight large range finders, all evidently stereoscopic, on the *Chapaev-* and *Sverdlov*-class cruisers.

Besides that equipment, the cruisers and the destroyer *Tallinn* have hemispherical stabilized directors mounted on a slightly conical tower and fitted with a radar antenna. Their characteristic shape is similar to that of the antiaircraft directors on battleships and heavy cruisers of the former German Navy where, as mentioned previously, they were known as *Wackeltöpfe,* or wobbling pots. However, whereas the German system operated optically, it may be deduced that the Russian fire-control system is partly electronic and partly electric. This deduction is made because the optical range finder, whose base is 13 feet, projects from either side of the director, and the parabolic radar antenna with adjustable elevation, projects from the front.* A similar but smaller and lighter director, mounted on a much narrower tower than those on the cruisers and on the *Tallinn,* is to be seen above the bridges of newer ships—so far on the *Kotlin*-class destroyers, *Riga*-class frigates, *Purga*-class tenders, and *Don*-class depot ships. This development of the *Wackeltopf* represents an effort to reduce top weight. The combined optical-electronic fire-control system

* Since Germany was delivering material to the Soviet Navy up to the spring of 1941, Soviet warships were equipped with *Wackeltopf* directors (without radar) during World War II. A cruiser—either the *Molotov* or the *Voroshilov*—stationed in the Black Sea had one by April 1944.

housed in the director is similar to its predecessor, but its optical base is only about 10 feet long. A radar antenna with a projecting feed horn which is also mounted on the director, together with the narrow, conical tower, gives the equipment the appearance of a wasp's head; hence, its code name. *Krupnyi*-class destroyers have a version of the Wasphead that has no radar antenna.

Cruisers have more optical range finders in their main turrets. On the *Chapaev* and *Sverdlov* classes they are about 30 feet long, but on the older ships they may be only about 26 feet. They project from either side of a turret and enable it to fire in local control, should the main director fail. The elevated turrets on the *Chapaev*s and *Sverdlov*s, the multi-purpose antiaircraft mounts on cruisers, and the main mounts on newer destroyers—*Tallinn* and *Kotlin,* for instance—all have electronic equipment. In each case, the radome projects like a wart, or frog's eye, from the starboard, forward corner of the turret or mount. On the triple turrets, it is mounted vertically, while on the multi-purpose mounts, it is tilted about 45 degrees forward. These radars for spotting the fall of shot might have been the forerunners of the Tellerform (or, dish-shaped) equipment, since the *Tallinn* originally had an almost identical tilted dome projecting from a housing mounted on a pedestal,* an installation which was later replaced by the Tellerform radar.

The Tellerform fire-control system on the modern warships was developed for the newer antiaircraft guns, and probably operates in the centimeter wave band. Its dish-shaped parabolic reflectors are unmistakable and give rise to its name. Doubtless, each equipment can be trained and elevated so that it can be used on either beam in conjunction with the appropriate twin or quadruple mount.

So far, two sizes of Tellerform have been developed: Tellerform-1, which is used only in connection with the 47-mm. quadruple and the 57-mm. single mounts; and Tellerform-2, which is used with all other 57-mm. mounts and the 3-inch twin gunhouses.

A new electronic fire-control system is in use in combination with 57-mm. twin gunhouses on *Moskva*-class helicopter carriers, *Kresta*-class guided-missile cruisers, *Poti*-class submarine chasers, and *Ugra*-class depot ships, and with 30-mm. twin gunhouses on small war vessels, such as the *Osa, Shershen,* and *Iurka* classes. This equipment looks like a searchlight, and is similar to the AN/SPG-55 detection radar on American ships fitted with Terrier missiles. It is obviously the successor to the Tellerform radars that appeared with the 57-mm. quadruple mount on the *Lama*-class missile supply ships and with the twin mount of similar caliber on the T-58 minesweepers.

There is nothing unusual about the fitting of other

* When this temporary director was first seen in a photograph, it was mistaken for an antisubmarine-rocket launcher, similar to the American Alfa.

equipment, such as radar aerials, whip aerials, and so forth. They follow general naval practice.

Until about 1953 or 1954, Soviet warships had considerably less radar equipment than did ships of the same age in Western navies. The Soviet lag in the development of radar came to light when the cruiser *Sverdlov* showed up at the Naval Review at Spithead, England, in 1953. Only in recent years have radars been in use in large numbers, and in variety of type and external dimensions.

All-round search antennas were first seen on the *Tallinn* in 1954, but it is only since 1956 that they have been normal equipment on Soviet destroyers, frigates, and other types. The shape of these antennas, which consist of a broad, sharply curved reflector of small vertical extent with two stabilizing vanes projecting from the rear in a V, makes them remarkable. The four known models of all-round search radar have been designated Head Net-1, Head Net-2, Head Net-3, and Head Net-4. The first three resemble one another in appearance and all have the characteristic vanes. Head Net-4, which has no vanes, seems to have been designed for small ships. It has been seen on *Poti*-class submarine chasers and on auxiliaries of the *Ugra* and *Lama* classes and, for a while, one was fitted to the mainmast of a *Krupnyi*-class guided-missile destroyer (see page 272). Much smaller, dish antennas, also without vanes, are fitted on the *Komar* and *Osa* missile patrol boats.

A larger and probably heavier antenna, the Big Net, is seen only occasionally, and is recognizable by its big elliptical reflector and large vanes. It was sighted first on the *Chukotka*-class, missile-tracking ships, and later on the *Dzerzhinski* missile cruiser. One or two other *Sverdlov*-class cruisers have been fitted with it and recently it has been observed on the mainmast of at least one *Kashin*-class, guided-missile destroyer, where it was most likely being used experimentally. The new *Kresta*-class cruisers may have had this antenna fitted while they were building. Head Net-3 with back-to-back antennas can be seen on at least one *Krupnyi* guided-missile destroyer, on the *Chazhma*-class, missile-tracking ships, and recently has been seen on *Kresta* cruisers. This type of antenna obviously doubles the data rate of other types, and one of the two Head Net-3 installations on the *Kresta* class can be elevated. The largest and most likely the heaviest antenna, which probably has 3-D functions (height-finding, range-finding, and bearing-finding), is installed in the *Moskva* helicopter carriers.

Modern fast patrol boats also have a radome on a special mast behind the bridge. The dome is purely protective and covers a rotating radar similar to the German 90-mm. type Berlin of 1944 and 1945. Most of the successors to this radome that have been seen are on fast patrol boats, but it has also been fitted on SO-I-class submarine chasers. The new radome has a larger diameter, but is much flatter.

Soviet Shipboard Radar Antennas

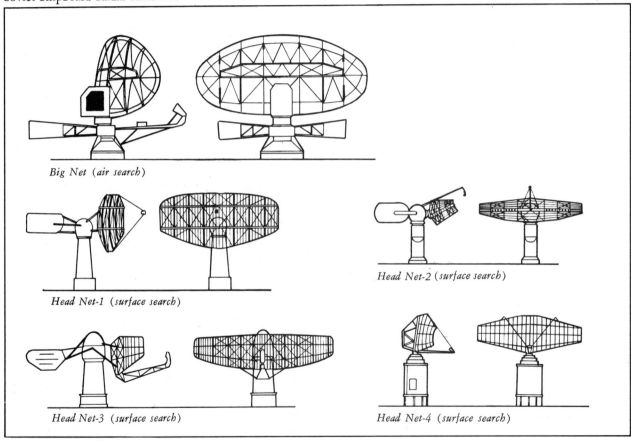

Big Net (air search)

Head Net-1 (surface search)

Head Net-2 (surface search)

Head Net-3 (surface search)

Head Net-4 (surface search)

A new piece of shipboard equipment is the so-called Uda-Yagi aerial, which consists of two X-shaped aerials mounted close together, and operates in the metric wave band for air early warning and surveillance. So far, it has been seen on *Chapaev-* and *Sverdlov*-class cruisers and on the *Tallinn*-class destroyer. The outward appearance of the antenna of the guidance systems on missile cruisers and destroyers varies considerably. No guidance system is visible on the Strela-equipped *Kildin* and *Krupnyi* classes or on the Styx-equipped *Komar*s and *Osa*s. On the other hand, the *Kynda* class has a fully trainable antenna system mounted on brackets projecting some distance forward or aft, as appropriate, from each mast. Since these antennas, which have the characteristic vanes, always appear as a double system, it may be inferred that one is for tracking the target, and the other is for tracking the missile.

Goa guidance equipment consists of several single antennas on a common mount that can be trained through 360 degrees.

Similar parabolic antennas on a common mounting are fitted on the cruiser *Dzerzhinski* for target acquisition and tracking in connection with the Guideline missile. On an elevated mounting abaft the forward stack, there is a large antenna that can be rotated and "wobbled" in order to obtain the range and altitude of target aircraft. The *Dzerzhinski* is the only Soviet vessel on which this layout has, so far, been seen.

Underwater Detection Systems

Underwater detection systems, called Tamir stations, were developed during—maybe, even before—World War II, but as yet no details are available in the West. A horn-like construction that projects from the bows of newer submarines is very likely an underwater detection device similar to the sonar equipment carried by NATO submarines.

CHAPTER 5

Ships of the Soviet Navy

All the important types of ship will be discussed in this chapter, the amount of space devoted to each depending upon its current operational effectiveness. More detailed information on each type is to be found in Appendix I.

Older classes of ship have been omitted from this book because either their continued existence cannot be confirmed, or they do not meet present-day requirements and can be ignored.

Aircraft Carriers

The Soviet Navy has no aircraft carriers. A few years ago, there was a rumor that two 55,000-ton carriers were being built in Black Sea yards, but there has been no confirmation of it, and there are no grounds for assuming that the Soviets intend to build any carriers.

Helicopter Carriers

Towards the end of September 1968, a Soviet naval vessel passed through the Bosporus en route to the Mediterranean. She was the helicopter carrier *Moskva,* a ship about which much had been said and that naval experts had been waiting for a year to see. The Soviets classify her as an ASW cruiser.

She might be described as a hermaphrodite: her unusually high, piled-up superstructure, which arises amidships and extends towards her bow makes that part of her look like a cruiser, whereas her after deck, used as a flight deck, makes her look like what she is—a helicopter carrier. She bears some resemblance to the Italian *Vittorio Veneto* and *Andrea Doria,* but she is more distinctly a helicopter carrier than they are. The ship she most closely resembles is the French *Jeanne d'Arc.*

The helicopter carrier Moskva *under way in the Mediterranean.*

According to information currently available, this class, which consists of the *Moskva* and the *Leningrad,* has a displacement of 18,000 tons: maximum displacement is listed as 20,000 tons, but might be somewhat greater. Over-all length is given as 670 feet, and that might be close to the correct figure: the helicopter deck is said to take up half the length. The beam appears to be about 88 feet but, since it is easy to see that the helicopter deck has an overhang, that figure can apply only to the after part of the ship.

The propulsion plant is believed to consist of steam turbines. The large conspicuous openings of the ventilation system lie somewhat forward under the funnel in the area of the bridge superstructure, with which they are combined, but on the port side only. The openings might, however, be air intakes and, if so, they would suggest gas-turbine propulsion. In any event, together with the inclined funnel, they show that the boilers or gas turbines are situated directly under the bridge structure.

The hull has a high freeboard, a flush deck, and a short fantail. The edges of the main deck have a quarter-circular profile and, instead of coming to a sharp point at the bow, the main deck is rounded. This is because the stem above the waterline is not pointed, as is the case on most Soviet warships, but also rounded. The cutaway stern, on the other hand, conforms to normal practice in Soviet warship construction. It is worth noting that because the high freeboard has obviated the necessity for much sheer, the fore part of the main deck rises only slightly. There are not many portholes but, just under the flight deck, there are some small openings at irregular intervals along the hull. The purpose of the openings is not clear: they look like ventilators for the dispersal of fumes when helicopters are being refueled in the hangar, yet seem too small to serve that purpose. There is no sign of aviation fuel pipes running along the ship's sides, as on many American aircraft and helicopter carriers. The helicopter deck extends over the fantail, where it rests on stanchions. The only elevator, situated directly under the funnel, is closed by doors on the helicopter deck side and is so narrow that it can accommodate only small helicopters: at first, it had been supposed in the West that it would be possible to load airplanes on it. On either side of the fantail, which serves as a boat deck, a motor launch hangs on davits.

Comparison between the *Moskva* class and the *Iwo Jima* class of American amphibious assault ships makes it clear that earlier estimates that the former would carry 30 helicopters per ship, were much too high. Ships of the *Iwo Jima* class were built along the lines of aircraft carriers and, consequently, have spacious accommodations for helicopters, but still the maximum number they can take on board is 32. Presumably, the hangar deck of the *Moskva* ends where the smoke or gas uptakes lead through it. True, it extends forward on both sides of the uptakes, but those extensions cannot go beyond where the ammunition elevators and the deck reinforcements of the 57-mm. AA gun mounts break through the deck. This means that, not counting the fantail or the space narrowed by the uptakes and the elevator, a maximum of 312 feet of the hangar deck is usable. If, then, the hangar deck is about 65 feet in width, the usable area is in the neighborhood of 20,000 square feet. In theory, this area is large enough to accommodate from 21 to 24 Kamov-25K helicopters, but in practice it is not, because the craft would be so tightly packed that it would be impossible to move one of them if, for example, it needed repair. It would seem that no more than 20 helicopters could be accommodated on the hangar deck.

Other armament aboard the *Moskva* serves exclusively for the defense of the ship. Starting at the stem, the following armament is recognizable: 2 12-barreled anti-submarine-rocket launchers, the after ones being slightly raised; 3 twin guided-missile launchers arranged one after the other on the centerline; 2 57-mm. twin AA mounts on the port and starboard upper decks, in the area of the superstructure. The first twin launcher behind the antisubmarine-rocket launchers is probably for antisubmarine-rocket torpedoes (very likely comparable to the American ASROC or the French Malafon), and the other 2 twin launchers seem to be for Goa surface-to-air missiles. Behind each of these launchers, characteristic flame-protection shields are recognizable. The enclosed 57-mm. mounts are placed diagonally to one another, the one on the port side being forward under the bridge, and the one on the starboard side farther aft under the funnel.

The superstructure follows the "new look" that has been noticeable for some years in Soviet naval architecture. The funnel deserves comment: it is conical and raked sharply aft; its side edges are sharply angular and its fin-shaped top projects aft; its athwartships projection also is conical, so that its base is the same width as the superstructure. The wide base was necessary to allow the helicopter elevator to be installed in it. Catwalks, the lowest of which is partly enclosed (presumably for housing the flight control), run around the after side of the funnel. A massive tripod lattice mast, whose legs are almost completely buried in the covering of the superstructure, towers above the funnel. The bridge descends forward in step form and has slanting fronts.

The electronic equipment installed is remarkable not

The Moskva *operating with her antisubmarine helicopters.*

only because there is so much of it, but because of how modern most of it is. A large antenna on the lattice mast, directed diagonally upward, probably serves 3-D functions and may be the successor to Big Net, heretofore the largest antenna in use on Soviet warships.

V-shaped fins on the back of the antenna are typical of Soviet equipment of this type. Below this large antenna is the standard Soviet surface-search antenna system. Two such antennas face one another on a single mount.

On the port side of the funnel, there are two pairs of electronic eyes, arranged not quite perpendicularly one above the other. There are none of these eyes on the starboard side. Such eyes were seen for the first time on *Kresta*-class cruisers. They look like ECM devices.

Two trainable structures, one behind the other, on the bridge structure, are, presumably, for target-finding and target-tracking electronics for the surface-to-air missiles. An unusual thing about them is that there are two parabolic antennas installed next to each other on the front wall of a box-like casing. Finally, on a console projecting offside on the bridge structure, there are the fire-control instruments for the 57-mm. guns. A small collapsible tripod mast just forward of the after guided-missile launcher is equipped with two direction-finder frames.

Ships of the *Moskva* class should certainly not operate alone. They will probably serve as command ships with a task group, such as the Soviet Mediterranean squadron. That squadron consists of cruisers, destroyers, frigates, landing ships, submarines, and so forth, but because there are no Soviet aircraft carriers, neither the Mediterranean squadron, nor any other Soviet group, could attain air supremacy when it was far away from its own

The Moskva *at anchor in the Mediterranean.*

bases. Even if vertical take-off and landing planes could be embarked in the *Moskva,* their number would be much too small to have any effect on a battle of any size or duration and, consequently, she could not come near to bridging the gap.

Battleships

The last two ships of the old *Gangut* class, the *Okt-iabr'skaia Revoliutsiia* (ex-*Gangut*) and *Sevastopol* (ex-*Pariskaia Kommuna*), were struck off the active list several years ago. Both were launched in 1911 and had approximately 23,500 tons standard displacement, 12 12-inch, 16 4.7-inch, 10 3-inch, and 17 37-mm. guns, 8.8 inches waterline armor, and a designed speed of 23 knots. They may have been broken up, or may be in use as training hulks. The third ship of this class, the *Marat* (ex-*Petropavlovsk*), was so heavily damaged off Kronstadt in 1941 that she was not worth repairing.

Two battleships, the *Sovetskii Soiuz* and the *Sovetskii Ukraina,* were laid down in 1938 but were never completed. In July 1945, the former was launched at the Ordzhonikidze Yard in Leningrad in order to clear her slip, and was so badly damaged during the war that her completion was out of the question: on 16 August 1941, the latter was blown up on her slip at the Marti Yard in Nikolaev. The *Novorossisk,* formerly the Italian *Giulio Cesare* handed over as part of the reparations called for by the Italo-Russian peace treaty, sank in the Black Sea in 1955, probably as a result of striking a mine.

Cruisers

The first new construction cruisers were begun during the second Five Year Plan (1933–38), because the cruisers then in service dated from the period of the First World War and, even after undergoing various forms of modernization, did not meet contemporary operational requirements. To begin with, the Soviets built "heavy cruisers," whose limitations of displacement and main armament caliber had been established by treaty at 10,000 tons and 8 inches, respectively. They did not build to those limits, but were content with a smaller type, whose displacement was about 9,000 tons and whose armament was 7.1-inch guns. This was the *Kirov* class, of which six ships were completed in two versions that differed in outward appearance. Their resemblance to contemporary Italian cruisers is unmistakable, the Italian firm of Ansaldo having been closely connected with their design and later with their construction. In addition to their main engines, they were fitted with diesel motors for economical cruising (approximately 17 knots), which considerably increased their radius of action.

Not until 1938, when they began to build the *Chapaev* class, did the Soviets adopt the general criteria for warship construction that were being followed by other nations. Instead of 7.1-inch guns, these ships were armed with more modern and efficient 5.9-inch guns in triple mounts, two forward and two aft, the most satisfactory layout. The first ship of the class was launched in 1941 but, due to the war, her completion was delayed for several years. Outwardly, the resemblance of this class to their predecessors, the *Kirov*s is slight, but nevertheless,

The cruiser Kirov *at Leningrad.*

The Kirov-*class cruiser* Slava *at anchor in the Mediterranean. Note the control-tower type of superstructure.*

they have the same typically Italian features as that class does. Especially characteristic are the "control tower" and the funnels, which are widely separated on account of the machinery layout. The latest stage of Soviet cruiser development is represented by the *Sverdlov* class that followed the *Chapaevs*. This class was designed immediately after the end of the war and, since 1948, has been built in large numbers. It first became known in the West in June 1953 when the name ship of the class, the *Sverdlov,* took part in the Coronation Naval Review at Spithead, England. The lines of the *Sverdlovs* are similar to those of the *Chapaev* class, but they have a higher freeboard and a cut-down quarterdeck.

At one time, it was thought that the Russians had a program for extensive conversion of the *Sverdlov* class, but this has not proved to be the case and only a small number of ships have been converted. The first conversion was the *Dzerzhinski* which, in 1961 or 1962, had a Guideline system fitted in place of her third 5.9-inch triple mount. It was probably an experimental installa-

The Sverdlov-*class cruiser* Dmitri Pozharski *off Vladivostok.*

The guided-missile cruiser Dzerzhinski *in the eastern Mediterranean.*

tion and consisted of a trainable twin launcher on a high deckhouse. The launcher looks very much like the Terrier/Talos launchers on contemporary American warships, and immediately behind it, there is a screen, about 26 feet high, apparently intended as a blast screen or deflector. Electronic equipment for target acquisition and missile guidance is most comprehensive. When the *Dzerzhinski* appeared in early 1962, the first Soviet shipborne surface-to-air missile system became known.

Another *Sverdlov*-class cruiser, the *Admiral Nakhimov,* is thought to have been similarly converted, but both her after mounts have been removed and replaced by a Strela installation, such as is fitted on the *Kildin*- and *Krupnyi*-class guided-missile destroyers. It could be that the *Admiral Nakhimov* is used to train personnel earmarked for ships of these classes, but since no photographs of her are available, all statements about her should be treated with reserve.

Whether or not other cruisers were converted is not known to Western observers, but it is not likely that such action would be taken now, as these vessels are obsolescent.

The Dzerzhinski *seen from the port quarter. Note the blast deflectors forward and aft of her Guideline missile launchers.*

Destroyers

The first class known to the outside world to have been built under Soviet rule was the *Leningrad* class. These vessels were not of a type regarded, at the time of their building, as destroyers, but rather as destroyer leaders. They followed closely the style of the French *Tigre*-class *contre-torpilleurs:* the two classes had similar main and torpedo armament but, not unnaturally, since French constructors were probably engaged in both the design and the building of the Russian ships, the resemblance went farther than that. The first ship of the *Leningrad* class, which was not very numerous, was laid down in a Soviet yard in 1935 and completed in 1937. These typical destroyer leaders differed in outward appearance from the average destroyer of their day, as indeed they do from those of today.

Shortly before the outbreak of the Second World War, a new class of single-funneled destroyers, which looked like Italian destroyers built at the same time, became known. This was the *Gnevnyi* class, whose name ship was laid down in the Zhdanov Yard at Leningrad in the middle of 1935, launched on 13 July 1936, and completed in 1939. She was lost during the war, and the class was later named after one of the other ships, the *Gordyi*. Twenty-six ships of the class were built (see page 23). The resemblance of these destroyers to Italian types is even more apparent when they are compared with the *Kondouriotis* class, which had the same arma-ment and were designed and built in Italy for the Greek Navy.

*Gnevnyi*s had the usual machinery layout, with all the engines aft of all the boilers, hence the single funnel, as opposed to the two widely separated funnels of the *Leningrad* class, which indicated that they had the so-called unit arrangement. The speed of the former class was little less than that of equivalent foreign construction, and their armament consisted of the same 5.1-inch single mounts as on the *Leningrad* class, two 3-inch antiaircraft guns, several 37-mm. weapons, and six torpedo tubes, whose outfit was six torpedoes in the tubes and six reloads.

The *Tashkent* and the *Opytnyi* were built more or less as experimental, high-speed ships, and they are no longer in service. From them, further development led to the *Sil'nyi* class, later designated the *Slavnyi, Strashnyi,* and *Storozhevoi* class, whose existence first became known in the West during the Second World War. The name ship, *Storozhevoi,* was laid down in the Zhdanov Yard, Leningrad, in 1936 and launched on 20 October 1937. The operational effectiveness of this class was about the same as that of the *Gnevnyi,* but their two widely separated funnels indicated that their machinery layout was different. It could be that they had the unit layout, for which the *Opytnyi* had, reportedly, been the experimental ship (see page 23). The siting of the 5.1-inch single mounts was the same as on the *Gnevnyi*

A Skoryi-class destroyer.

class. Three or four ships, among them the *Storozhevoi,* were later fitted with a twin mount in place of the two forward ones. These mounts were introduced on the *Otlichnyi* class, and were adopted for all subsequent classes. This modification appears to have been made on the *Sil'nyi*s only for research purposes.

Externally, there are only minor differences between ships of this class—the experimental installations of the 5.1-inch, twin mounts on the forecastle, some variations in antiaircraft armament, and some ships had no mast forward of the after funnel.

Plans for a class of similar but bigger destroyers were

drawn up shortly before the outbreak of the Second World War. This was the *Otlichnyi* class, known for short as the O class, because the names of all its ships began with that letter. Building began in 1939, and the first ships were launched in 1941. Their completion was considerably delayed by the war, and most of them were not finished until after 1946. The *Otlichnyi*s bore a strong resemblance to the preceding *Sil'nyi*s, but their entire main armament was twin-mounted. Also new, was the tripod mast behind the bridge, a feature now common to all destroyer classes, the older ones having had them fitted during modernization. In contrast to preceding classes, the number of torpedo tubes was increased from six to eight, although the much smaller, experimental *Opytnyi* had eight tubes. Plainly, the *Otlichnyi*s were the immediate forerunners of the *Skoryi* class.

After the war, when destroyer construction began again, it was on a larger scale than before. Even before the *Otlichnyi*s, whose completion had been delayed by the war (the *Ognevoi* was the only one completed during the war), went into service, there were plans for a new class of destroyer that would incorporate, as far as limitations on size and dimensions permitted, the changes dictated by wartime experience. This class, known as the *Skoryi* class, is an enlarged version of the *Otlichnyi* class and not, as some German writers have maintained, a development of the German 1936A destroyer. The first *Skoryi*s were launched in 1949 or 1950 and commissioned in 1951 or 1952. They were armed with four 5.1-inch in twin mounts, two 3.3-inch, and seven or eight 37-mm. antiaircraft guns. Although the *Skoryi*s have two more torpedo tubes than the *Otlichnyi*s and four more than the *Sil'nyi*s and *Gnevnyi*s, they do not have more torpedo armament, because, in contrast to those earlier classes, they do not carry reload torpedoes. It can even be said that they have less, for the *Gnevnyi* and *Sil'nyi* classes carried a total of 12 torpedoes, while the *Skoryi*s carry only ten: however, the ten tubes of the *Skoryi*s are, of course, always ready for immediate action. Navies of the satellite states and of states friendly to the Soviet Union have been provided with ships of this class (see pages 178–9).

The next class of destroyer to become known to Western observers represented a radical departure from anything that the Soviets had built theretofore. It was first sighted in 1955, and is known to the West as the *Tallinn* class. Its hull form is completely different from previous Soviet destroyer construction in that it is flush-decked. The layout of the superstructure displays some noteworthy features, and another change is in the guns—the 5.1-inch main armament is in stabilized mounts, very similar to the heavy antiaircraft armament of the later cruisers. In fact, the *Tallinn* is the prototype for "new Russian" ideas in shipbuilding.

Significantly bigger than the *Skoryi*s, this class seemed, at first, to be a type of destroyer leader, yet the

The Nastoichivyi, *only destroyer of the* Tallinn-*class.*

strong torpedo armament of ten tubes tended to contradict that supposition. It can be assumed, therefore, that it represented a Soviet attempt to develop an especially fast destroyer that incorporated all the latest technical improvements for which the *Skoryi*s were too small. The conjecture that this class would be represented by more than one ship was current for several years, but that now seems most improbable: it is virtually certain that the *Tallinn* is an experimental ship, the only one of her class, just as the *Opytnyi* was.

Only a short time after the *Tallinn* appeared, another new destroyer was seen off the island of Kotlin, to the

A Kotlin-*class destroyer to which a helicopter deck has been added.*

west of Leningrad, and her class was consequently designated *Kotlin*. Although this class has some things in common with its immediate predecessor—a flush deck and the positioning of its main armament—the layout of its superstructure is quite different: it is reminiscent of the *Skoryi*s. The *Kotlin*s may well represent the present-day, standard Soviet destroyer, with which it was intended gradually to replace the older ships of the *Skoryi* class. The fact that *Kotlin*-class destroyers have appeared not only in the Baltic but also in the Arctic, the Far East, and the Black Sea lends credence to that theory. Apparently, however, no more *Kotlin*s are being built, and their place is most likely being taken by new types of guided-missile destroyers.

Comparison of the New Classes of Destroyer

Hulls. Nautical publications do not seem to be in complete agreement as to the actual length of either the *Tallinn* or the *Kotlin,* but the hull length generally given for the latter, 129 meters (423 feet), is based on an examination of good photographs and the known dimensions of certain items—for example, the twin mounts are slightly more than 26 feet long—and can be taken as a close estimate. Similar examination of photographs of the *Tallinn* reveals a ratio of about 16.2:1 between turret length and ship's length, whereas in the case of the *Kotlin* it is about 15.7:1. It follows that the two ships cannot be the same length and that the *Tallinn* can be assumed to be more than 423 feet long. Nautical publications in all countries agree with that contention, but the length of the *Kotlins* is the subject of much dispute in the German technical press. It is more difficult to check beam dimensions, but both correspond quite well to the length/beam ratio of high-speed warships—approximately 09.6 to 10.2.

The *Skoryi* class was the last Soviet destroyer class to be built with a raised forecastle. This feature was seen for the first time in Soviet warship construction on the *Otlichnyi* class, but in that class there was little or no sheer. The raised forecastle probably resulted from efforts to obtain the highest possible speed in heavy seas.

In the *Tallinn* and *Kotlin* classes, Soviet shipbuilders went a step further: they built them as flush-deckers, thus obtaining a higher freeboard aft of the forecastle. However, it should be noted that the *Tallinn*'s hull is an enlarged version of the *Skoryi* hull with the raised forecastle being extended right aft, which explains why the midships freeboard of the former is about half a deck higher than that of the *Kotlins.* The hulls of these ships differ considerably from one another: the *Tallinn* is significantly longer and, above all, beamier than the *Kotlin* class.

Both have a sheer, which, on the *Tallinn,* commences at about the forward edge of the bridge, whereas on the *Kotlin* it commences farther aft, roughly abreast the forward group of torpedo tubes. From the following comparison, it can be seen that the *Kotlins* have the highest sheer:

Class	Commencement of Sheer (measured from bow)	Height of Sheer (forward freeboard less midships freeboard)
Skoryi	about 56 feet	about 4 feet
Tallinn	about 131 feet	about 10 feet
Kotlin	about 196 feet	about 15 feet

From the design point of view, the sheer is particularly noteworthy for its lack of harmony and beauty. Instead of being a smooth, continuous curve, it starts with a sharp bend (on the *Kotlins* there is even a second bend farther forward), then runs obliquely upwards (see page 26).

All three classes are, for the most part, electrically welded, the *Skoryi*s obviously somewhat less so than the others. *Kotlin*s have only a few side scuttles, at about the level of the upper messdeck, whereas it can be seen that the *Skoryi*s and the *Tallinn* have them at the level of the lower messdeck as well.

Anchors on the *Skoryi* class and on the *Tallinn* are stowed at forecastle level (see page 23). On the *Kotlin*s, they are in the hawsepipes, as is more usual, presumably because the freeboard forward is considered to be high enough to prevent the bow wave from reaching them.

For operations in Artic waters and in the Baltic, *Skoryi* destroyers were strengthened against ice, apparently by having extra plates welded to the stem after the ships had been completed. Such strengthening must have been fitted to the two later classes while they were building because it is not as noticeable from the outside.

A basic characteristic of all the newer Soviet destroyers is the severely raked, but straight, bow which, on the *Kotlin*s, has been carried to extremes. The *Skoryi*s and the *Tallinn* have transom sterns, while the *Kotlin*s have the same stern as the *Krupnyi* guided-missile destroyers and the *Kynda* and *Kresta* guided-missile cruisers—its upper part is round. Besides the openings for minelaying, the *Tallinn* and the *Kotlin*s both have a third, somewhat deeper, opening exactly on the centerline, intended for a stream anchor. Only these two classes have propeller guards, probably because they have divergent shafts.

Main Machinery. There are many gaps in available information about main machinery. All three classes have two sets of geared turbines fed by six water-tube boilers. The working pressure of the boilers appears to be relatively low in order to provide greater reliability and simplicity of maintenance and operation. Their output does not approach that of boilers common in the German Navy up to 1945.

Both *Kotlin*s and *Skoryi*s seem to have the unit arrangement for their machinery. But, although the principle of that arrangement may have been retained in the *Tallinn,* she almost certainly has a different layout. The great distance between her funnels indicates that both engine rooms are between the boiler rooms, making the sequence from aft, boiler/machinery/machinery/boiler, instead of machinery/boiler/machinery/boiler, as it is in the other two classes. It indicates also that the *Tallinn*'s machinery does, in fact, produce the 100,000 shaft horsepower (SHP) for the maximum speed of 40 knots that has been mentioned repeatedly for many years by both domestic and foreign publications. This is consistent with continuing Russian attempts to develop a high-speed destroyer for series production, to wit, the *Novik,* the *Opytnyi,* and the *Tashkent.* An increase of 30,000 SHP—almost 50 per cent of a *Skoryi*'s power—is the high price paid to achieve an extra four knots of

A midships view of the Nastoichivyi (Tallinn *class*), *showing her main-battery director and Uda-Yagi radar antenna.*

speed. Naturally, the more powerful machinery would require more space and may account for the hull of the *Tallinn* being more than three feet higher than those of the *Skoryi* and *Kotlin* classes. Moreover, it may be the real reason for the poor stability the *Tallinn* is reported to have and which is attributed by most technical publications to the high mounting of the *Wackeltopf* director. In fact, close comparison reveals that the director of the *Kotlin*s is almost as high as that of the *Tallinn*. The latter has greater diameter and is, consequently, heavier, but most of that weight increase is offset by the smaller after superstructure of the *Tallinn*.

Fire-Control and Electronic Equipment. Skoryi-class destroyers were the last to be built with a twin range-finder director above the bridge: the *Tallinn* has a *Wackeltopf* director, the *Kotlin*s have the newer Wasp-head equipment. On the other hand, both of the later types received light antiaircraft armament controlled by gunnery radar with dish antennas (see page 68), instead of the after, single, range-finder, antiaircraft directors fitted on the *Skoryis*. On the *Kotlin*s one antenna was mounted above the bridge in front of the Wasp-head, and another on an elevated platform between the mainmast and the funnel, while on the *Tallinn* one was mounted above and behind each twin turret.

In their original form, the *Skoryis* did not have this radar, but they are being modernized and it is now being fitted to control the 47-mm. single, antiaircraft mounts.

Large, all-round search radar aerials were fitted on the *Tallinn* and *Kotlin* classes right from the start, but the *Skoryis* are receiving them only during modernization.

The Uda-Yagi early warning radar fitted only on the *Tallinn* is new, but the remaining arrays of radars, whip aerials, and so forth on all three classes are quite usual.

A view from the forecastle of a Kotlin-*class destroyer, showing her forward 5.1-inch dual-purpose guns.*

Armament. Main armament consists basically of four guns in two twin mounts, one forward and one aft. The *Skoryi* class had 5.1-inch, low-angle guns with limited capacity for barrage fire against air targets. They are mounted in twin gunhouses that may be lightly armored on the front and sides. The main armament of both the other classes consists of dual-purpose, 5.1-inch guns in twin gunhouses. Their gunhouses are similar to those on the *Chapaev-* and *Sverdlov*-class cruisers, but they look somewhat longer, because there is a canvas-covered, steel framework at the back of them. There is a door at the side of the gunhouse, so this structure cannot have anything to do with access to it, and, presumably, its function is to catch empty cartridge cases.

For defense against high-flying aircraft, the *Skoryi*s use the 3.3-inch, twin, antiaircraft mounts on the after superstructure. Later classes have not been armed with these guns because the role of defending against high-flying aircraft has, to some extent, been taken over by dual-purpose weapons. Light antiaircraft armament is different on all three classes. The *Skoryi*s have 37-mm. single and twin mounts (both these and the 3.3-inch guns are being replaced by new 57-mm. guns) while, since the *Tallinn,* 47-mm. quadruple mounts with shields have been fitted. The siting of the mounts and the arcs of fire of those guns on the *Tallinn* are not as satisfactory as those on the *Kotlin* class (see page 42).

Torpedo armament is identical on all three classes and consists of ten tubes in two quintuple mountings, whose torpedoes are probably not bigger than the standard 21-inch. Reload torpedoes are not carried, as they were on the earlier classes. Recent modernization of some *Kotlin*s has included removal of the after tubes and extension forwards of the after deckhouse. These alterations may have been made in connection with the trials of antisubmarine torpedoes, an operation that requires preparation space, and that could be made available only by the removal of the tubes. In the course of their modernization, the *Skoryi*s have had their forward tubes removed.

Both conventional and guided weapons are in use for antisubmarine warfare. The *Skoryi* class was, and still is, fitted with single-barrel throwers and, in some cases, with simple launchers for depth charges, but the Russians turned to special antisubmarine mortars for the *Kotlin*s (see page 50).

Antisubmarine, guided-missile launchers were first seen on the *Tallinn.* A pair of launchers, presumably for shipboard trials, was mounted aft on the upper deck (see page 51). Almost identical equipment in a 16-barreled mount has now been fitted on both the *Skoryi* and the *Kotlin* classes but, in contrast to the *Tallinn,* these mounts are forward of the bridge, on either side of the antiaircraft gun deck above "A" turret.

Kotlin-class destroyers have been seen with an elevated platform aft for a KA-15 helicopter.

All three classes have minelaying tracks extending from the stern to the vicinity of the forward torpedo tubes. The rails are not fastened on the deck, as they are in some vessels belonging to other navies, but are set into it, thus, they are not a hazard to the crew when, for instance, they are hurrying to action stations. The tracks slope downwards over the stern, and the maximum outfit of mines for all three classes is about sixty. Because of the positioning of the after antiaircraft mounts on the *Tallinn,* her sets of tracks could not make a straight run: they had to be diverted around either side of the mounts and meet at a midships turntable.

Superstructure. The basic layout of the upperworks of the *Skoryi* and *Kotlin* classes resembles that of an average destroyer—bridge/mast/funnel/torpedo tubes/midships superstructure/mast/funnel/torpedo tubes/after superstructure—but the upperworks of the *Tallinn* consist of two large and two small structures, which give her a quite different appearance. The torpedo mounts between the funnels are separated by one of the smaller structures. So far, this layout is unique in destroyer construction, but it is similar to the one planned for the German reconnaissance cruiser project of 1939–40. The mainmast is sited forward of the after funnel on all three classes, a feature often found in the warship construction of other navies.

A striking feature of all three classes is that they have short, squat funnels with black cowls, the after funnel being a little shorter than the forward. Their rake is considerable and has become characteristic of present-day Soviet warship construction. The external appearance of the funnels contributes to the sleek look that these ships have. Around the forward half of both their funnels the *Kotlin*-class destroyers have prominent and unusual excrescences, whose purpose may well be to protect the boiler-room air intakes (see page 27).

Variations in the masts are worth noting: both the *Skoryi* and the *Kotlin* classes have tripod masts, but they are quite different from one another. Originally, the *Skoryis*' had the main leg forward on the centerline and the two supporting legs extended aft. On the *Kotlins*, it is just the reverse: the foremast has two main legs athwartships and one forward supporting leg on the centerline, while the mainmast has a vertical main leg and two after supporting legs. With the exception of the mainmast of the *Skoryi* class, all masts have horizontal and diagonal bracing for extra stiffness. Equipment is mounted on the masts in the normal way, but a special feature consists of direction-finding loop aerials, most of which are sited on the foremast but some are on the mainmast. The *Tallinn* has a tall, raked pole mast which, although it has short supports fitted, still cannot be described as a tripod (see page 28). Equipment is mounted in the normal way on this mast also.

Davits are generally used for hoisting and lowering boats, but, besides davits, the *Tallinn* has a king post and

derrick on either side of her upper deck, immediately abaft the bridge. The *Kotlin*s also have derricks but theirs are attached to the foremast supports (see page 29). Boats are stowed in the usual manner, on the upper deck, whence they can be lowered by the davits or derricks. On the starboard upper deck of the *Skoryi*s, two boats are stowed one above the other near a pair of davits: the cradle of the upper one is set somewhat inboard so that either boat can be lowered or hoisted, as required.

All three classes have open bridges, and some of the ships have platforms towards the sides, from which the usual equipment projects. *Skoryi*s and *Kotlin*s have bridges that are basically similar, but the *Tallinn*'s bridge is unusual because the tall, conical tower for the *Wackeltopf* director projects from it. A long platform, mounted well up the mast, connects the bridge with the director tower.

The *Kotlin*s have a bulwark, about 52 feet high, abreast the bridge superstructure, as has been common on American destroyers for about two decades. The after superstructure of the *Skoryi* and *Kotlin* classes serves mainly as a platform for medium and light antiaircraft weapons, and is the same size on both classes. On the

A midships detail of a Kotlin-*class destroyer. Note the tripod-mount mainmast and the dish-shaped fire-control radar.*

Tallinn, similar weapons were originally mounted on the small deckhouse situated between the torpedo mounts. The guns were 25-mm. in twin mounts, but they have since been removed, and additional aerials mounted in their place.

Summary of Performance

An over-all evaluation of these three classes of Soviet destroyers follows:

Hitting Power. Main armament is numerically the same on all three, but it must be assumed that the *Skoryis'* 5.1-inch, low-angle guns are inferior to the faster firing and more accurate 4.7–5.1-inch guns of the two more recent classes, and that their antiaircraft armament is not as conveniently positioned as is that of the *Kotlins.* Furthermore, the 3.3-inch antiaircraft guns of the *Skoryis* do not perform as well as the dual-purpose guns of the later classes. All three classes have identical torpedo armament and seem now to have the same antisubmarine armament.

Resistance to Battle Damage. Nothing definite can be said on this subject, but it can be assumed that the watertight subdivision is sufficient to guarantee satisfactory stability in case of damage.

Speed. Available data cannot be checked for accuracy. Maximum speeds are of secondary interest as they can be reached only under favorable, generally nonoperational conditions and, especially in the shallow waters of the Baltic, can be maintained for only short periods. Of greater interest are the maximum sustained speeds, which are usually from six to four knots less than maximum speeds. Assuming a maximum speed of 36 knots, these Soviet destroyers can be credited with maximum sustained speeds of from 28 to 32 knots.

Endurance and Seaworthiness. Since figures on radius of action and fuel capacity are not available, it is impossible to make a critical comparison. As regards seaworthiness, the *Kotlin* displays the most advanced features of any conventional destroyer yet seen. The *Tallinn's* obvious lack of stability has prevented her from being a success, and could be the main reason why she has not gone into series production.

The *Kotlins* appear to be the most modern and successful class of conventional destroyer ever developed by the Soviets. One factor seems to have been constant in Soviet destroyer development since the 1930s: the desire to produce general-purpose ships suitable for all tasks. Development to that end has been interrupted only by attempts to produce exceptionally fast prototypes, such as the *Opytnyi,* the *Tashkent,* and the *Tallinn.*

Opposite: A port-quarter view of a Kotlin-*class destroyer, showing her after 47-mm. quadruple mount and 5.1-inch twin gun mount.*

A Kildin-*class guided-missile destroyer lying to in the eastern Mediterranean.*

Guided-Missile Cruisers and Destroyers

The first ships to be armed with missiles were conversions from the conventionally armed *Kotlin*-class destroyers. Beginning about 1957, from four to six uncompleted vessels of this class were modified and completed as guided-missile destroyers. A magazine, measuring approximately 36 x 14 x 23 feet, was built aft, and a launcher for the Strela surface-to-surface missile was fitted nearer the stern. The installation was the same type as that fitted on the *Krupnyi*s, a later class, built to be missile ships. The converted *Kotlin*s had their main

gun armament—two 5.1-inch twin mounts—removed, and their 47-mm. quadruple antiaircraft mounts replaced by the more efficient 57-mm. version, but not always in the same positions. In the course of the conversion, antisubmarine torpedo tubes were fitted, together with an antisubmarine rocket launcher on the forecastle.

These conversions are known as the *Kildin* class, and their prototype, the *Kildin-I,* retained the characteristic *Kotlin* funnels and Wasphead gunnery director above the bridge. The *Kildin-II* and the *Kildin-III* are variations: they have narrower funnels and no Waspheads.

A Krupnyi-*class guided-missile destroyer in the Baltic. Note the massive Strela missile launchers.*

A Kotlin Sam *guided-missile destroyer with canvas over her Goa missile launchers and radar.*

Evidently, the *Kildin*s were produced in order to provide a platform for the thorough testing of the weapon system intended for the *Krupnyi*s, built as guided-missile destroyers and first seen at the Leningrad fleet review in 1967. The latters' hulls and superstructures are similar to those of the *Kotlin* class, but their missile installations consist of two launchers, one forward and one aft, and a magazine to hold 12 missiles—double that of the *Kildin* class. The rest of the armament, 16 57-mm. antiaircraft weapons, six antisubmarine torpedo tubes, and two groups of antisubmarine rocket launchers, is similar to that of the *Kildin*s. There is a helicopter platform over the fantail, and it is believed that the helicopter is used for missile guidance.

As can be seen from the masts and their associated antennas, the *Krupnyi*s carry more comprehensive electronic equipment than the conventionally armed destroyers. The forward mast has been raised, as on the *Kildin* class, presumably in order to extend the radar horizon and, thus, the range of the missiles. For strength and freedom from vibration, a quadrupod lattice mast has been fitted.

In June 1962, a missile-armed version of the modified *Kotlin* class—NATO designation *Kotlin Sam*—was seen. Except for a strengthened mast, the forward part of the ship remains the same, but the after part presents an entirely new appearance. A missile magazine, measuring about 65 x 29 x something over 13 feet high, with a trainable twin launcher on top, has been fitted. This was the first confirmed sighting of a Goa installation.

The after funnel has been moved slightly farther aft and its shape has been changed, presumably because of the possibility of jet blast from the launcher behind it. Where the mainmast used to be, there is now a tower-like structure with an extra-large, target-acquisition and tracking radar, and the foremast now carries a large, all-round search radar. Both groups of antisubmarine rocket launchers and the forward group of torpedo tubes have been removed, as has the original armament, with the exception of the forward 5.1-inch mount and the forward 47-mm. quadruple antiaircraft mount. However, the space left by the removal of the beam quadruple mounts was never used for any other purpose and they have now been put back. These ships seem not to

have been put to their best use following their conversion and, if that is so, the reason may be that there were problems of stability and top weight, probably caused by the size of the "radar tower."

It is almost certain that the *Kotlin Sam* constitutes no more than an intermediate step in design and is intended mainly for shipboard trials of the Goa missile. No more *Kotlin*s are likely to be so modified.

An early milestone in the development of Soviet guided-missile ships was the *Kynda*-class cruiser, first seen toward the end of 1962. The first keel was laid down in June 1960 at the Zhdanov Yard, Leningrad. April 1961 has been mentioned as the date of launching, while the seagoing trials are estimated to have begun in June 1962. The second ship of the class is thought to have been launched in November 1961 and completed in August 1962. A third, named the *Variag,* entered service with the Pacific Fleet in August 1962. It is understood that there are now four ships of this class. In appearance, they are quite unlike the *Kildin*s and the *Krupnyi*s, and are clearly the first of a new line of development. Consequently, it may be concluded that the *Kildin*s, and certainly the *Krupnyi*s, were intermediate types and that no more of them will be built. (It would not be difficult, from a technical standpoint, to equip the *Krupnyi* class with the Shaddock system that is fitted on the *Kynda* class but, so far, there is nothing to indicate that such conversions are being made.)

The Kynda-*class guided-missile cruiser* Variag *in the Pacific.*

Especially noteworthy is the comprehensive and well-balanced armament of the *Kynda* class, consisting, as it does, of Shaddock surface-to-surface and Goa surface-to-air missiles, multi-purpose guns, and antisubmarine weapons. The main armament is clearly the Shaddock, for which there are two groups of four launching tubes. The outfit of missiles is believed to be two per tube—one in the magazine and one in each tube. On the forecastle, there is a twin Goa launcher mounted on a low platform, forward of which there are two antisubma-rine rocket launchers. A group of triple antisubmarine torpedo tubes is situated amidships, on either side, abreast a gap in the superstructure. Rails between the mounting indicate that the torpedoes are supplied from a common preparation space and can be launched from either group, as required. The rails cannot be intended for mines, because the stern from which the mines would have to be laid is one deck lower. Abaft the after Shaddock mountings, there are two superimposed, 3-inch, twin mounts. Right at the stern, the deck is

A midships detail of a Kynda-*class cruiser. Note her enclosed quadrupod masts and multiple launchers for Shaddock missiles.*

A Kashin-*class guided-missile destroyer.*

marked out as a helicopter platform. At one time, the *Kynda* class was thought to have gas-turbine propulsion, but this has now proved not to be the case.

The penultimate development in this type of ship is the *Kashin* class of destroyers that first appeared in 1964. In contrast to the *Kyndas*, they resemble the *Krupnyi* class in that they are flush-decked, but they have a higher freeboard, both midships and aft. The stem is not straight, but gently curved, and has a considerable overhang above the waterline, a feature that has

been taken to indicate the presence of a bow sonar set. *Kashins* are interesting on two counts: first, their appearance, which leads to conclusions concerning their propulsion machinery, and, second, their weaponry.

Their appearance is dictated by the arrangement of their four funnels in two athwartship pairs, the after pair being sited unusually far aft. Individual funnels are squat and are canted outboard so that each pair forms a V. Together with large air intakes, one to starboard of the forward pair and one to port of the after pair, these

A midships detail of a Kashin-*class guided-missile destroyer, showing the unusual two-abreast arrangement of the funnels.*

funnels are characteristic of gas-turbine propulsion. Longitudinally, each one is divided in two, and their V-form layout was presumably adopted to prevent the hot exhaust gases from corroding the electronic equipment mounted on the centerline: numerous openings in each funnel admit cooling air and provide more protection. Since their first appearance both pairs of funnels have been raised somewhat, the forward pair rather more than the after pair, and it may be assumed that this was done to ensure that the gases would be led well clear of the upper deck.

The weapon system of the *Kashin*s, which consists of Goa surface-to-air missiles, multi-purpose guns, and antisubmarine weapons, is designed primarily for the engagement of air targets, thus filling a gap that was becoming increasingly serious. There are missile magazines both forward and aft on the upper deck, and fully trainable twin launchers are mounted on them. It seems that the target-acquisition and tracking equipment needs to be as high as possible, and consequently the bridge has become a tower-like structure, far higher than on earlier vessels. The forward set of equipment is mounted on that structure, while the after set is mounted on a similar, but lower, tower aft. Gunnery radars are mounted lower down on the towers.

*Kashin*s are fitted with quite powerful antisubmarine weapons, consisting of a quintuple torpedo mounting on the upper deck, between the mainmast and the after "radar tower," and four groups of rocket launchers, two on either side, abreast each tower.

The *Kresta* class represents the latest in guided-missile ships. Judging by their appearance, they do not seem to be in any way inferior to their Western counterparts. Their derivation from the *Kynda* class is unmistakable, especially the hull and the tall pyramid mast. However, their missile system is quite different from that of the *Kynda*s: they have four Goa and four Shaddock launchers, whereas the *Kynda*s have two of the former and eight of the latter. As on the *Kashin* class, the *Kresta*s' Goa launchers are mounted fore and aft, on deckhouses that are presumably magazines. Their Shaddock launchers are in pairs (as on J and E class submarines) on either side of the bridge, and they can be trained through a little more than 100 degrees, from dead ahead to just abaft the beam. The smaller number of launchers is no disadvantage if they can carry more missiles than can the *Kynda* class, and that would appear to be the case, because the magazine extends the whole width of the ship, from the bridge forward to just aft of the forward Goa launcher. What is on top of the magazine is not clear, but it could well be equipment for embarking missiles, including a lift. Also noticeable, is the fact that the launchers are mounted lower than are those on the *Kynda*s, the base and training mechanism presumably being below deck level. The upper deck immediately behind the launchers is designed to deflect blast.

A Kresta-*class guided-missile cruiser.*

This new arrangement of the Shaddock launcher makes it unnecessary to have more than one mast: on its forward side are the missile-guidance antennas, already familiar on the *Kynda* class and, projecting a little from either side, are some discs that may be a development similar to the American AN/SPS32 and 33 radars to be found on the nuclear-powered aircraft carrier USS *Enterprise* and cruiser USS *Long Beach*. These antennas (probably ECM) are mounted rigidly on the sides of the superstructure and radiate forward and on either beam.

The mast of the *Kresta* class is combined with the funnel into a compact structure. The funnel is divided longitudinally and what are, in effect, twin uptakes bend outboard near the top, probably because of the large, all-round, air-surveillance radar mounted on a conical base projecting from between them. Plating that connects the two uptakes across their after ends, blanks off the space between them. Typical air-intake slits can be seen on the sides of both funnels in ships of this class.

Kresta-class vessels are the first Soviet warships to have a helicopter hangar. It is situated aft, and opens onto the quarterdeck, where a flight deck is marked out.

Twin-mounted, 57-mm. guns are on raised platforms on either side of the after superstructure. They are the same guns as are fitted on the *Poti*-class submarine chasers and *Ugra*-class depot ships, and their mounts can be trained through a little less than 180 degrees. Associated fire-control equipment is on a platform abaft the funnels.

On either side of the upper deck, just abaft the funnel, there is a group of tubes, presumably for antisubmarine torpedoes, and there are antisubmarine rocket launchers on the forecastle and on either side of the helicopter hangar.

When compared with the *Kynda* class, there is little new about the rest of the electronic equipments. Besides a Big Net surveillance radar between the uptakes, the pyramid mast carries the usual array of antennas, two of them mounted on a common base. From photographs, it appears that at least one of them is rotatable about a second axis. The acquisition and tracking radars for the Goa system are probably the same as on the *Kynda* and *Kashin* classes.

The *Kresta*s' propulsion system is believed to be a combination of gas-turbine and diesel engines, a system first used in a warship of this size on the *Kashin*s.

These three latest classes of Soviet guided-missile vessels are particularly interesting because they tend to demonstrate Russian confidence in the effectiveness of their surface-to-surface missiles—weapons not to be found in Western fleets; and because—again in contrast to the latter—they carry a comprehensive variety of weapon systems, and are thus able to operate independently over wide areas. Furthermore, the role of each is clearly defined: one ship of the *Kynda* and *Kresta* class, together with one or two of the *Kashin* class, would form a powerful task group and, while the *Kynda* or *Kresta* engaged surface targets, the *Kashin*s would be responsible for providing antiaircraft defense.

The emphasis placed on surface-to-surface and surface-to-air missiles leaves little doubt that such groups are intended for use against the large NATO carrier groups, in case the latter were ever required to combat Soviet aggression.

From the way in which the *Kresta*s' missile systems have been changed from those of the *Kynda* class, it can be assumed that the former are intended to minimize the disadvantages of operating in waters where intensive air operations could be expected, for example, in both the Baltic and the Mediterranean.

*Opposite: A midships view of a **Kresta**-class cruiser. Note her massive pyramid mast and twin launchers for Shaddock missiles.*

Frigates

The forerunners of the present-day frigates were the *Shtorm* class, whose construction began in 1929 and was completed between 1931 and 1937, when the last one went into service. Seven of the 18 vessels known to have been built were stationed in the Baltic, two in the Black Sea, six in the Far East, and three were allocated to the Northern Fleet. Their displacement was just under 500 tons, their top speed was only 24 knots, and their armament consisted of three 3.9-inch guns, four 37-mm. antiaircraft weapons, and three torpedo tubes. Seven or eight members of the class were lost during the war; the others were in service for some years, but they would, by now, be obsolete and must have been broken up.

In 1935, two Italian-built patrol boats, the *Kirov* and the *Dzerzhinski,* arrived in the Far East. At first they served with the frontier guard, but later were incorporated into the fleet. They were diesel-engined and could reach 20 knots. They displaced 810 tons, and were armed with three 3.9-inch guns, four 45-mm. antiaircraft guns, and a number of smaller machine guns. Other vessels of the same pattern were probably built in Soviet yards, although this is now disputed. It may be that the three *Albatross*-class ships, whose presence in the Black Sea was reported but whose existence was never confirmed, were of this type.

It was not until 1938 that an independently developed class of escorts began to be built. This was the *Iastreb* class—NATO designation *Ptisi*—three of which were completed during the war. In dimensions and gun armament, they were similar to the Italian-built class but were significantly faster and their torpedo armament was more like that of the older destroyers and torpedo boats. Torpedoes have appeared on all subsequent classes of escort vessel right up to the present time. In this respect, they correspond to the escorts that were developed by the Anglo-Saxon navies during the war, and are now classed as frigates.

Iastreb-class ships displaced 842 tons and had turbine propulsion that gave them a top speed of 30 knots. Originally, they were armed with three 3.9-inch guns, four 37-mm. antiaircraft guns, and three torpedo tubes, but in the course of time their armament was reduced to two 3.9-inch guns, the antiaircraft weapons, and no torpedo tubes. Possibly consisting of a total of seven ships, this class was in service until 1962, at the latest.

In 1954, the first postwar design—the *Kola* class—made its appearance. Technical publications have often stated that their construction was based on that of the German fleet torpedo boats of 1939. Although both classes have a flush deck, they differ significantly. Not only do the *Kola*s have a "knuckle" low down on their hulls, which the German vessels did not, but the latter had quite different, more harmonious lines than the Soviet class, and their armament layout was different (see page 25). The *Kola*s have considerable combat

A Riga-*class frigate.*

potential and, under certain circumstances, they could put up a successful resistance against a larger surface opponent, but their lack of radar and modern fire-control equipment makes them weak in antiaircraft defense. They are much more like small destroyers than were the earlier escorts, and are of an obviously well-balanced design. The entire class seems to be stationed in the Arctic, where the demands made upon the seakeeping qualities of such ships are greater than they are in, for instance, the Baltic. They are in no way suitable for Atlantic conditions and, apparently, are not intended to

be. Their tasks are probably the security of the Arctic sea routes and the surveillance of the long, heavily indented coastline.

The next class of frigate was the *Riga,* which appeared in two versions and first became known in 1956. Its flush deck, high sheer commencing with a sharp bend, and severely raked stem made its lines distinctly "new Russian." Those features, together with the well-designed forward frames, made it obvious that much effort had been put into producing a hull that would enable the weapons to be used in poor weather and sea

A Mirka-*class frigate in the Mediterranean.*

conditions. Considerable numbers of this class were built and many have been transferred to satellite navies. For their size, they are powerfully armed but at the cost of less speed than the *Kola*s have. They, too, are armed with torpedoes and basically have a greater resemblance to a destroyer than to a modern frigate.

Looked at from the viewpoint of a coastal-minded navy and considering warfare in restricted waters, such as the Baltic, this rigid adherence to the torpedo may not be so mistaken or old-fashioned as comparison with Western frigates might make it appear. Operating, as

they do, mainly in restricted waters, the Soviets do not have to reckon with a powerful submarine threat, as must the great sea powers which operate in the open oceans. The latter are forced to give overriding priority to antisubmarine weapons for their destroyers and frigates, in spite of the fact that their underwater targets will be more scattered than will those of the Soviets. Naturally, today, there are certain limitations on the validity of that theory, but when the above-mentioned Soviet escorts and conventional destroyers were planned, such considerations may have been decisive.

Development since 1960 has produced ships that are most accurately described as corvettes. Among them are the *Petya* class of 1965 and the *Mirka* class that appeared in that year, both of which have diesel/gas-turbine propulsion.

It is thought that some of the *Petya* class were built in Kaliningrad (Königsberg) and some in Nikolaev, and that its first representative was launched not later than 1961. They are flush-decked, have a sheer at both the bow and the stern, and a bow bulwark as additional protection. They also have a raked stem and a square stern, to which mining rails lead. The superstructure is limited and is dominated by the bridge and a tripod lattice mast. Farther aft, there is a low funnel with a trapezoidal ground plan, which actually consists of two uptakes in a common casing. Short, high bulwarks abreast and on either side of the lengthy bridge superstructure, provide protection in heavy seas. The bridge superstructure extends above the actual bridge and probably houses the command position. Forward, this position is totally enclosed, but aft it is open. Above this again, is a circular platform, on which a typical Teller-form antiaircraft gunnery radar is mounted.

The very low funnel has a large air intake on its after side and, apparently, serves only the gas turbines: the diesel exhausts are led over the ship's side in the vicinity of the torpedo tubes.

So far as can be seen, the armament consists mainly of guns—two 3-inch twin gunhouses. Between the funnel and the after gunhouse, there is a quintuple antisubmarine torpedo mounting, and there are two groups of antisubmarine-rocket launchers on the bridge deck, and two aft.

Main machinery is probably a multiple installation consisting of two diesel engines and two gas turbines. The diesels would be for cruising, and a gas turbine would be used for high speed.

All in all, those ships with their economical use of material appear to have turned out well. In the confined waters of the Baltic, they are capable of undertaking a variety of operations, since they have weapons to combat submarines, aircraft, and light surface forces. They are not big enough to carry any but conventional weapons.

Their unconventional design makes the *Mirka* class conspicuous. Probably because the gas turbines are situated right aft, the hull is about 8 feet higher there than elsewhere. From this raised after part, two air intakes project, while exhaust gases leave via two vents in the stern that can be closed by flaps. Basically, this arrangement is similar to that on, for example, the British Brave-class fast patrol boats and ensures that people working on the upper deck are not affected by the dangerously hot exhaust gases. On the other hand, the exhaust vents of the *Petya* class are amidships, and are bound to affect people on the upper deck.

Perhaps because the *Mirka*s' fire-control equipment is

required to serve both gunhouses, the mast is considerably aft of the normal position immediately behind the bridge. This unusual arrangement reduces the size of the blind sector astern.

In armament and other respects, the *Mirka*s are similar to the *Petya* class and what has been said about the latter applies to the former.

Armed Motorboats

Before and during the Second World War, large numbers of armed motorboats went into service with the Soviet Navy, not only in coastal waters, but on rivers and lakes. To begin with, many of them were under the command of the MVD border guards but, in time, most of them were transferred to the Navy. The most impressive were the improvised motor gunboats (*Bronekatery*) armed with one, and some of them with two, turrets of the type fitted to the T-34/76 tank (earlier, the T-26 tank turret had been used). The turrets were mounted on the fore deck and were trainable. Most of the boats so fitted were in the Baltic and the Sea of Azov, but some were to be found on rivers. They were better armed than the German R and S boats and their high speed often enabled them to evade large warships. Some motorboats were also fitted with free-flight rockets and intervened effectively in land warfare.

So little is known about postwar development of this type that nothing more can be said on the subject.

Fast Patrol Boats

Along with submarines and mines, fast patrol boats are weapons much favored by the Russian Navy and, since the end of the Second World War, great emphasis has been placed on their development and construction. According to over-all estimates, there are now available more than 500 of them. The importance attached to these vessels is understandable: during the war they were the German Navy's most formidable opponents, being mainly responsible for the Russian Navy's otherwise modest offensive operations in coastal waters.

None of the fast patrol boats (or motor torpedo boats) developed and built before the war, the best-known of which was the G-5 class developed from the British 55-foot Thornycroft type, is still on the active list. The same may apply to the wartime P-2 class, which in recent years has been seen only with the Polish Navy.

The first motor torpedo boats to be built after the war were the P-4 class. They began building in 1952 and there are probably only a few of them left. They were forerunners of the P-6 class, about 500 of which are believed to have been built between 1953 and 1960. Many have been transferred to other navies, but even so the Soviet Navy still has about 400 in service. In contrast to the light-metal construction of the P-4, the later class is wooden. The external appearance of the later P-6s is almost the same as that of the earlier ones: only the antiaircraft weapons which, either from considera-

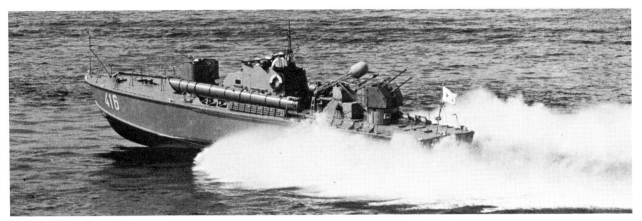

A P-6 fast patrol boat at Leningrad. Her radar mast has been lowered, probably to permit passage under a low bridge.

tions of space or of the helmsman's view, had been mounted asymmetrically on the earlier boats, and the radar have been altered.

Between 1956 and 1960 a number of P-6s were converted to submarine chasers and renamed the MO-VI class. Their torpedo tubes have been removed, but they carry a fairly large number of depth charges.

During the years from 1956 to 1960, the P-8 and P-10 classes, based on a common design, made their appearance. There were not, however, many of them, presumably because they were experimental types. Both have combined diesel/gas-turbine propulsion and the

uptake is, therefore, abaft the command position. The P-8s have hydrofoils, but their bridge layout, masts, and so on, are so similar to those of the P-6s that it cannot be stated with certainty whether they are converted P-6s or a separate development.

On the other hand, it is known that between 1959 and 1961 a number of P-6 boats were fitted with guided-missile systems. These are known as the *Komar* class. The first of them were seen at Leningrad in July 1961, and the Soviet Navy is, so far, the only one that builds fast patrol boats armed with guided missiles. These conversions carry a fixed launcher, which consists of an oval

P-10 fast patrol boats.

tube containing two launching rails, secured by a lattice mounting on either side of the bridge. The launcher has an elevation of about 20 degrees and the inner cross section is diamond-shaped. The tube is intended to protect the missile from the weather, but as there is no means of closing the front end of it, spray can enter and reach the missile skin. A connecting cradle between the rails is shaped to allow room for the missile booster.

Because of their small size, all the classes of fast patrol boat so far mentioned are suitable only for coastal use in fairly calm seas.

In 1960 a significantly larger boat appeared. This was the *Osa* class which, from the outset, was intended to carry guided missiles and in fact its missile armament is twice that of the *Komar* class. Its launchers, which can be completely sealed, are situated in pairs on either side of the upper deck, the after pair firing over the forward pair. Behind each pair, there is a plate to deflect the blast over the side during the missile launch. So far, two versions of the *Osa* class have appeared and, apart from an antiaircraft, fire-control system mounted on an elevated platform aft, they differ only in minor details.

Osa-class guided-missile fast patrol boats.

A Shershen-*class fast patrol boat.*

Units of both the *Komar* and *Osa* classes have been transferred to other navies, and this fact, coupled with lack of evidence that further development is under way, may mean that these small missile vessels have not fulfilled the hopes of their designers. Any development in this direction will receive great attention.

The *Shershen* class which, to all intents and purposes, is a conventionally armed version of the *Osas*, is now in service. They are said to be gas-turbine-driven and to carry four torpedo tubes and four 30-mm. antiaircraft guns. Their armament, their size, and the seagoing quali-

ties that the latter probably gives them, invite comparison with the *Jaguar* class of the Federal German Navy, as whose potential antagonists they may well be regarded. With this in mind, it is surprising that a number of them have been given to the Yugoslav Navy.

Finally, the *Pchela*-class hydrofoils, first seen in the Baltic and the Black Sea in 1965, must be mentioned. Boats of this class are intended as inshore submarine chasers, and carry neither torpedoes nor missiles. In them can be seen the beginning of a new era in Soviet hydrofoil construction.

Pchela-*class hydrofoil fast patrol boats.*

An SO-I fast submarine chaser belonging to the East German Navy.

Submarine Chasers

The oldest submarine chasers are the *Artillerist* class, which date from the Second World War and are now obsolete. They are so similar in appearance to the American PC submarine chasers developed at the beginning of the war that they can be regarded as a Russian version of them. There is disagreement as to how many units the class contained, and figures anywhere from 6 to 36 have been mentioned.

In the early postwar years, the *Kronstadt* class was developed from the *Artillerist* class and was built in large numbers, apparently in two versions. One version has fewer depth charges than the other, and is suitable for minelaying; the other is definitely a submarine chaser with a more powerful antisubmarine armament of depth-charge throwers and stern launching ramps. So far as can be judged from details hitherto divulged, the *Kronstadt* class represents a well-balanced construction especially as regards speed and armament. Of course, its small size makes its employment beyond coastal waters scarcely possible, and that may be the reason why it has been seen mostly in the Baltic and in northern waters,

A Poti-class submarine chaser, seen during the 1967 Navy Day review at Sevastopol.

A **Stenka-***class fast submarine chaser.*

although many have appeared with other navies, including the Cuban and the Indonesian.

The SO-I class was designed as a successor to the *Kronstadt* and, like it, is motor-powered. Its most interesting feature is its armament, which consists of depth-charge ramps aft, and four quintuple, antisubmarine rocket launchers mounted on the forecastle; for defense it carries two of the familiar 25-mm. twin mounts. This class, which can be intended only for use in confined waters, is probably being built in large numbers, and is being delivered to the satellite navies. Some SO-Is have recently been modernized to the extent of having anti-submarine torpedo tubes fitted in place of the after 25-mm. mount.

In 1964 the *Poti* class came to light. Although it could be classed as a large version of the SO-I class, its lines are very much like those of *Mirka*-class frigates, and both classes have gas-turbine propulsion machinery aft. The after deck of the *Poti*s is raised in a fashion similar to that of the *Mirka,* and the same air intakes project from it, while exhaust vents can be seen at the stern. Their antisubmarine weapons consist of torpedo tubes and rocket launchers, and for self-defense they carry twin-mounted 57-mm. guns.

Besides the MO-VI class, which are converted P-6 fast patrol boats, there are from three to five *Stenka*s, a new class of submarine chaser, whose displacement is 210 tons, standard.

Minesweepers

Mines have played an important part in Soviet naval thinking, especially concerning such areas as the Black Sea and the Baltic, where the shallow water is suitable for mine warfare. In the First World War the Russian Navy achieved considerable success with mines. During the Second World War, however, it had less success, largely because the Soviets had not put much emphasis on mine development. Today, the scant attention that had been paid to mine research is frankly admitted in Soviet military literature.

Thus, although influence mines were, apparently, known when the Soviet Union entered the war in 1941, none existed. The only mines available were moored types with vibration exploders.

Apart from a few left over from World War I, the only minesweepers available at the beginning of World War II were the new *Fugas* class. This class had begun building in 1934 and, by the summer of 1941, 39 of them had been delivered. Displacing 440 tons, they had a maximum speed of 18 knots, were armed with one 3.9-inch and two 37-mm. antiaircraft guns, and were the first Soviet warships to be powered by diesel engines. About the beginning of the war, two turbine-powered ships of the *Vasili Gromov* class were added to the minesweeper fleet. Building of these had begun in 1938 and from two to four of them may have been delivered by the end of the war. They were obviously intended mainly for use in the Baltic and, with their maximum speed of 24 knots, it would seem that their task was the defense of fast fleet units. Their displacement was 600 tons standard, and they carried two 3.3-inch guns, plus three 37-mm., and a number of other automatic weapons for antiaircraft defense.

Besides converting tugs, trawlers, and other types of fishing vessels into minesweepers, the Soviet Navy put a large number of minesweeping launches into service during the war, but it is assumed that, as soon as the war ended, all these craft returned to their normal tasks. In spite of the efforts the Soviets made, they needed far greater numbers of minesweepers than they could provide, and the deficiency had to be made up by their allies, who transferred a large number of vessels under the terms of the Lend/Lease Agreement.

The United States provided 34 ships of the *Admirable* class and 49 YMS, Britain provided 5 motor minesweepers, and Canada made available 10 ships of the Lake class. After the war, the Soviet Navy was able to add more than 100 large and small German vessels to its minesweeping fleet. Thus, it acquired a motley collection of minesweepers that varied, not only as to origin, but as to age, condition, and technical development. Apart from the Lend/Lease ships, which were returned, they all remained in service for a long time, and some were still steaming at the end of 1959 or the beginning of 1960. It was the same with the remaining units of the

Fugas and *Vasili Gromov* classes; today, some of them may be in use as training hulks, but they are no longer of any operational value.

In 1944 the first inshore minesweeper of the T-301 class, built in inland yards under a crash program, went into service. Construction of this class may have commenced as far back as 1941, for at the outbreak of war, there were a number of uncompleted vessels which might have been *Fugas* or *Vasili Gromov* class, or even the first of the T-301 class. Between late autumn 1944 and the beginning of 1945, 18 T-301-class vessels were completed in the Baltic area alone and, by August 1945, seven or eight more were completed in the Far East. By 1955 or 1956, when construction of this class ended, probably more than 200 of them had been built. It is unlikely that more than 50 are still in commission: some of them were transferred to other navies, and the rest are assumed to have been broken up. This class appeared to be uncomplicated, rugged, and well able to fulfill its mission. Over the years, technical improvements were made, but the basic design remained the same.

Building of the first postwar design, the T-43 class, began in 1947 or 1948 and continued until 1956 or 1957, and it is estimated that, at the present time, some 175 of them are in existence. Several of them have been handed over to other countries, and approximately 140 remain in Soviet service. They are of steel construction and are suitable for operation on the high seas.

A modified T-43 minesweeper.

Apart from minor changes, two distinct modernization schemes have been confirmed. The order in which they were introduced is not known, as both were first seen in 1963 or 1964. One scheme involved a thorough-going modernization and, outwardly, these vessels now resemble the more recent T-58 class. Their original armament has been replaced by more powerful antiaircraft guns and better electronic equipment, while the funnel has been moved forward somewhat and the bridge enlarged. Although they still have their distinctive masts, it is now difficult to distinguish, especially from a distance, between modernized T-43 and T-58 minesweepers.

The second modernization scheme involved the conversion of a number of vessels of this class for future use as radar early warning ships. While their general outline is not greatly changed, a quadrupod lattice mast with a big, rotating, parabolic reflector has been erected abaft the funnel. The mast is partially clad, and the radar offices may be situated inside. This large and heavy antenna may have had an adverse effect on the athwartships stability of these relatively small ships.

A T-43-AGR radar picket ship.

A new inshore minesweeper, the *Sasha* class, began to enter service in 1957, and may have been designed as a successor to the T-301. The flush-decked hull of this class was a new feature for minesweepers, and to ensure good seakeeping a large sheer was necessary. As on the *Kotlin*-class destroyers, the sheer does not commence in a gradual curve, but in a quite definite bend with a second bend farther forward, so that the freeboard at the bow is twice what it is midships. A compact superstructure enables the sweep deck to commence immediately abaft the funnel and, consequently, it is large enough to accommodate all the equipment a modern minesweeper requires to handle a variety of mines. Compared with similar vessels of other nations, these small ships are quite heavily armed: on the forecastle is a 57-mm. antiaircraft gun, without a shield, that could probably successfully engage light surface forces, while between the mast and the funnel the superstructure has been extended to form a platform for two 25-mm. twin antiaircraft mounts.

In 1958 the T-58 class was ordered as a successor to the T-43. As far as the hull and the propulsion machinery are concerned, the T-58 is similar to its predecessor, but its armament is quite different. In addition to four 57-mm. antiaircraft guns, there are antisubmarine rocket launchers abreast the bridge. Recently, ships of this class have been seen with fire-control equipment above the bridge and, according to British reports, in 1961 in Leningrad three of them were converted into submarine rescue ships, and have since been designated the *Valdai* class by NATO. Two large davits for a rescue chamber have been installed, one on the port side abaft the funnel, and the other right aft.

Rather surprisingly, until 1963 the Soviet Navy stuck to steel construction for its minesweepers, but in that year it adopted wooden construction for the *Vanya* class of coastal minesweepers. Comparison between the *Vanya*s and the numerous NATO *Bluebird* class reveals no

A T-58 minesweeper.

major differences. The former have no funnel, and above the open bridge there is a narrow lattice mast with crosstrees and radar.

The sum of all postwar minesweeping experience has probably been incorporated into the new, oceangoing *Iurka* class, intended as a replacement for the T-58 class. Since this new class was designed to meet the requirements of high-seas operations, the forecastle extends well aft and the freeboard is quite high. It is remarkable that the Soviet designers, having adopted wooden con-

struction for the *Vanya* class, went back to steel for the *Iurka*s. The latter were very likely designed at about the same time as the *Kynda* class of guided-missile cruisers, since they have the same unusual funnel—its longest dimension runs athwartships instead of fore and aft, a form that makes it look, when viewed from forward or aft, bigger than it really is. If this funnel design was not dictated by the machinery layout, it must have been used in order to provide more deck space abaft the funnel and to reduce the silhouette.

Landing Ships

For their very limited amphibious operations in World War II, the Soviets pressed into service all manner of small, shallow-draft vessels from coastal minesweepers to fast patrol boats. They had no specialized ships for such operations, and during the early postwar years, lack of information on the development or construction of landing vessels made it seem unlikely that the situation was to be remedied.

It was not until 1957 or 1958 that a craft designed for amphibious operations appeared and, even then, only one unit of its class, the MP-2, was built. At about the same time, a second class, the MP-4, became known. It may be that this class, which consists of converted old coasters, actually preceded the MP-2 class but did not become known until later. After that came the MP-6 class, which were converted *Bira*-class freighters, then the MP-8 class which, like the MP-2, was specially designed for amphibious operations, and whose external appearance indicates that it is an enlarged version of the MP-2.

The next vessel of this type to appear was quite different from anything the Soviets had produced up to that time. This was the MP-10, quite plainly an improved version of the well-proved German *Marinefährprähme* (or prams) of World War II, large numbers of which fell into Russian hands at the end of the war. A further development is the *Polnochnyi* class, which is known to have been built in Polish shipyards and is believed to be in service with the Polish, as well as the Soviet, Navy. A new class of landing ship is the SMB-I, an improvement over the MP-10s. Little is known about the *Vydra* class, which have a 500-ton, deep-load displacement.

Far in advance of any previous Soviet designs are their first large landing ships, the *Alligator* class. They displace 4,000 tons, in contrast to the 2,000 tons that had previously sufficed.

All classes, except possibly the MP-4s, have their propulsion machinery aft and are diesel-powered. The bridge and command positions are also well aft, leaving most of the fore part of the ships available for cargo. There are vehicle ramps behind the bow doors, but the *Alligator* has a stern ramp as well, so that loading and unloading can be done at either end.

No definite information regarding the capacity of the various classes is available, but by comparing them with similar sized vessels of other navies, the following estimates can be made. It would appear that the MP-2, MP-4, and MP-6 classes can carry from six to eight tanks. The MP-10 class are really ferries, and would be called into use when beach conditions made it impossible for the larger classes to discharge their loads directly on shore. In that event, these very shallow-draft vessels would load troops and equipment and convey them to the beach. It is assumed that the *Alligator* class, which

Landing ships of three classes, MP-8, Polnochnyi, *and* Alligator, *in an amphibious exercise in the Baltic.*

can carry a complete motorized rifle battalion, has been, or shortly will be, put into series production.

All these facts point towards a new maritime strategy, particularly in the Baltic area, where there is already capacity for an assault lift of 7,500 men. Recent amphibious developments can have only one purpose—seizure of the exits from the Baltic.

Support Ships

In the first years following the war, the Soviet Navy's small fleet of support vessels consisted mainly of merchant types (freighters, for example) that had undergone a minimum of conversion to fit them for naval use. Virtually none of its ships had been designed and built for the task. Valuable acquisitions—not least as proto-

The Mahomet Gadzhiev, *a* Don-*class depot ship, crossing the Bosporus.*

types from which to learn—were the modern submarine and fast patrol boat tenders that came into Russian hands after the German capitulation. They were the *Otto Wünsche* and the *Waldemar Kophamel,* built between 1938 and 1942 at the Howalt Shipyard in Kiel, displacing 4,700 to 5,000 tons, and powered with diesel engines, and the *Adolf Lüderitz,* built by the Neptun Shipyard in Rostock between 1938 and 1940, displacing 2,900 tons and also diesel-powered. In Soviet service,

these ships became the *Paysherd,* the *Kuban,* and the *Pechora.* Since no pictures of these three ships are available, it is not known whether they have been converted or modernized. In fact, it is not known whether they are still in commission.

Enormous numerical expansion of the Soviet fleet has made greater demands upon the support ships than before. New construction failed to keep pace with the increase in the numbers of submarines and minor war vessels which, therefore, remained largely dependent on shore bases, a situation that, in the nuclear age, it is best to avoid. Presumably because shipbuilding capacity was entirely taken up with the production of fighting ships, especially submarines, the building of specialized support ships could not be permitted, and the Soviet Navy was forced to make do with more merchant ship types. East Germany contributed several large *Atrek*-class depot ships, but they hardly filled the need, and, anyway, they had been built as freighters.

Another stopgap was the conversion in 1958 and 1959 of a number of coal carriers that had been built in Polish shipyards just after the war for the Soviet Navy. They became the *Tovda* class. A second funnel was added and the two original masts were replaced by a single tripod. The hold forward of the bridge was retained and is probably used for the stowage and maintenance of torpedoes. The chances are that these ships have extensive workshops.

In 1959, soon after those conversions had been made, a new class of support ship, the *Purga,* appeared. It cannot be said with certainty that the *Purga*s were, from the outset, intended to fill the support role. From their bows, it might be inferred that they were designed as icebreakers and completed as support ships in order to meet changed needs—a need, perhaps, for tenders that could cope with ice conditions in the Arctic.

Information on the *Don* class first came to hand in

A Don-*class depot ship, showing her lifting gear.*

A **Lama**-*class missile supply ship.*

June 1961. Auxiliaries of this class are larger and probably much better than any the Soviets had before. Characteristic of the class is the 100-ton, heavy lifting gear above the curved stem, and the bridge situated well aft with a lengthy hold forward of it. The lifting gear appears to be intended for at-sea propeller and rudder repairs to submarines. The hold is probably a torpedo stowage, and on either side of the coamings there are cranes for lifting the torpedoes from the hold onto cradles. The latter run on tracks to the vicinity of the funnel, where a heavy crane then lifts the torpedoes outboard to the waiting submarine. At least one of the

Dons has had a helicopter platform fitted aft, and her old 3.9-inch guns removed.

The new *Uda* class have turned out to be submarine supply ships. Of tanker-like construction, with the main machinery aft, they have fittings that can only be for replenishing ships at sea. They probably supply stores, such as ammunition, as well as fuel oil.

Towards the end of 1964, two more classes of support ships, the *Lama* and the *Ugra,* were identified. Both are submarine tenders apparently for high-seas operations, a clue to their task being provided by their extensive antiaircraft armament. Their designers obviously had in mind the large and omnipresent Western aircraft carrier forces.

Present-day strategic concepts are quite clearly displayed in the *Lama* class, which are comparable, not so much in their size as in their task, to the big American nuclear-submarine tenders. Their large midships section, or hangar in which missiles are stowed, indicates that they were especially designed and, from a technical point of view, they are exceptionally interesting. Two sets of narrow-gauge tracks run out of the hangar on to the well deck, where they end in turntables, between which there is a cross-connecting track. The deck over the missile stowage contains a lift that measures no more than 23 x 23 feet, and is probably intended for transporting missile sections to and from the hangar. (It should be remembered that the Sark and Serb missiles,

with which Soviet submarines are armed, are 49.2 and 35.1 feet long, respectively.)

At the forward end of the hangar, there are two trainable luffing cranes for hoisting missiles out to the submarines. They are housed in the horizontal position and, judging from their massive construction, their working load is probably not less than 20 tons. Presumably, the missiles are transported from the hangar on cradles running on the tracks, then lifted by one of the cranes and lowered vertically into the launching tube of the submarine secured alongside. In the ship's side, there are a number of fairleads for securing lines.

Between the cranes is a simple mast with a derrick, whose purpose may be to lift the missile when it is being transferred from one side to the other as, certainly in the case of the Sark, the well deck is far too narrow for this to be done in any other way. After the missile has been lifted, the cradle is probably moved, via the turntables and cross-connecting track, and the missile is then lowered again. The cranes are unusual in that, when stowed, their jibs are on the deck, and the upper portion of the king posts is apparently collapsible. The reason for this arrangement is probably that it allows more room for training the foremast derrick which would otherwise be restricted.

The *Ugra* class is unmistakably the successor to the *Don* class. They have the same torpedo stowage forward of the bridge, but have only one crane, situated on the

An Ugra-*class depot ship.*

starboard side. A diagonally-positioned, movable ramp on the port side is used when torpedoes are being put in and taken out of the stowage. Very likely, lack of space for a loading hatch is responsible for this arrangement. Other supplies are probably stowed in the after part of the ship, where there may also be workshops. There appears to be a lift immediately aft of the after antiaircraft mount. Since British reports have mentioned a

helicopter platform at the stern, it seems reasonable to suppose that it is a lift, which would facilitate the movement of heavy stores to the helicopter. Such stores could then be loaded in, or slung beneath, the helicopter and transported to the waiting submarine.

Another recent development is the *Oskol* class of repair ships, said to have been built in Poland. They have a helicopter platform on the forecastle, but otherwise are built along the lines of merchant ships, with the engines aft.

The main objective of present-day Soviet support-ship construction is plainly to provide support to their submarines, particularly on the high seas. This support would make them less dependent on shore bases, and would prolong their endurance. Of course, there is an enormous difference between a supply ship that must remain on the surface and one that need not. Nevertheless, it seems as if the Soviets are basing their ideas on the experience of the German submarine service during World War II, when, for example, the stores provided by a single Type XIV supply U-boat enabled 12 Type VII U-boats to remain at sea four weeks longer than they could have done without such support. Thus, it is easy to see to what extent a large support ship can affect the endurance of its associated submarines.

Since conventionally-powered boats still predominate in the submarine fleet, fuel oil is the biggest item to be supplied. Other important stores include ammunition, provisions, and fresh water, which even nuclear submarines must have if their sea time is to be extended. A new aspect of the supply mission is the replenishment of missile armament, and whether nuclear or conventionally-powered submarines are involved, this item is particularly important because Soviet submarines carry significantly fewer missiles than do American Polaris boats.

Special-Purpose Ships

Most important among the ships of this type are the four *Chukotka*-class, missile-tracking ships, first seen at the beginning of 1960, about 700 nautical miles south of Midway and 1,200 nautical miles west of Pearl Harbor. They are converted freighters of about 4,000 gross register tons each. Forward of the superstructure of three of them, there are three radar aerials which, having appeared at a time when the Soviets were conducting comprehensive missile-firing tests in the Pacific, are presumed to be for tracking ballistic missiles. The fourth ship does not have the radar aerials and appears to be a floating helicopter base, whose task is probably to recover missiles or space capsules after splash-down. Of course, the other ships also are equipped with helicopters. The existence of any armament on board could not be confirmed, and apparently they are not under naval command, but are operated by a nonmilitary research organization.

Two more ships of this type, the *Chazhma* and the *Chumikan*, have been added since 1960. They are both converted freighters, and carry a distinctive giant radome above the bridge. Most probably, they also are controlled by a nonmilitary authority.

The very latest development is the newly completed *Astronaut Vladimir Komarov*, named after the astronaut who died in a space accident in 1967. With her three radomes, she is larger than any of her predecessors.

A Chukotka-class missile-range instrumentation ship participating in ballistic-missile tests in the Central Pacific.

The missile-range instrumentation ship Astronaut Vladimir Komarov.

Training Ships

Apart from the warships that are used solely or occasionally for training, there are in use a number of training ships, some of which are so old that they are immobile. One of the oldest is the cruiser *Aurora,* now part of the tradition of the Soviet Navy, for it was she that fired the first shot in the October Revolution. Today she is something of a national monument, and lies stationary in Leningrad, where from time to time she is open to the public. To be posted to this ship for training is regarded by cadets as a mark of special distinction.

Icebreakers

The severity of the Russian climate is responsible for the large number of icebreakers. They are not under command of the Navy, but of the Chief Administration of the Northern Sea Route, and although, in compliance with the Hague Convention, they are unarmed, they count as auxiliary war vessels. Some of them seem to have been recently assigned to the newly formed task groups of the Northern Fleet.

The nuclear-powered *Lenin* is the largest icebreaker in the world. After World War II, six large icebreakers

The Murmansk, *one of four icebreakers of the* Moskva *class.*

An icebreaker of the Dobrynia Nikitich *class.*

were built as reparations by the Finnish Sandvikens Yard. From them, the icebreaker fleet reaches back, via the former German ships (see page 320), to the turn of the century, when the *Iermak,* the world's first large icebreaker, was built under the aegis of the Tsarist Admiral Makarov. Most of the big icebreakers carry one or two helicopters for ice reconnaissance.

Four new icebreakers are planned, but it is not known whether work on them has yet begun. The first two will probably be larger than any that have been seen hitherto: they will be nuclear-driven, will displace 25,000 tons, and the name ship of their class will be the *Arktika.* The other two will probably have conventional propulsion and displace 12,000 tons.

Since 1961, a new class of small icebreakers, the *Dobrynia Nikitich* class, has been built. Nine of these vessels are believed to have been completed, and three may be under naval command.

Submarines

Since about 1950, submarines have been the predominant arm of the naval forces of the Soviet Union. From year to year that arm grows stronger, and the Western powers become increasingly disturbed by it. Covert activities are very much in accord with Russian character, and appreciation of that fact explains why the Russians have long attempted to use the area beneath the surface of the sea for war vessels.

Early Development

According to contemporary sources, the first efforts to do so took place in the time of that naval enthusiast, Tsar Peter I. Thereafter, development proceeded, via the most curious suggestions and constructions, to the practicable submarine, and is linked inseparably with the names of Schilder, Spiridonov, Aleksandrovski, Bauer, Dzhevetski, Poukalov, and Bubnov, to mention only a few. The bold ideas of these pioneers, most of whom were Russian, were frequently frustrated by a lack of understanding on the part of those in authority. It was only in times of emergency—during the Crimean and Russo-Turkish wars, for instance—that these inventors and engineers were remembered and given freedom of action, in the hope that, with minimum resources, they would produce weapons to defend against enemy surface fleets. In its early days, the submarine was regarded, by the Russians at least, as just such a weapon; the concept that it should be employed solely as a defensive weapon was in keeping with the continental outlook that is deeply rooted in the Russian mind and has, in the past, given defense of the coastline priority over offensive operations.

In December 1900, Bubnov, an enthusiastic and gifted engineer and an expert on the subject of ship stability, was appointed chief constructor of submarines in the Baltic shipyards. His first boat, the research submarine *Del'fin*, which had an internal combustion engine for surface use and an electric motor for use when submerged, was launched in 1903, and went into service shortly afterwards.

At about the same time, increasing tension with an expansionist Japan prompted the Russians to strengthen their Navy, in the first instance by means of submarines. Russian submarine development was, however, moving only slowly towards the construction of an operational type, whereas abroad, especially in the United States and Germany, development was more advanced. Consequently, it was to those two countries that the Russians turned for help. They entered into both purchasing and building agreements with them. Among the American boats, those built by Simon Lake were favored by the Russians and they bought several from him, the first of which, the *Protector*, was renamed the *Osetr*. Between 1904 and 1907, no less than 16 submarines were acquired from foreign sources, while in the same period, Russian shipyards delivered only eight.

It is interesting to note that the Krupp-Germania shipyard in Kiel received its first order for a submarine not from the German, but from the Russian, Navy. In 1902 that yard built a 16-ton submarine, the *Forel'*, in whose extensive trials a Russian commission took part. The three boats that were purchased in 1904 as a result of that participation constituted the *Karp* class, whose displacement was 210 tons on the surface and 240 tons submerged.

At the beginning of 1904, a second submarine, based on the *Del'fin* but significantly improved, was started, but when the Russo-Japanese War broke out on 8 February of that year, the only operational submarine in the Russian Navy was the *Del'fin*. During February and March, the construction of five more submarines was pressed forward with great haste, and towards the end of the year five boats, including the *Del'fin*, were transported to the Far East for use in defense against the Japanese.

That war left the Russian Navy so weakened that drastic measures had to be taken to build it up and, since submarines were a type of vessel that could be built in a relatively short time, a program for building them was undertaken. First, the experimental boat *Minoga* was built, followed in 1908 by the improved *Akula*. These two boats were the links in the chain of development that led to the *Bars* class, which were built under the direction of Bubnov shortly before the First World War and became, to all intents and purposes, the standard Russian submarine. In 1912, Russian constructors produced plans for a large submarine-cruiser,[17] which was far ahead of her time, and whose characteristics were:

Displacement: 4,500 tons, surfaced; 5,400 tons, submerged.
Length between perpendiculars: 400 feet.
Beam: 34 feet.
Draft: 5 feet.
Horsepower: 4,400.
Speed: 26 knots, surfaced; 14 knots, submerged.
Submerged Endurance: 275 nautical miles at 6 knots.
Armament: 2 4.7-inch guns in a turret on the upper deck, 36 torpedo tubes with 60 torpedoes, and 120 mines.
Armor: 2 to 3 inches.

Development of the submarine as a minelayer was a Russian idea, born during the siege of Port Arthur in the Russo-Japanese War. A railway engineer named Naletov who lived in Port Arthur saw the Russian battleship *Petropavlovsk* sink on 13 April 1904 after entering a secretly laid minefield, and conceived the idea that submarines could be used as minelayers. No one was interested in his idea so, at his own expense, he built a small submarine, but she sank after an accident during her first trial. Undeterred, Naletov built a second and better boat of about 25 tons. Although he got no support from higher authorities, he got effective assistance from subordinate establishments. However, in spite of all efforts, his boat could not be completed before the port was surrendered. A year later, Naletov produced plans for a new project—a 300-ton submarine minelayer. In 1906, his design was submitted to a naval technical committee which, thus, for the first time, became aware of the possibility. The committee took a whole year to consider and, eventually, to approve the project, but in October 1908 the construction of the world's first submarine minelayer was begun. She was named the *Krab* and her exploits in the First World War created a sensation. Even today, the Russians take pride in the *Krab* and her achievements.[18]

Following the success of the *Krab,* two *Bars*-class submarines, the *Ersh* and the *Forel',* were converted to minelayers during the war.

In 1910 another Russian engineer, named Bard, had a project for a submarine minelayer whose speed and outfit of mines would enable her to lay a circle of mines around an enemy fleet before that fleet was aware of its predicament. The latter would then be so hindered in movement that it could be destroyed by torpedoes. This fantastic project never materialized because the means of propulsion then available could not provide the necessary speed.

First World War and the Revolution

At the beginning of the First World War, the Russian Navy had 28 submarines, only four of which were fit for operations, and they were deployed as follows: 12, including the four operational ones, in the Baltic; 4 in the Black Sea; and 12 in the Far East.

By the time of the armistice in 1917, this number had been increased by more than 50 boats, including three that had been built for the Army and intended for the defense of Kronstadt.

To be sure, the shallow waters of the Baltic are by no means ideal for submarine operations, but on top of that, the Russians had neither operational experience nor a maritime strategy that could lead to a successful submarine campaign. The tempo of operations was not stepped up until after 1915, when five British boats were transferred and, even then, they were responsible for most of the success that was achieved.

Throughout the war, Russian submarines in the Baltic sank only seven merchant ships and brought in three more as prizes. The record in the Black Sea was even less impressive, only a few small Turkish ships being sunk. But the submarine minelayer *Krab* twice managed to penetrate the Bosporus and laid more than 120 mines, causing considerable damage to and confusion among Turkish coastal shipping. No submarines were stationed in the Arctic until 1917.

Then came the Bolshevik Revolution, in the course of

which several submarines were lost. A number of boats were under construction at the time, and those that were not willfully destroyed were broken up or left to rot. When the Revolution became a civil war and the Allies intervened, the new rulers at once began to man some of the available boats and to use them against the Allied naval forces, which soon put most of them out of action: 13 submarines were sunk in Sevastopol Harbor, and four in the Baltic, while another fell into Finnish hands and was interned. Four boats joined the White Russian forces and belonged to the so-called "Wrangel Fleet" which, after the collapse of the White Front, sailed to Bizerta, where it was interned. The only success that the Bolshevik submarines could claim was the sinking of the British cruiser *Victoria* on 31 August 1919.

Between the Two World Wars[19]

By the end of 1921 when the civil war was virtually ended, the Soviets had 15 submarines left, most of which were of the Bubnov type. Ten of them were in the Baltic, and five in the Black Sea. They were very soon worn out and scarcely mobile, but a Ten Year Plan for the renewal of the Navy, whose main objective was the building of submarines, could not be started until 1928.

In 1929 the first of six D- or *Dekabrist*-class submarines appeared. They were intended for use on the oceans and were, for the most part, based on contemporary Italian construction (see page 29). Shortly afterwards there followed the 25 L-class (*Leninetz*) boats, whose design was based on the British L class, one of which was sunk off Kronstadt in 1919 and raised by the Russians in 1928. The *Leninetz* boats proved to be the most successful class developed at the time. On the other hand, the three P-class (*Pravda*) submarines were quite definitely failures and spent most of their time on transport tasks. Finally, a medium-sized type for limited oceangoing use, the SC class, was built in several variations, and by 1941 nearly 100 of them had been built.

The second building period began in 1933, when orders were given for a small submarine for defensive operations in coastal waters. This was the M class (*Maliutka*) which appeared in considerable numbers from 1934 onwards. Prefabrication was used for the first time; sections were completed at inland yards and assembled at yards that have access to the sea. This practical method of construction made it relatively easy to disassemble the boats and transfer them from one area to another by inland means. It had been planned to mass-produce M-class submarines in the event of war, but because the necessary material was required for more urgent armament production, that was not done. During the Second World War, this class proved to be particularly satisfactory in restricted and shallow waters.

A new class of oceangoing submarine, the S class, appeared in 1935 and more than 50 of them were built.

It was very similar, not only in appearance, but in its high speed, to the slightly older German 1-A boats. In order to bypass the terms of the Versailles Treaty, the prototype 1-A-class submarine was designed by an undercover German design office in Holland and built with German finance and under German direction in a Spanish shipyard in 1928. It is not impossible that the Soviet espionage service which, even at that time, was operating most efficiently, managed to get the plans.

The last prewar Russian construction, the K class, first appeared in 1936 and was intended for oceangoing use, but was built only in small numbers. Its characteristics seemed to be generally good, especially its diving time of 50 seconds. This was a tremendous advance, as the much smaller L-class boats required 150 seconds, and the similar-sized P class required 90 seconds. By 1939 the Soviet submarine force of nearly 200 boats was the strongest in the world. The second strongest was the Italian, with 98 boats: then came the United States with 96, France with 79, Great Britain with 62, Japan with 60, and Germany with 45.

In the Baltic alone, the Russians had 75 submarines. This large fleet was only moderately successful against Finnish shipping during the Russo-Finnish War, obviously because the principles of command under which it operated were those of the First World War. Throughout the campaign, Soviet submarines sank only four merchant ships and one armed yacht. The latter was sunk by a torpedo, but the former all fell victim to gunfire from surfaced submarines. At the beginning of February 1940, the freezing up of the Baltic brought a halt to Soviet submarine operations.

Second World War

On 21 June 1941, the day of the German attack on the Soviet Union, the Soviet Navy had 276 submarines in service and 51 under construction, and they were deployed as follows: 76 (+ 34 under construction) in the Baltic; 45 in the Arctic; 68 (+ 10 under construction) in the Black Sea; and 87 (+ 7 under construction) in the Far East.

Work on the submarines still in the shipyards soon had to be abandoned because the major yards either were besieged and all available manpower was needed for their defense, or they had been captured by the Germans. For instance, only 20 of the boats building at Leningrad had been completed by the end of the war.

The Soviets tried to concentrate their submarine operations in various areas, particularly in the Arctic.[20] In the Arctic, where there was no lack of worthwhile targets and where the geographical situation was favorable, lay the best hope of conducting successful submarine warfare, and the transfers of submarines to that area indicate that the Russians intended to take advantage of their opportunities. Before German air attacks at the end of August 1941 inflicted severe damage on the

White Sea Canal—the Finnish advance to the Svir River finally made it unusable—20 S-, K-, and L-class boats, completed but not operational, were moved, via the Canal, to the White Sea, and during 1942 and 1943, six more boats were transferred from the Far East, via the Pacific, the Panama Canal, and the Atlantic.

However, Soviet strategic concepts were demonstrably poor and, just as in the Russo-Finnish War, the operational and tactical control of the submarines was unimaginative. The commanders were bound by detailed orders and were not free to act as changing situations dictated. There was no co-ordinated control from the shore, and each vessel was allocated a specific area within which it had to remain. This method of operation was not abandoned until quite late in the war: it was given up, first, in the Arctic and, towards the end of the war, in the Black Sea and the Baltic. That there was a new concept could be inferred from the fact that several submarines co-operated in attacks on convoys and from similar changes in tactics.

At first, the presence of Soviet submarines in the Baltic caused some disruption to German shipping, but when the Soviets lost the westward bases they had gained by occupying the Baltic states, their naval forces were practically penned in the Gulf of Finland. In 1942 some submarines did break through the barrages erected by the Germans and the Finns and reach the Baltic, but they did not achieve much, and the submarine campaign did not come to life again until 1944 or 1945, when the Soviets were able to remove the barrages.

Although opportunities were plentiful, the Soviet Navy achieved little success against enemy shipping. The sinkings of the refugee ships *Wilhelm Gustlov, General Steuben,* and *Goya,* which cost the lives of 15,000 people, were isolated successes made possible by the chaotic conditions following the Russian breakout from the Baranov bridgehead in January 1945.

Soviet submarine activities in the Black Sea were just as unsatisfactory as they were in the Baltic. No doubt one reason for the opportunities there not being exploited was that submarines were used for such special missions as running supplies to Sevastopol during the lengthy siege of that city, and for landing reconnaissance and sabotage groups on enemy-held coasts.

Soviet submarine losses were quite heavy: they totaled about 40 per cent of the number of boats in service at the outbreak of the war. Success was costly. As the following table shows, one submarine was lost for each ship sunk in the Baltic, and the ratio in the Black Sea was worse. It was best in the Arctic.

Successes and Losses of Soviet Submarines 1941–45

	Baltic	Arctic	Black Sea	Total
Warships and Merchant Ships Sunk	51	45	32	128
Submarines Lost	51	25	34	110

Soviet submarine crews were obviously not well enough trained and their great fighting spirit, demonstrated by the reckless breakouts into the Baltic in 1942, was not a substitute for training. Their boats and hardware, however, proved to be robust and reliable.

Buildup Since 1945

When the war ended and eastern and middle Germany were occupied, not only large quantities of shipbuilding material, but shipyards and workshops, some intact or only slightly damaged, fell into Russian hands. A still more important acquisition was the great number of experts in submarine construction: technicians, scientists, and skilled workers. The Soviets did not hesitate to make use of the human material for military purposes. At the same time, they could not fail to learn from the comprehensive documents concerning German submarine construction and operations, to which they fell heir.

With all these spoils in hand, the rebuilding of the Soviet submarine force could be begun. Of greatest interest were the German Types XXI, XXIII, and XXVI, which had the potential to revolutionize submarine operations, for they came closer to being true submersibles than any previous type. Thus, the four completed Type XXI and one completed Type XXIII boats and the numerous prefabricated sections that were captured were especially welcome. In addition, at the Schichau yard in Danzig there were between five and eight Type XXI boats under construction. These, the Soviets were able to complete with the help of the "conscripted" German experts. It is not known how many prefabricated sections were found.

According to recent estimates, the Soviets may have had 190 submarines left at the end of the war; that figure includes those that had been started before or built during the war, and the three British submarines —the *United,* the *Unison,* and the *Unbroken*—transferred to the Soviet Union in 1944 as the V-2, V-3, and V-4. Fifty or 60 of the 190 were only partially mobile or operational and must have been struck off the active list after the war's end. Against this, 17 German and 2 Italian submarines were taken over: so, at the beginning of 1946, there were between 150 and 160 operational submarines.

The Soviets certainly did not break up all their decommissioned boats, but make use of them in other ways. They could, for instance, convert them into floating "loading points" for conventional submarines. Those still capable of diving, which no doubt most of them are, could, in case of nuclear attack, submerge and be safe from blast, heat, and radiation. Such "loading points" could, conceivably be stationed at secret bases, especially in the Arctic and Antarctic.[21]

It is reported that some—perhaps 20—nonoperational submarines have been transferred to the Caspian Sea where they are said to be used for training crews. While

A W-class submarine during an air-sea transfer.

the old boats are certainly suitable for training purposes, it seems doubtful that the dying, shallow Caspian Sea is the ideal practice area.

Up to about the end of 1950, only some 50 new submarines were completed, and they were most likely improved versions of types developed by the end of the war. During that period, most of the Soviet submarine yards as well as the industries supplying components had to be rebuilt and consequently were not working at full efficiency. It must also be borne in mind that captured and dismantled equipment played a big role in reconstruction, and the Russians needed time to familiarize themselves with it. Moreover, most of the submarines built before and during the war had to be converted and modernized: the most important thing was to increase their battery capacity. Some of them were fitted with snorkels. It was mostly the large types that underwent such modifications.

New Submarines

First of the postwar construction was the W class, designs for which are said to have been completed by the beginning of 1944. Since the existence of this class was not confirmed until 1956, research and development, and the trials that followed, must have required a great deal of time. Hydrodynamically, their hull form appears to be as satisfactory as that of the German Type XXI. Today, numerous W-class boats are in service and,

A W-class attack submarine of the Black Sea Fleet.

although other classes have been developed since, they remain the standard class of Soviet submarine.

Its radius of action indicates that the W class is intended for oceangoing operations using torpedoes. Z-class submarines, whose existence was disputed in the West for a long time, are, as far as can be judged from external appearances, a slightly enlarged version of the W class. The hull shows the same construction as the W class, and cannot deny its descent from the German Type XXI any more than can the Ws. The shape of the

conning tower, also influenced by the Type XXI, is the same as that of the W class. Also like the Ws, the Zs were originally equipped with light antiaircraft weapons, which have since been removed.

The first Z-class submarine is believed to have been started by 1951 and commissioned in 1954. It is reported that 18 boats of this class were built at the Sudomech yard in Leningrad, from which it might be concluded that this yard was responsible for the construction of the entire class. The Z class was obviously

1 midships view of a Z-class attack submarine.

A Z-V-class ballistic-missile submarine.

intended for oceangoing torpedo warfare, but it is certain that a few of them, known as the Z-V class, have been armed with guided missiles. The addition of two missile-launching tubes built into the lengthened and heightened conning tower (see page 57) was probably carried out at the Zhdanov yard in Leningrad.

The Z-V-class boats, the first Soviet ballistic-missile submarines, were succeeded by the somewhat larger G class, whose construction was begun in 1958 or 1959 and which was intended from the outset to carry ballis-

tic missiles. In contrast to the Z-V class, the G-class boats were fitted with three launch tubes, and unconfirmed reports state that there is a version with four.

Another class of submarines that appears to have been influenced by German developments is the Q class. If, as French sources estimate, they have three shafts, it may be that the center shaft has a propulsion unit based on the German Walther system, which would allow them to attain a high submerged speed—for a limited time. It has not been possible to confirm that this is so, but the

A G-class ballistic-missile submarine. One of the missile launch tubes in the conning tower is open.

A Q-class attack submarine at a naval review at Leningrad.

reported submerged speed of 16 knots makes it certain that, like the Type XXI, they have considerable battery capacity. The Q class, of which there are supposed to be about 50, is a medium type for limited oceangoing use and could be of value in the Baltic and Black seas.

Two new classes of conventional submarines are the Fs and the Rs. Reports from the Eastern bloc maintain that these classes have an even more satisfactory hull and many other improvements. All the F-class boats, developments of the Z class, were built at the Sudomech yard in Leningrad. The R class consists of a number of converted Z-class submarines, apparently intended less for torpedo attacks on surface vessels than as hunter-killers against enemy submarines. It may be that they represent a Soviet attempt to develop a weapon to counter American Polaris submarines. An elliptical cylinder—a snorkel, perhaps—that projects from the conning tower is in three sections and is probably telescopic. By being telescopic, it could be protected from the risk of damage at high speeds.

An R-class attack submarine.

An F-class attack submarine putting to sea.

The last class with conventional propulsion was the J class, whose construction was commenced in 1960. They are thought to be experimental boats used for testing the weapon system later incorporated into E-class nuclear submarines.

It is extremely likely that all Soviet submarines can carry mines in place of torpedoes, and can launch them from the torpedo tubes. Almost certainly, the mines are a development of the German torpedo-tube mine, three of which can be carried in and launched from each tube. There is no evidence that the Soviet Navy has any special minelaying submarines.

Since the war, the Soviets have built several types of midget submarine, probably for offensive use in coastal waters. The first sighting of these types was during fleet maneuvers in April 1957. The incentive to build such craft was, no doubt, provided by the operations of German, British, Japanese, and Italian midget submarines during the Second World War. Three types are believed to be in existence, one being carried by a "mother" submarine (like the Japanese "Kaitens" during the war in the Pacific), while the other two types are transported to their operational area by special surface vessels. So far, the following details concerning these types have become known:

	2-Man Type	3-Man Type	4-Man Type
Surface Displacement (tons):	20.0	30.0	25.0
Length (feet):	39.0	59.0	69.0
Beam (feet):	5.0	8.0	6.0
Draft (feet):	6.0	?	9.0
Surface Speed (knots):	6.5	14.0	10.0
Submerged Speed (knots):	4.0	?	8.0

Except that the 3-man type is believed to carry two torpedoes, nothing has been said about their armament, but it may be taken as almost certain that they can carry two, or perhaps four, torpedoes or else mines. The latter are probably carried outboard on both sides of the pressure hull, as they were on the German "Seehund" miniature submarines.

Nuclear Submarines. Until early in 1963, there had been no public confirmation of the existence of Soviet nuclear-powered submarines. Repeated Soviet announcements that such boats were in service with their Navy seemed to be propaganda. For example, as long ago as the end of 1958, in an article in *Krasnaia Zvezda,* the Deputy Chief of the Soviet General Staff, Army General Aleksii I. Antonov, referred to the existence of nuclear submarines, and on the occasion of Red Navy Day, 30 July 1961, the Commander-in-Chief of the Warsaw Pact Forces, Marshal Grechko, declared that from then on, the basis of the Soviet Navy would be "modern submarines with atomic power and missiles of various types." In view of the fact that, since 1959 or so, Khrushchev had repeatedly asserted that the Soviet Union possessed a number of nuclear submarines, Western observers expected to see at least one of them during the Fleet Review on the Neva River in July 1961, but they were disappointed.

Since the submarine was at the core of Soviet maritime strategy, the possibility that adoption of nuclear power would eliminate one of its major weaknesses, must have given the Soviet Union and its Navy the incentive to begin this revolutionary development. That the Soviets were capable of using nuclear energy as a means of propulsion had been demonstrated by the construction of the icebreaker *Lenin.* Moreover, they were already engaged in research into nuclear-powered

An N-class nuclear-powered attack submarine in the Gulf of Mexico.

land vehicles and aircraft. Among other things, a nuclear-powered locomotive had been mentioned and it appeared that efforts to produce a nuclear-powered flying boat had been going on for some years. No doubt, the Soviets saw in the latter, with its theoretical independence from fuel supplies, a vehicle that could be used for long-range, oceanic reconnaissance. Having no carrier-borne aircraft, they had no means of conducting such reconnaissance.

Plans for nuclear-powered submarines to be built raised a technical problem of major importance: how to design and build a reactor large enough to be efficient, but small enough to require only such shielding arrangements as would be compatible with the weight and space limitations of a submarine. It was much easier to develop a reactor for the icebreaker *Lenin,* for instance, because size and weight did not play such a decisive role. No doubt, this complication was at least partly responsible for the time the Russians lost before 1962 and which it will now be hard for them to make up, for by that time, the Americans had a proven force of nuclear submarines.

Shortly after the Twenty-second Communist Party Congress, held in late 1961, an interesting report published in the newspaper *Izvestiia,* stated that "no small difficulties faced the Soviet constructors when they commenced the development of nuclear submarines. The reactors had to be fitted into the smallest space possible, shielding arrangements had to be produced and equipment developed to turn nuclear energy into mechanical, that is, propulsive, energy." The article confirmed the suspicion expressed by the present author not only in this book but elsewhere as early as 1959.[22]

There must have been many difficult technical problems to solve, or the most powerful submarine service in the world would have been the first to have nuclear submarines. As it was, the first nuclear-powered Soviet vessel followed five years after the first American nuclear submarine, the *Nautilus,* had been commissioned, and then she was not a submarine, but the icebreaker *Lenin.*

It is unlikely that any of the Soviet nuclear submarines now in existence had been completed by the summer of 1961, since none was included among all the new construction that was shown for the first time on the occasion of the Fleet Review on the Neva.

Failure to recognize early the significance of nuclear-powered submarines would appear to be another reason why the Soviets fell behind in developing them. In the usual Soviet way, a scapegoat was named—ex-Minister of Defense for the Soviet Union, Marshal Zhukov. *Izvestiia* suggested that Zhukov "had denied the importance of technical progress," while in the same breath it styled Khrushchev "father of the Atomic Submarine Fleet which today guards the borders of the Soviet State, for only he had attended to the matter."

Izvestiia further reported that the Soviet nuclear submarine has a "blunt nose like a transport aircraft and a small, very powerful tail similar to the tail fins of a huge sturgeon." This indicates that the hull is whale-shaped, like that of the American submarines *Albacore, Skipjack,* and *Thresher,* for example, a form that reduces drag and significantly increases submerged speed.[23] According to *Izvestiia,* these Soviet submarines have a speed "higher than that of the fastest ocean liner," and their size corresponds to that of conventional submarines. It is interesting that *Izvestiia* named Lev Zhultov as the commanding officer of one of the nuclear submarines, apparently the first of the class, and described him as "a veteran of the Soviet atomic fleet."

At the end of January 1963, Moscow caused a stir among the experts by publishing a report on the polar voyage of the nuclear submarine *Leninskii Komsomol.* During an exercise in locating and engaging enemy

An H-class nuclear-powered ballistic-missile submarine in Arctic waters.

submarines before they could reach Soviet waters, this boat was stated to have transited the polar region beneath the ice and to have reached the North Pole.

At the same time, *Krasnaia Zvezda* published the first picture of a Russian nuclear submarine. The illustration depicted a vessel of the N class, whose whale-shaped, or "teardrop," hull indicated that she is capable of making a high speed, and whose streamlined conning tower is situated unusually far forward. N-class submarines were

designed to detect and attack enemy submarines; in other words, they are hunter-killers. Their propulsion machinery was said to be very noisy, but it may be that that defect has since been rectified.

The H class, ordered in 1959 or 1960, is a logical development of the G class, which it closely resembles. Neither this class nor the later E class has a whale-shaped hull. The latter appeared in two versions, both carrying antiship, guided missiles.

Strength of the Submarine Force

By the end of 1957, it was assumed that the development of nuclear submarines would shortly cause the series production of conventional submarines to end. This assumption was proved wrong two years later, when there were reports of increased activity in Soviet shipyards building submarines. At first, it was thought that failures in nuclear-submarine development had necessitated renewed or continued construction of conventional boats. Now, it is certain that the activity was concerned with the conversion of a number of large conventional submarines to guided-missile and hunter-killer boats in order to counterbalance, quantitatively at least, American progress. Apparently, the construction of conventional boats was limited, probably to the latest classes, while development work on nuclear submarines was being energetically pressed forward.

The strength of the Soviet submarine force cannot be assessed without taking into account the number and efficiency of shipyards building submarines. To start with, it must be emphasized that the number of yards engaged on submarine construction is relatively small. Because of transport restrictions, inland yards can build only submarines up to about 500 tons. Larger boats must be built in yards that have access to the sea, although prefabricated sections can be delivered to them from the inland yards. The following yards are known to be building submarines: the Marti, Ordzhonikidze, Sudo-

An E-II nuclear-powered guided-missile submarine.

mech, and Zhdanov yards in Leningrad; the Marti yard in Nikolaev, and other yards in Odessa and Sevastopol; the naval yards in Tallinn, Izhorsk-Kolpino, Komsomolsk, Sovetskaia Gavan, and Severodvinsk; and three or four inland yards.

An estimated average of 65 boats is built annually by those yards. That figure is not far off the 70 boats per year mentioned by Khrushchev during his visit to England in 1956. Although the Arctic and Far Eastern yards have recently been significantly extended and modernized at great expense, their capacity is still considerably less than that of the yards situated on the two land-locked seas. Weather conditions, which affect both the delivery of material and the actual construction, are mainly responsible for the difference in capacity. Baltic shipyards, mostly those in Leningrad, are still building the majority of Soviet submarines.

General Review

It would be scarcely possible to conduct a submarine campaign along the lines of the German one of 1939–1945 with the oceangoing submarine fleet that now exists. This point of view is reinforced when it is remembered that the components of the fleet are widely dispersed, and that about half of the submarines concerned are stationed in land-locked seas from which it would not be easy, in the event of war, for them to escape. A submarine campaign would have to be directed against Western shipping engaged in transporting supplies to Europe; but long passages to operational areas, lack of reliable Soviet air reconnaissance over the oceans, and the defensive capacity of Western forces, could well limit the success of such a campaign.

These considerations do not apply to the operations of missile-armed submarines, which could present a serious threat to the exposed centers of the West. Those boats that are nuclear-powered would be extremely difficult to combat.

Today, Soviet submarines visit the oceans of the world more frequently than they ever did before. During voyages of several weeks' duration, the crews gain experience in all aspects of submarine operations, observe shipping, and become familiar with conditions that they might encounter in war. It has become routine for the boats to operate in groups, and they constantly practise co-operation with the air forces and with replenishment ships. Hydographic units—survey ships—are everywhere, and their task is to procure oceanographic and nautical information necessary for submarine operations. There can be no doubt that the Soviets have studied the causes of their limited success in submarine warfare during the two world wars and are trying to eliminate them.

Their lack of success in the past cannot be used as a yardstick to measure future operations. In both world wars, Russia was fighting a continental power, Germany, and victory could be gained only on land. As far as can be foreseen, any future conflict would pit Soviet submarines against the world's strongest naval powers: consequently, Soviet leaders have taken appropriate steps to strengthen the submarine.

A C-class nuclear-powered guided-missile submarine, a type first seen in 1969.

Modern submarines, which spend most of their time below the surface and have a much greater radius of action than their predecessors had, require the submariner to be capable of swift appraisal of and reaction to situations that arise and, above all, to have a high degree of self-discipline. These are not characteristics for which the average Russian is renowned, anyway, and the Communist system, which breeds mistrust between superiors and subordinates, inhibits initiative, and adheres to inflexible dogmatism, militates against his acquiring them.

It is true that so long as the Communist ideology holds sway there will be some problems in this area.

On the other hand, the seaman of yesterday—and it cannot be said that the Russians have no vocation for the sea—is, to a greater and greater extent, being replaced by the highly qualified technician, and the Russians have been educated in technology for nearly half a century. Consequently, it would be foolish, even dangerous, to bank on the Soviets not having appropriate manpower for their submarines.

Activities of the Soviet Fleet

The Soviet Fleet no longer restricts its activities to home waters, as it used to do. For some years now, its submarines have been making long-range voyages on a scale previously unknown, and there are Russian submarines constantly in every sea. As their crews familiarize themselves with operational and weather conditions in far-off areas, the boats and their equipment are being subjected to exhaustive tests. It is reported that many of the boats carry scientists who make the oceanographic research required for modern submarine warfare. It is not uncommon to see submarines, mostly off Newfoundland and Alaska, practising at-sea replenishment by taking fuel and stores from fishing vessels. Judging by the frequency with which submarines are seen under way on the surface, a number of problems do arise in the course of all this training.

Surface ships cruise, either singly or in groups, under simulated war conditions. The Northern Fleet places special emphasis on training cruises along the Northern Sea Route. Inadequate base and dockyard facilities in the Arctic and the Far East may be one reason for the frequency with which ships are transferred from one fleet to another.

Major fleet exercises take place once a year in each of the four fleets. In order to achieve the closest possible co-operation between the services, the exercises, especially the amphibious operations which are practised in-

Petya-class frigates sortie during a Baltic Fleet exercise.

tensively, are frequently combined with Army maneuvers. Great importance is attached to sea-air co-operation, particularly with units of the naval air forces. Satellite navies often participate in the large-scale exercises.

Besides amphibious operations, high priority is given to convoy exercises and to scouting sweeps by the task groups. A typical group would consist of some cruisers, eight to ten destroyers, a similar number of frigates, four to six submarines, and replenishment ships equipped with helicopters. The submarines usually operate with the frigates and helicopters, while the cruisers and destroyers accompany the replenishment ships.

Frequent exercises conducted by the river flotillas are also intended to ensure the closest co-operation with the land forces. During such exercises, the formation and defense of bridgeheads, supply and transport operations, and the defense of river crossings play an important part.

Gun and torpedo firings, as well as blockade exercises, are conducted as often as possible, and include competitions, in which special distinctions are awarded to the best ships.

Soviet warships undertake political missions in the form of visits to foreign ports, and for some time now they have been visiting member states of the Western alliances as well as satellite countries. Most of these missions have been carried out by a *Sverdlov*-class cruiser and a number of destroyers, the first having been made by the *Sverdlov* herself when she attended the Coronation Fleet Review at Spithead, England, in June 1953. Thereafter, the Soviet Navy commenced a busy schedule of visits which, in most cases, were reciprocal. The Soviet port usually open to foreign vessels was Leningrad, but French ships and ships from the United Arab Republic were privileged to enter Sevastopol. Among the Soviet excursions were:

1953: October
> Vice Admiral V. A. Parkhomenko with the cruisers *Frunze* and *Kuibyshev* and four destroyers to Rumanian and Bulgarian ports.

1954: July
> Rear Admiral G. S. Abashvili with the cruiser *Ordzhonikidze* and two destroyers to Helsinki.
>
> *August*
> Rear Admiral V. F. Kotov with the cruiser *Admiral Ushakov* and four destroyers to Stockholm.

1955: October
> Admiral A. G. Golovko with the cruisers *Sverdlov* and *Aleksandr Suvorov* and four destroyers to Portsmouth, England.

1956: April
> N. A. Bulganin and N. S. Khrushchev to Great Britain in the cruiser *Ordzhonikidze* with two destroyers.

The Sverdlov-*class cruiser* Ordzhonikidze *and two* Skoryi-*class destroyers visit Copenhagen, Denmark, in August 1956.*

1956: May–June

Admiral V. A. Kasatonov with the cruiser *Mikhail Kutusov* and two destroyers to Yugoslav and Albanian ports.

June

Vice Admiral V. A. Chekurov with the cruiser *Dmitri Pozharski* and two destroyers to Shanghai.

1956: July

Rear Admiral V. F. Kotov with the cruiser *Sverdlov* and two destroyers to Rotterdam.

July–August

Admiral A. T. Chabanenko with the cruiser *Oktiabr'skaia Revoliutsiia* and two destroyers to Göteborg and Oslo.

1956: August

Admiral A. G. Golovko with the cruiser *Ordzhonikidze* to Copenhagen.

1957: October

The cruiser *Kuibyshev* and two destroyers to Yugoslav ports, and Vice Admiral V. F. Kotov with the cruiser *Zhdanov* and one destroyer to Syrian Latakia and Yugoslavia.

1958: August

Admiral N. M. Kharlamov with the cruiser *Ordzhonikidze* and two destroyers to Helsinki.

September

The cruiser *Oktiabr'skaia Revoliutsiia* and one destroyer to Stockholm.

1959: November

Admiral V. A. Fokin with the cruiser *Admiral Seniavin* and two destroyers to Djakarta.

1962: June

Three attack submarines and the depot ship *Viktor Kotelnikov* to Stockholm.

1963: November

Captain 1/R B. I. Bukovski with the surveying ships *Zenit* and *Azimut* to Bergen.

1964: May

Admiral A. E. Orel with the cruiser *Komsomolets* and two destroyers to Copenhagen.

June

Admiral S. E. Chursin with the cruiser *Mikhail*

Kutusov and two destroyers to Yugoslavia.

August

Vice Admiral G. K. Chernobai with the cruiser *Dzerzhinski* and one destroyer to Constanta.

August

Vice Admiral V. F. Chalyi with the cruiser *Mikhail Kutusov* and one destroyer to Bulgarian ports.

September

Captain 1/R B. I. Bukovski with the surveying ships *Zenit* and *Azimut* to Dakar and Casablanca.

October

. Vice Admiral S. M. Lobov with the cruiser *Murmansk* and one destroyer to Trondheim.

1965: February

Rear Admiral G. F. Stepanov with the destroyer *Naporistyi* to Massawa, Ethiopia.

1966: January

Rear Admiral V. S. Sysoev with the destroyer *Plamennyi* to Massawa.

August–November

Vice Admiral G. K. Chernobai with the guided-missile destroyer *Boikii*, the frigate *Pantera*, two attack submarines, and the depot ship *Mahomet Gadzhiev* to United Arab Republic and Algerian ports.

October

Captain 1/R S. Sokolan with the destroyer *Naporistyi* to Toulon.

1967: January

Rear Admiral G. A. Gromov with the guided-missile destroyer *Gnevnyi* to Massawa. (Admiral Gorshkov, Commander-in-Chief of the Soviet Navy, also present.)

June–October

Rear Admiral I. N. Molodtsov with a force of warships at Alexandria during the Arab-Israeli conflict.

June–July

Rear Admiral V. P. Beliakov with the cruiser *Kirov* and one destroyer to Stockholm.

1968: February

Admiral S. E. Chursin with the guided-missile cruiser *Groznyi,* one destroyer, the depot ship *Dmitri Galkin,* and three attack submarines to Yugoslavia.

March–April

Admiral N. N. Amel'ko with the cruiser *Dmitri Pozharski,* the guided-missile destroyer *Gordyi,* and a smaller guided-missile ship to Madras and Bombay. (Admiral Amel'ko and the *Gordyi* departed on 6 April for arrival at Vladivostok on 1 May.)

April–July

A detachment under the command of Rear Admiral N. I. Khovrin in the *Dmitri Pozharski* toured the Indian Ocean and put in to ports in Somalia, Yemen, Aden, Iraq, Pakistan, and Ceylon. The detachment was fueled by the oiler *Poliarnik.*

April

Captain 2/R A. P. Ushakov with the guided-missile cruiser *Groznyi* to Latakia.

May–June

Rear Admiral V. M. Leonenkov with the hydrographic ships *Fedor Litke* and *Aleksei Chirikov* to Massawa.

October

Vice Admiral B. F. Petrov with the guided-missile cruiser *Groznyi,* the guided-missile destroyer *Gnevnyi,* and two attack submarines to Casablanca.

November–December

Captain 1/R S. Korostylev with the guided-missile cruiser *Admiral Fokin,* one destroyer, and the supply ship *Dunai* to Mombasa.

December

Captain 1/R V. A. Merzliakov with the depot ship *Ivan Kucherenko,* two attack submarines, and an oiler, the *Alatyr',* to Dar-es-Salaam.

1969: January–February

Captain 1/R S. Korostylev with the guided-missile cruiser *Admiral Fokin,* the guided-missile destroyer *Gnevnyi,* the destroyer *Vdokhnovennyi,* the supply ship *Dunai,* and the transport *Ul'ma* to Aden, Hodeida (Yemen), and Mombasa.

An Oskol-class repair ship and two F-class attack submarines moor at Algiers in August 1968.

1969: January

Captain 1/R A. A. Trofimov with the hydrographic ships *Semen Cheliushkin* and *Andrei Vil'kitski* to Colombo.

January

The guided-missile destroyer *Gnevnyi* to Massawa.

February–March

Captain 1/R V. Platonov with the guided-missile destroyers *Boikii* and *Neulovimyi,* one attack submarine, and a fleet oiler to Conakry, Guinea, and Lagos, Nigeria.

April

Captain 1/R S. E. Korostelev with the guided-missile cruiser *Admiral Fokin,* the guided-missile destroyer *Gnevnyi,* and the oiler *Alatyr'* to Port Louis, Mauritius.

July

Rear Admiral B. Drugov with the cruiser *Komsomolets* to Helsinki.

July

Rear Admiral Stepan S. Sokolan, of the Black Sea Fleet, with the guided-missile cruiser *Groznyi,* the guided-missile destroyer *Bedovyi,* one destroyer, two attack submarines, the submarine tender *Tobol,* and the tanker *Lena* to Cuba.

July–August

Captain 1/R T. A. Liashko with the guided-missile destroyer (?) *Upornyi* and the tanker *Egorlyk*

to Zanzibar.

August

Vice Admiral V. S. Sysoev, Commander of the Black Sea Fleet, with the cruiser *Dzerzhinski* and four escorts to Varna.

August

Rear Admiral Stepan S. Sokolan with the guided-missile cruiser *Groznyi* to Fort-de-France, Martinique.

August

The guided-missile destroyer *Bedovyi* and the tanker *Lena* to Bridgetown, Barbados.

August

Captain 2/R A. Moshnin with the hydrographic ship *Pamiat' Merkuriia* to Pantelleria.

Ships' companies behave well in foreign ports. Shore excursions, when permitted, are made in small groups and supervised by several officers.

Soviet warships frequently observe exercises being conducted by Western fleets. Whenever the Bundesmarine conducts exercises, some Soviet ships are on the scene, apparently for the purposes of causing confusion among the participating forces and picking up information about frequencies, methods of communication, detection techniques, and anything else they can. An incident that occurred in the autumn of 1960 attracted considerable attention: the cruiser *Oktiabr'skaia Revo-*

Guided-missile warships in Cuba in July 1969: a Kildin-*class destroyer; a* Kynda-*class cruiser; and a* Kashin-*class destroyer.*

A Kashin-class guided-missile destroyer shadows the carrier USS Franklin D. Roosevelt *in the Mediterranean.*

liutsiia and two destroyers, returning from a cruise in the North Atlantic, met some units of the Bundesmarine exercising in the Baltic. In defiance of all the accepted standards of good seamanship and manners, the Russians steamed right through the middle of the German formation, passing within less than ten meters of some of the German ships. They maintained complete radio silence, but operated their detection equipment and aerials.

The frequency with which Soviet submarines appear in the waters off the missile research center at Cape Kennedy, Florida, needs no explanation. During the Cuban crisis, in the autumn of 1962, numerous Soviet submarines, some of them ballistic-missile carriers, were in the waters off the east coast of the United States. There was similar activity in the Middle East during the summer of 1967. Admiral Thomas H. Moorer, then American Chief of Naval Operations, estimated that some 35 to 40 Soviet warships were, at that time, in the Mediterranean, a number of them spending several weeks in Port Said and other Egyptian ports. They were obviously intended to bolster the morale of the Arab states, and to bring pressure to bear on Israel.

"Reduction" of the Soviet Fleet

A few years ago, Khrushchev claimed that the Soviet Union intended to scrap about 90 per cent of its cruisers, and on 31 January 1959 the Soviet news agency, Tass, reported that the Soviet Forces were in the process of being reduced by about 300,000 men. There have certainly been reductions in numbers since 1956, and a quantity of obsolete weapons and equipment has been removed from service. In reality, however, the Soviets have increased their firepower by the introduction of weapons recently perfected and put into series production, and they have streamlined the organization of their forces.

In 1956 there was a report that many ships had been taken off the Navy's active list. The ships concerned were, without exception, obsolete or obsolescent, and only very few of them were scrapped: most of them were put to use as tenders, and so forth. Many ships of all types and classes were transferred to the satellite navies (see pages 177–9), while others were handed over to civil authorities. In all, 5 cruisers, 25 destroyers, 67 escort and similar vessels, 59 submarines, 90 minesweepers, minelayers, and patrol craft, about 100 old transports, training ships, coastal patrol boats, and other craft were involved. If Soviet sources are to be believed, 2 battleships and 3 cruisers were scrapped: 375 ships of the Baltic and Black Sea fleets (including the Caspian, Volga, Dnepr, and Danube flotillas) alone, were paid off. How many ships of the Northern and Pacific fleets were affected has not been disclosed.

There was a corresponding reduction of manpower in the naval land forces: in the case of the coast defense forces, this was probably because missiles replaced artillery. According to Western estimates, the total reduction, including redundant seagoing personnel, amounted to between 200,000 and 250,000 men. Of these, 100,000 were immediately directed into the shipbuilding industry, 80,000 into the building and extension of harbors and similar installations, and 50,000 into transportation on inland waters.

Measures affecting the 9th Minelaying Brigada in Batumi and the 17th Minesweeping Brigada in Poti provide an example of how a reduction can, in fact, represent an increase in combat effectiveness. The 18 minelayers and 45 minesweepers with which those two units, respectively, were equipped, were all mothballed. Some men were released from the Navy, but the long-service men were drafted to the newly formed 20th Minelaying and Minesweeping Brigada. This unit is said to consist now of 24 new minesweepers that are also suitable for minelaying, escort duties, antisubmarine warfare, and similar tasks. Furthermore, they are faster than the craft they replaced.

Clearly, what was termed a "reduction" has strengthened the Soviet Navy.

Summary of the Ships of the
Soviet Fleet as of 1 January 1969

Characteristics are given only for ships and vessels not discussed in the text or in Appendix I. There may be many ships, old and new, not known to the West. Consequently, the following summary should be treated with reserve, especially where small craft are concerned.

2 Helicopter Carriers
  2 *Moskva* class

18 Cruisers
  2 *Kirov* class
  3 *Chapaev* class
  13 *Sverdlov* class

10 Guided-Missile Cruisers
  4 *Kynda* class
  5 *Kresta* class
  1 *Dzerzhinski* class

27 Guided-Missile Destroyers
  5 *Kotlin-Sam* class
  4 *Kildin* class
  8 *Krupnyi* class
  2 *Kanin* class
  10 *Kashin* class

70 Destroyers
  50 *Skoryi* class
  1 *Tallinn* class
  22 *Kotlin* class

117 Frigates
  10 *Kola* class
  50 *Riga* class
  35 *Petya* class
  22 *Mirka* class

53 Ballistic-Missile Submarines
  10 Z-V class
  30 G class
  13 H class

45 Guided-Missile Submarines
  6 W class, Single-Cylinder and Twin-Cylinder
  6 W class, Long Bin
  8 J class
  25 E class

255 Attack Submarines
  145 W class, including Radar Picket Submarines and W class, Canvas Bag
  25 Z class
  15 Q class
  40 F class
  15 R class
  15 N class

A Kanin-*class guided-missile destroyer. These converted* Krupnyis *are among the latest of Soviet warship types.*

152 Guided-Missile Fast Patrol Boats
   42 *Komar* class
  110 *Osa* class

.. Armed Motorboats

400+ Fast Patrol Boats
   .. P-4 class
   .. P-6 class
   .. P-8 class
   .. P-10 class
  25+ *Shershen* class
  25+ *Pchela* class

270+ Submarine Chasers
  100 *Kronstadt* class, including *Libau*-class communi-
     cations vessels
   90 SO-I class (fast boats)
   80 *Poti* class
   .. MO-VI class (fast boats)
  3 to 5 *Stenka* class (fast boats)

319 Minesweepers
   36 T-301 class
  130 T-43 class
   20 T-58 class
   50 *Sasha* class
   35 *Iurka* class
   48 *Vanya* class

179+ Landing Ships
  16 MP-2 class
  28 MP-4 class
  10 MP-6 class
  18 MP-8 class
  40 MP-10 and SMB-I classes
  40 *Polnochnyi* class
   7 *Alligator* class
  20 *Vydra* class

... Landing Craft

700 (approx.) Auxiliaries:
Communications and Picket Ships, Tenders, Depot Ships, Repair Ships, and Minelayers
  .. *Libau* class
  .. T-43-AGR class
  1 *Paysherd,* formerly German S-boat tender *Adolf Lüderitz:* built, 1939–40; 2,900 tons standard; 23 kts.; 4 4.1-inch guns.
  2 *Pechora* and *Kuban,* formerly German U-boat tenders *Otto Wünsche* and *Waldemar Kophamel:* built, 1939–41; 4,700 to 5,000 tons standard; 20 kts.; 4 4.1-inch AA guns.
  1 *Angara,* formerly German fleet tender *Hela:* built, 1939–40; 2,115 tons standard; 19 kts.; 2 4.1-inch guns.

1 *Purga* class
6 *Atrek* class
4 *Tovda* class
6 *Don* class
3 *Ugra* class
5 *Dnepr* class
1 or 2 *Alesha* class
4 *Oskol* class—may be more
3 *Lama* class

Fleet Oilers and Supply Ships
29 *Khobi* class
.. *Nercha* class
.. *Iakhroma* class
.. *Vodolei* class
3 *Pevk* class
4 *Uda* class—may be more

Net-Layers (in peacetime, Cable-Layers also) and Others
18 *Neptun* class: built, 1957–60; 700 tons standard; 12 kts.; no armament.
3 *Ladoga* class: built, 1941; 350 tons; 9.5 kts.; 3 45-mm. AA guns.
.. *Sura* class: built, 1964; 3,150 tons standard; 12 kts.; no armament.

Submarine Rescue Ships
10 *Valdai* class

Salvage Ships and Tugs
4 *Pamir* class
6 *Prut* class
.. *Orel* class
8 *Okhtenshiy* class—may be more
1 *Kommuna:* built, 1912–13; 2,400 tons standard; 8 kts.; no armament. Twin-hulled submarine-lifting ship, can lift 1,000 tons. Stationed at Kronstadt.

Surveying Ships
10 *Samara* class
1 *Aitodor:* built, 1963–64; 1,217 tons gross.
3 *Okean* class: built, 1937–38; 1,500 tons standard; 14 kts.; in peacetime, no armament, in war, can lay mines.
1 *Ekvator,* formerly the German *Meteor:* built, 1915; 1,200 tons standard; 14.5 kts.; probably no armament.
1 *Chukcha:* built, 1920; 2,700 tons standard; 10 kts.; no armament.
3 *Partizan* class: built, 1937; 1,300 tons standard; 9.5 kts.; no armament.
1 *Lebed':* built, 1931; 1,100 tons standard; 12 kts.; no armament.
4 *Gidrofon* class, formerly U.S. *Admirable*-class minesweepers: built, 1942–43; 650 tons standard; 15 kts.; no armament.

Icebreakers
  1 *Volynets:* built, 1914; 4,000 tons standard; 13.5 kts.
  1 *Malygin:* built, 1916; 2,070 tons standard; 13.5 kts.
  1 *Vladimir Ilyich:* built, 1917; 6,260 tons; 12 kts.
  1 *Sibiriakov,* formerly the Finnish *Jääkarhu:* built, 1926; 4,825 tons standard; 15 kts.
  1 *Polluks,* formerly the German *Pollux:* built, 1943; 4,500 tons standard; 13 kts.
  1 *Aliosha Popovich,* formerly the German *Eisvogel:* built, 1941; 2,090 tons standard; 13.6 kts.
  1 *Ilya Muromets,* formerly the German *Eisbär:* built, 1941; 1,918 tons standard; 13.6 kts.
  2 *Admiral Lazarev* class: built, 1937–39; 1,100 tons standard; 15 kts.
  1 *Peresvet* class
  3 *Kapitan Belousov* class
  4 *Moskva* class
  5 *Dobrynia Nikitich* class
  1 *Lenin* class
  2 *Arktika* class—one under construction, one planned
  2 ships planned

Training Ships
  1 *Tovarich,* formerly the German *Gorch Fock:* built, 1933; 1,350 tons standard; 8 kts.; no armament; sail training ship.
  4 *Praktika* class: 300 tons; sail training ships.
  1 *Neman,* formerly the German *Isar:* built, 1930; 3,850 tons standard; 12 kts.; no armament.

Research Ships
  2 *Chazhma* class
  1 *Astronaut Vladimir Komarov* class—one more may be under construction
  4 *Chukotka* class
  1 *Mikhail Lomonosov:* built, 1956; 13 kts.; no armament.
  1 *Baikal:* built, 1964; no other data.
  1 *Ob:* built, 1953; 12,000 tons gross; 15.5 kts.
  1 *Sevastopol:* built, 1951; 2,450 tons; 10 kts.
  1 *Vitiaz:* built, 1939; 5,750 tons; 14.5 kts.
  2 *Sergei Vavilov* class: no other data.
  2 *Severianka* class: research boats, *see* W-class submarines.

Opposite: A C-class nuclear-powered missile submarine.

Ships Transferred To Other Navies

Albania
  4 W-class submarines
 12 P-4-class fast patrol boats
  4 *Kronstadt*-class submarine chasers
  6 T-301-class minesweepers
  2 T-43-class minesweepers
  1 *Atrek*-class depot ship
  1 *Khobi*-class fleet oiler

Algeria
  6 *Komar*-class, guided-missile fast patrol boats
  1 *Osa*-class, guided-missile fast patrol boat
  8 P-6 fast patrol boats
  2 SO-I-class submarine chasers

Bulgaria
  2 *Riga*-class frigates
  2 W-class submarines
  8 P-4-class fast patrol boats
  2 *Kronstadt*-class submarine chasers
  6 SO-I-class submarine chasers
  4 T-301-class minesweepers
  2 T-43-class minesweepers
 22 Patrol boats

Cuba
    18 *Komar*-class, guided-missile fast patrol boats
    12 P-4-class fast patrol boats
    12 P-6-class fast patrol boats
     6 *Kronstadt*-class submarine chasers
    12 SO-I-class submarine chasers

Cyprus
     6 P-4-class fast patrol boats

East Germany
     4 *Riga*-class frigates
    12 *Osa*-class, guided-missile fast patrol boats
    27 P-6-class fast patrol boats
    12 SO-I-class submarine chasers

Egypt
     4 *Skoryi*-class destroyers
     7 W-class submarines
     5 R-class submarines
     1 M-V-class* submarine
     8 *Komar*-class, guided-missile fast patrol boats
    12 *Osa*-class, guided-missile fast patrol boats
    36 P-6-class fast patrol boats
     3 *Shershen*-class fast patrol boats
     8 SO-I-class submarine chasers
     2 T-301-class minesweepers
     6 T-43-class minesweepers

    2–3 *Polnochnyi*-class landing ships
    18 SMB-I-class landing ships
        A few *Okhtenshiy*-class tugs

Finland
     2 *Riga*-class frigates

India
     2 *Petya*-class frigates
     4 F-class submarines
     6 P-6-class fast patrol boats
     2 *Polnochnyi*-class landing ships
     1 *Ugra*-class depot ship (submarine tender)
     6 Patrol boats

Indonesia
     1 *Sverdlov*-class cruiser
     7 *Skoryi*-class destroyers
     7 *Riga*-class frigates
    12 *Komar*-class, guided-missile fast patrol boats
    24 P-6-class fast patrol boats
     8 *Kronstadt*-class submarine chasers
     1 T-301-class minesweeper
     6 T-43-class minesweepers
    12 Patrol boats
     1 *Atrek*-class depot ship
     1 *Don*-class depot ship
     2 Oilers

Iraq
12 P-6-class fast patrol boats
3 SO-I-class submarine chasers

North Korea
2 W-class submarines
39 P-4-class fast patrol boats
4 *Artillerist*-class* submarine chasers
2 T-43-class minesweepers
8 *Fugas*-class* minesweepers
4 Patrol boats

North Vietnam
12 P-4-class fast patrol boats
3 P-6-class fast patrol boats
3 SO-I-class submarine chasers

Poland
4 W-class submarines
6 M-V-class* submarines
2 *Skoryi*-class destroyers
12 *Osa*-class guided-missile fast patrol boats
20 P-6-class fast patrol boats

Red China
4 R-class submarines
3 M-V-class* submarines
4 S-class* submarines

4 *Gordyi*-class* destroyers
6 *Kronstadt*-class submarine chasers
2 SO-I-class submarine chasers
6 *Artillerist*-class* submarine chasers
2 T-43-class minesweepers
A large number of fast patrol boats and small craft

Rumania
4 *Osa*-class, guided-missile fast patrol boats
8 P-4-class fast patrol boats
3 *Kronstadt*-class submarine chasers
22 T-301-class minesweepers

Somalia
12 P-6-class fast patrol boats
2 Patrol boats

Syria
10 *Komar*-class, guided-missile fast patrol boats
15 Fast patrol boats (class not known)
2 T-43-class minesweepers

Yugoslavia
7 *Osa*-class, guided-missile fast patrol boats
6 *Shershen*-class fast patrol boats

* This class is no longer operational in the Soviet Navy.

Opposite: The pilot of a Beriev-12 amphibian briefs his crew before flight.

CHAPTER 6

Naval Air Forces

Organization

The table of organization of Soviet military aviation shows an unusual structure, for besides the air forces under the command of the Army and the Navy, there are air forces that are completely independent and have clearly defined missions.

The Army Air Forces, whose task is tactical support of the Army, have almost two-thirds of the military aircraft of the Soviet Union.

The Long-Range Air Force has a strategic role and can be equated with the U.S. Strategic Air Command.

The Home Air Defense Force includes the warning and reporting system, the fighter command, and antiaircraft defenses (guns and missiles).

The Air Transport Force has as its primary mission the deployment of airborne troops.

The role of the Naval Air Forces is tactical. Originally, the forces included fighter units, but in 1960 they were withdrawn and, probably in order to consolidate air defense under one command, most of them were transferred to the Home Air Defense Force. Some units, however, did go to the Army Air Forces. These transfers markedly reduced the numerical strength of the Naval Air Forces which, today, stands at about 770 aircraft, as against approximately 3,500 in 1960. Each of the four main fleets is allocated an air corps, which in turn is divided into a number of air divisions of two or three air regiments. An air division may comprise about 100 aircraft, an air regiment 25 to 30. Regiments are specialized according to the role of their aircraft, that is, there are bomber regiments, reconnaissance regiments, and so forth. No regiment is known to have more than one role.

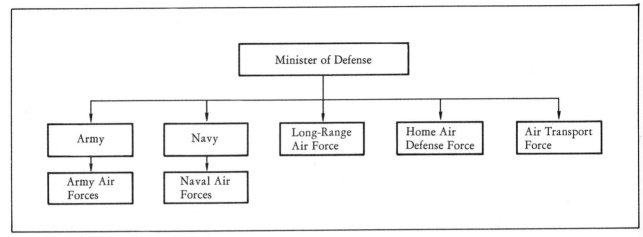

Organization of Soviet Military Aviation

At this writing, the numerical strength of Soviet air power is estimated at approximately 20,000 aircraft, allocated as follows:

Army Air Forces: 9,000 aircraft (fighters, fighter bombers, reconnaissance planes, and bombers).

Naval Air Forces: 770 aircraft (reconnaissance planes, bombers, and helicopters).

Long-Range Air Force: 1,500 aircraft (bombers and tankers).

Home Air Defense Force: 7,000 aircraft (fighters).

Air Transport Force: 1,500 aircraft (transports).

Operations and Training

The Naval Air Forces' operational tasks are clearly defined. First, they are required to conduct long-range, maritime reconnaissance aimed at providing intelligence for the deployment of surface forces and, most important, for the direction of submarines to enemy targets, either convoys or fleet formations. Of almost equal importance, is the mining, possibly with nuclear mines, of enemy harbors, bases, and sea lanes. In this connection, it should be remembered that the whole of Europe lies within reach of the Soviet Naval Air Forces.

Next among their tasks come nuclear and conventional attacks on ports, naval installations, and enemy shipping in restricted waters, such as the Mediterranean and the English Channel. The oil refineries and terminals of the Middle East can be reached relatively quickly from bases in the southern part of the Caspian Sea area, and attacks upon those targets could destroy a large part of the West's oil supplies. In home waters, an increasingly important mission for the Naval Air Forces is antisubmarine warfare, especially against American Polaris submarines. No longer are antisubmarine operations conducted only by shore-based aircraft: warship-based helicopters now participate.

In Arctic waters, ice reconnaissance is important, particularly along the Northern Sea Route which, it must be expected, will be used increasingly for the transfer of naval units. In this task, also, helicopters perform excellent service.

There is close liaison between the naval and other air forces and, in general, co-operation between them is good. Co-ordination is facilitated by the fact that, with few exceptions, the types of aircraft in service are standard in all the air forces, thus simplifying not only production and the provision of spares, but the training of flight and technical personnel. Information is exchanged freely, probably so that if an emergency makes it necessary for one of the forces to undertake the tasks of another, that force will be prepared.

A Northern Fleet aircrew leaves its bomber after a mission.

Training is comprehensive and emphasizes ability to conduct day and night operations in all weathers, irrespective of the type of aircraft to be flown or the role to be played. Energetic efforts are being made to equip the aircraft with radar and other systems appropriate to their various roles.

In each of the four fleet commands, the Naval Air Forces have their own advanced schools, such as the Levanski School in Nikolaev for officers and pilots, a school for technical officers in Perm, and a school for communications officers in Novaia Ladoga.

Aircraft

Although it is true that most of the aircraft in service with the Naval Air Forces are, basically, the same as those in use with the other air forces, they are, naturally, modified to meet the requirements peculiar to air-sea warfare: for instance, they have more radar and other specialized equipment and extra fuel tanks. Special types of aircraft for the sole use of the Naval Air Forces have been developed in only small numbers.

The Naval Air Forces' longest-range aircraft is the Miasishchev-4, which has for some time been the standard strategic bomber of the Long-Range Air Force. Apparently, a whole series of this type has been equipped for maritime operations, and will be used primarily for long-range maritime reconnaissance and for directing submarines to convoys. Another of its

Miasishchev-4 Bison long-range bombers.

important tasks will be making strikes against enemy shipping. In its role as a strategic bomber, its normal range is almost 9,000 miles, but the version that serves in the naval role probably has a greater range—maybe, 10,000 miles. Consequently, a big percentage of the oceans of the world can be covered by this aircraft: for instance, the entire North Atlantic, from the Kola Peninsula; a broad area of the Pacific, from the Far East; and almost all the Indian Ocean and neighboring areas, from the Turkmen Republic.

In the independent Long-Range Air Force, the newly operational Miasishchev-200 and Tupolev-24 are replacing the Miasishchev-4. The relatively minor Naval Air Forces are not likely to be allotted many of those aircraft for some time.

Besides the Miasishchev-4, the Naval Air Forces have a number of old types that were also originally developed for the Long-Range Air Force, the oldest being the Tupolev-4, produced just after the Second World War and, unmistakably, a copy of the American B-29 Superfortress. Today, the Tupolev-4 could be used for long-range reconnaissance and possibly also for minelaying. Special versions of the newer Tupolev-16 and Tupolev-20, armed with guided missiles apparently for use against surface and subsurface targets, have appeared with the Naval Air Forces. Both these aircraft and the Miasishchev-4 can probably be armed with nuclear weapons.

A Miasishchev-200 Bounder long-range jet bomber.

A Tupolev-95 Bear long-range bomber on a reconnaissance flight over the Mediterranean.

The Naval Air Forces also have a number of light bombers that may be capable of making torpedo, as well as bombing, attacks. Now that the use of guided missiles offers greater likelihood of success, the importance of the short-legged torpedo is decreasing.

There is a definite shortage of flying boats. The jet-engined Beriev-10, very similar to the American Martin Seamaster and first seen at the Tushino air show in the summer of 1961, is the only modern flying boat in service with the Soviet Naval Air Forces. The designs of

G. M. Beriev span the years since 1932, when his first flying boat, the Beriev-2 (MBR-2) with a range of something over 1,000 miles and a top speed of 195 miles per hour, flew for the first time. When the Beriev-4 appeared in 1940, it attracted attention because of the pronounced angle between its longitudinal axis and the thrust line of its engines.

Numbers of Consolidated PBY Catalinas were received from America during the war, and some of them are still in service.

Beriev-10 Mallow jet-propelled flying boats.

In the foreground, a Beriev-12 Mail turboprop amphibian awaits take-off at a Soviet air show.

In 1949, the Beriev-6 long-range, flying boat, intended mainly for antisubmarine operations and, apparently, a Russian version of the American Martin PBM Marlin, went into service. A turbo-prop version of this aircraft—either a prototype or a conversion—was seen at Tushino in 1961.

A jet-engined flying boat, the Beriev-8, developed from the Beriev-6, was first seen in 1951. It was a forerunner of the Beriev-10, and did not go into series production.

In August and September 1961, it was claimed that Soviet test pilots had set several world records for jet-propelled flying boats, including the following altitude records:

Empty	14,742 meters*
With 5,000-kilogram** payload	14,042 meters
With 10,000-kilogram payload	12,700 meters
With 15,000-kilogram payload	12,120 meters

* 1 meter = 39.37 inches
** 1 kilogram = 2.2 lbs.

An average speed, with a 5,000-kilogram payload, of 875.86 kilometers per hour was claimed. A speed of 910 kilometers per hour, reportedly reached in August 1961, was also claimed as a world record. The aircraft in which that feat was achieved is probably intended for long-range, maritime reconnaissance and antisubmarine operations.

In recent years, strenuous efforts have been made to equip the Naval Air Forces with helicopters, whose main task will be antisubmarine warfare. Helicopters will, however, also be used for reconnaissance, including ice reconnaissance, and air-sea rescue duties. They are ideal ship-to-ship liaison aircraft.

Soviet destroyers have been recently equipped with helicopters. The first trial shipboard installation to become known was an elevated platform over the fantail of a *Kotlin*-class destroyer. The helicopter she carried was a KA-15.

Postwar Naval Aircraft

(Details of the most important types may be found in Appendix II.)

Beriev-2 (MBR-2): NATO designation Mote. Pusher-type flying boat. 850-HP engine in a nacelle above the fuselage. Obsolete. Only a few in service.

Beriev-6: NATO designation Madge. Piston-engined flying boat.

Beriev-8: NATO designation Mole. Flying boat. Jet-propelled version of the Beriev-6. Probably never went into production.

Beriev-10: NATO designation Mallow. Jet-propelled flying boat.

Beriev-12: NATO designation Mail. Flying boat. Turboprop version of the Beriev-6.

GST: NATO designation Mop. American amphibian Consolidated-28 built under license as the GST. Deliveries under Lend-Lease included later versions, among them the amphibian PBY-6A and the flying-boat versions PB-2B and PBN. Some have been fitted with modern radar, and are in use today.

Il'yushin-4: NATO designation Bob. Bomber with twin piston engines of 1,100 HP each. Development started in 1939, series production in 1942. Many converted to torpedo bombers and are still in service, mostly on reconnaissance and patrol duties.

Il'yushin-28: NATO designation Beagle. Light jet bomber.

Miasishchev-4: NATO designation Bison. Long-range reconnaissance bomber.

Miasishchev-200: NATO designation Bounder. Long-range jet bomber.

Tupolev-Antonov-8: NATO designation Mug. Twin-engined flying boat. Obsolete.

Tupolev-4: NATO designation Bull. Long-range reconnaissance bomber.

Tupolev-10: NATO designation Frosty. Twin-engined jet attack aircraft with swept-back wings. Army Air Force version designated Brawny. First sighted 1949. Probably only a limited number built.

Tupolev-14: NATO designation Bosun. Jet bomber.

Tupolev-16: NATO designation Badger. Heavy jet bomber.

Tupolev-24: NATO designation Blinder. Medium jet bomber.

Tupolev-95: NATO designation Bear. Long-range bomber.

Kamov-10: NATO designation Hat. Small, one-man helicopter. 56-HP engine with two co-axial, counter-rotating, three-bladed rotors. Open pilot's seat in a simple steel-tube fuselage. Two large pontoons for landing on water or dry land. First sighted in 1950. Used extensively by the Navy for reconnaissance.

Kamov-15: NATO designation Hen. Helicopter.

Kamov-20: NATO designation Harp. Helicopter.

Kamov-25K: NATO designation Hormone. Helicopter.

Mil*-1: NATO designation Hare. Helicopter.

Mil-4: NATO designation Hound. Helicopter.

* Mikhail L. Mil, designer.

Aircraft Carriers

The fact that the Soviet Navy has no aircraft carriers limits the maritime capability of the Soviet Naval Air Forces. There has been Soviet interest in carriers and, in fact, one was laid down at the Marti Yard in Leningrad in 1939 or 1940, but she was not completed. After the war, but still in Stalin's time, plans were drawn up for the construction of carriers to operate with the newly laid-down cruisers. But after Stalin's death, the plans were canceled because, on the one hand, expertise was lacking and, on the other, it would take an immense amount of time before the ships became operational. The Soviets had no experience of their own, and they could no longer expect their former allies to provide technical advice or to transfer a carrier to them. They had captured the one and only German carrier, the *Graf Zeppelin:* however, not only was she too outdated from a technical standpoint to provide the necessary knowledge, but she had been so badly damaged by explosives towards the end of the war that she was really little more than a hulk. The Russians did make her seaworthy, and they loaded her hangars with captured equipment, mainly machinery. In the late summer of 1947, when she was on her way to Leningrad, she sank.

Even if the Russians did build carriers—and there is no question about their technical ability to do so now—it would take several times as long to bring them to operational efficiency as it would to build them. Starting

A Tupolev-16 Badger medium-range bomber on a reconnaissance flight over the Western Pacific.

Kamov-25K Hormone antisubmarine helicopters landing on the helicopter carrier Moskva.

with propeller or, at the very most, slow types of jet aircraft, they would have to proceed step by step in carrier flying operations, and only after acquiring experience with those craft, could they begin to think about operating with modern jet aircraft. Furthermore, the first carrier they built would, undoubtedly, have any number of unforeseen shortcomings which could be rectified only during the construction of later ships. It would take many more years to build the next carriers and make them operational. For large ships, such as carriers, the timetable from design to operation, is estimated at:

First ship

Design—	approximately 1 year
Construction—	approximately 2 years
Fitting-Out—	approximately 2 years
Trials—	approximately ½ year
Work-Up—	approximately 2 years
Total—	7½ years

Subsequent ships

Design—	approximately ½ year
Construction—	approximately 2 years
Fitting-Out—	approximately 1½ years
Trials—	approximately ½ year
Work-Up—	approximately 1 year
Total—	5½ years

In other words, it would be 13 years at the least before they had even a few operational carriers.

Such a development period would make it well-nigh impossible for the Soviets to overtake the enormous lead that the NATO fleets have, not only in numbers of aircraft carriers but, even more important, in operational efficiency. This may explain their assertions that they do not need carriers because their ballistic missiles can reach the enemy continent, and their repeated insistence that the missile-armed submarine is a far more effective weapon than the aircraft carrier. Such assertions are only partially valid, for in an ocean war the carrier is a very effective, fast-moving, long-range weapon. For a navy that must reckon on having to face the great maritime powers, the aircraft carrier is absolutely essential, whether for using its aircraft to direct submarines towards enemy convoys, for the surveillance of sea areas, or for the protection of its own surface forces and replenishment ships. The Soviet lack of carriers is an important factor in estimating the military strength of the West. Recognition of this fact is doubtless responsible for Soviet pronouncements that "large ships," by which they mean aircraft carriers, are outdated and worthless.

These arguments are advanced for psychological reasons: they are an attempt to disguise Soviet shortcomings and to prevent the enemy from enjoying a feeling of superiority in certain types of weapon.

Thus, the main strength of the Soviet Naval Air Forces is tied to its own and satellite land bases. Of course, most of the Western world, including all Europe, the Mediterranean area, the Near and Middle East, large parts of the Arctic, and the North Pacific Ocean, is within range of those bases. Nevertheless, the Soviets could neither conduct nor support a naval campaign such as the one the Americans conducted in the Pacific from 1942 to 1945.

Opposite: A PT-76 amphibious tank backs into a Polnochnyi-*class landing ship of the Baltic Fleet.*

CHAPTER 7

Naval Land Forces

Branches

Naval land forces are divided into naval infantry, naval pioneers, coast defense forces, and rear services. Since the main mission of naval infantry and naval pioneers is to conduct amphibious operations, their organization and armament are the same as those of the army. Naval pioneers include frogmen and clearance divers.

Coast defense forces appear to have undergone extensive rearmament, with guided missiles replacing artillery. Antiaircraft guns are probably the only type still in use, but even these are being replaced, to a greater and greater extent, by fixed and mobile surface-to-air missile systems. Units equipped with such systems are most likely incorporated into what is called the Home Air Defense Force. If that is so, the chances are that there are no longer any coast defense batteries in service. Instead there are a number of completely motorized regiments, which operate under naval control and can be relatively quickly deployed to important areas.

Some of these coast defense regiments have been armed with the Kennel, which is also in use as an air-to-surface missile. In the coast defense role, this weapon is mounted on a trailer and towed by a special vehicle. There are two versions of the trailer: the older one carries a launcher that has to be raised to the vertical before the launch, while the newer one serves as its own launcher. The Kennel missile is being replaced by the Shaddock, which is carried in a cylindrical container on an eight-wheeled ZIL-135 vehicle. This container has to be brought to the vertical before the weapon can be launched.

195

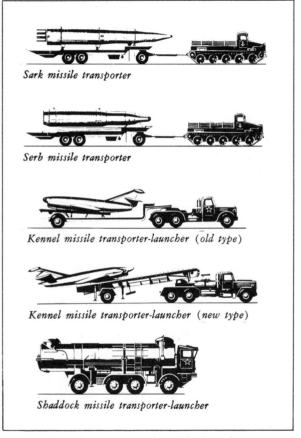

Sark missile transporter

Serb missile transporter

Kennel missile transporter-launcher (old type)

Kennel missile transporter-launcher (new type)

Shaddock missile transporter-launcher

Soviet Missile Transporters and Mobile Launchers

Although the Sark and Serb missiles that have been displayed at Red Square parades in recent years are clearly under naval control, they cannot be assumed to belong to the coast defense regiments. They are mounted on special trailers towed by heavy tractors, but have no launching arrangements, and are probably for display purposes only.

Rear services include people employed at arsenals, depots, bases, and other short establishments. This branch includes also mobile units equipped with land vehicles and harbor craft, such as tugs and lighters.

Very little is known about the strength, command structure, or organization of the naval land forces.

Amphibious Operations

Soviet amphibious operations are frequently conducted by combined military and naval forces, and are just as thoroughly considered and planned as any other combined operation. Naval infantry and pioneers are used to make the initial assault and secure a beachhead, while army troops not specifically trained in amphibious operations are used to make follow-on attacks and to extend the beachhead. All participating forces take part in the planning for an amphibious assault, but the senior naval officer afloat is in over-all command until such time as the assault commander, who also controls air and naval gunfire support, reports that the beachhead has been taken.

A tank gains the beachhead during amphibious maneuvers in the Baltic.

In large amphibious operations, at least one battalion of naval infantry is allocated to each army division to form the spearhead of the assault. Landings are usually made on a broad front by platoons, and consist of three phases, each one of which has a specific objective to be attained.

Naval infantry, equipped with light automatic and recoilless weapons and light grenade throwers, are the first to land. Bypassing enemy strongpoints, they occupy the beachhead and organize perimeter defense. On the flanks, they maintain close contact with the hedgehog positions.

Amphibious vehicles run ashore from an MP-4 landing ship of the Pacific Fleet.

The second group to land, the naval pioneers, equipped with technical devices and explosives, clear mines and other obstacles, under covering fire provided by the infantry.

The third group consists of military units in first and second echelons. Armed with heavy weapons, their missions are to reduce enemy strongpoints bypassed by the naval infantry and to consolidate the beachhead for an advance to specified objectives.

Reconnaissance and mine-clearance parties are sent in if enemy resistance is anticipated. Should such resistance be based on prepared positions, mine-clearance parties are landed under cover of darkness, some eight to ten hours before the assault is made. If, on the other hand, resistance is expected to be improvised and to be in no greater strength than infantry units, the naval infantry usually lands without prior reconnaissance.

To sum up, the task of the naval infantry is to seize the beachhead and hold it until the army units have landed. As soon as the Army is established, the mission of the naval infantry ends.

Responsibility for transporting the entire assault force, complete with weapons and equipment, rests with the amphibious forces, as does responsibility for re-supply of the beachhead with fuel, ammunition, provisions, and so forth. Special emphasis is placed on the importance of landing armored vehicles and motor transport without problems.

Amphibious Vehicles

The land forces have been acquiring amphibious vehicles for some years, and the following are in use:

Amphibious Tank PT-76
  Weight, 16 tons; length, 22 feet; width, 10 feet; height, 10.5 feet; 328 HP; speed, 30 mph; crew, 3; armor, 20 mm. maximum; armament, one 3″/48 gun with a 7.62 mm. machine gun on the same mount. Water-jet propulsion. Amphibious Tank PT-85 is similar, but has a 3.3″ gun.

Armored Personnel Carrier BTR-50 (P)
  (Developed from the PT-76). Weight, 16 tons; length, 22 feet; width, 10 feet; height, 6.5 feet; 320 HP; speed, 30 mph; crew, 1 driver and 14 troops; armor, 20 mm. maximum; armament, one 12.7 mm. machine gun or one 14.5 mm. Z-PU1 cannon. Water-jet propulsion.

Amphibious Vehicle 6 x 6 (BAV)
  Copy of the American DUKW. Length, approx. 29.5 feet; width, approx. 8.2 feet; payload, 3–4 tons; water speed, approx. 6 mph; 6 wheels. Propellers under the stern.

Tracked Amphibious Vehicle K-61
  Weight, 10 tons; length, approx. 29.5 feet; width, approx. 10 feet; height, approx. 6.5 feet; water speed, about 6 mph; 2 propellers under the stern. Stern door acts as loading ramp for small vehicles, for guns up to about 4.8″ caliber, or for up to 32 troops. Payload, approx. 5 tons.

Tracked Amphibious Vehicle GAZ-47
  Payload, approx. 1 ton.

Amphibious Vehicle GAZ-46
  Externally similar to the American jeep.
  Propeller for use in water. Payload, approx. 1,764 lbs.

CHAPTER 8

Bases and Ports

The relative importance of Soviet bases and ports depends largely upon their geographical situation. Naturally the most important ports are those that have unrestricted access to the high seas, namely those in the Arctic and the Far East. However, as centers of warship-building, they are less important than the bases on the Baltic and Black seas, whose shipyards are more efficient. Arctic and Far Eastern bases have quite a small building capacity and, in the event of war, could not be relied upon to maintain a shipbuilding program sufficient to support an oceanic naval campaign.

Leningrad, with its extensive shipbuilding industry, is the center of Soviet warship construction. Since submarines of almost any size can pass through the White Sea Canal, which was opened in 1933, boats can be transferred to the Arctic—so long as the canal is not damaged.

Thanks to the co-operation of the Polish and East German satellites, a chain of Soviet bases extends to the western Baltic. In view of the fact that, in winter, the ports of the eastern Baltic are closed by ice, use of the western ones is an indisputable advantage.

It is understandable that the Soviets should have given unrestricted priority to the extension of their Arctic bases, for despite their severe climatic conditions, they offer secure access to the high seas. At the present time, the most important bases are Murmansk and Poliarnyi, both of which are completely ice-free and, since the war, have been developed at considerable expense. A series of bombproof shelters for submarines and small warships has been blasted out of the rocky coastline.

201

Next in importance, so far as access to the ocean is concerned, are the Pacific bases. Even before the Second World War, they had been extended, and a new center of shipbuilding had come into being. The main means of transportation for material and equipment is, of course, via the Trans-Siberian Railway, which was double-tracked by 1938. Since 1945, some 2,825 of its 4,347 miles of track have been electrified. The more important bases and ports—Khabarovsk, Komsomolsk, and Sovetskaia Gavan—have also been linked by double-tracked railways. The Northern Sea Route, open only in the summer months, appreciably supplements the Trans-Siberian Railway.

The Baikal-Amur Railway, which leaves the Trans-Siberian Railway at Taishet and runs via Nikolaevsk to Komsomolsk, was started before World War II and was built mainly for naval purposes. Had this railway not existed, work in the Pacific shipyards could not have continued at all during the war. Most of the necessary material had to come from plants in the Ural Region, and the shortage of railway cars caused numerous delays in deliveries. Nevertheless, the construction commenced before 1941 was completed, whereas almost all work in the European yards was halted for nearly two years. Three destroyers and six submarines of the Pacific Fleet were transferred to the Arctic to help in the European theater: the former traveled via the Northern Sea Route, and the latter via the Panama Canal and the Atlantic.

Supplies for the Pacific bases had to be moved over the limited rail facilities available, from centers in the interior of Russia, and the severe Siberian winter hampered the efficient functioning of the bases.

Being encircled by Soviet territory, the Sea of Okhotsk is not only the ideal exercise area for the Soviet Pacific Fleet, but it is a good jumping-off point for a Soviet naval campaign in the Pacific. It can be readily understood, therefore, why bases on that sea have been and are being urgently built up. As yet, however, no spur line links them with the Trans-Siberian Railway. The Amur River is the vital artery of communication.

Black Sea bases, on the other hand can have little or no influence on an oceanic naval campaign. Passage from the Black Sea to the Mediterranean is via that bone of contention, the Bosporus, which is under the control of Turkey, a member of NATO, and can be effectively blocked. The centuries-old effort of the Russians to expand towards the Mediterranean has become even more intensive in recent years, and has met with some success. In certain circumstances, the base and repair facilities of the United Arab Republic would be available to the Soviets. Due to their breach with Albania, the rulers in Moscow in 1961 had to give up the submarine base that was built on the island of Saseno shortly after the Second World War (see page 238). Saseno, formerly held by Italy, is well situated strategically, and from it the Strait of Otranto and, thus, the whole of the

Cargo ships follow an icebreaker's path into Riga during winter operations in the Eastern Baltic.

Adriatic, can be controlled. Consequently, the Soviets put a great deal of work into the base there: they built a number of bombproof shelters and three airfields in the vicinity of Valona. Presumably, the latter were needed for supplying the base, since there is no overland connection between Albania and the Soviet Union.

To summarize: the bases on the Baltic and Black seas would be of little importance as regards maritime operations in the event of war. Their exits to the oceans are narrow and are controlled and defended by members of

NATO. The Arctic and Pacific bases, on the other hand, would be of great strategic importance. However, they are, of course, exposed to weapons of mass destruction, and would appear to be very tempting targets. In addition, it could be difficult to supply them in wartime, not only because of climatic conditions, but because of enemy activity. Furthermore, naval forces stationed at these bases do not have year-round freedom of action and, during the ice-free period, they would be able to operate only so long as the bases remained in being.

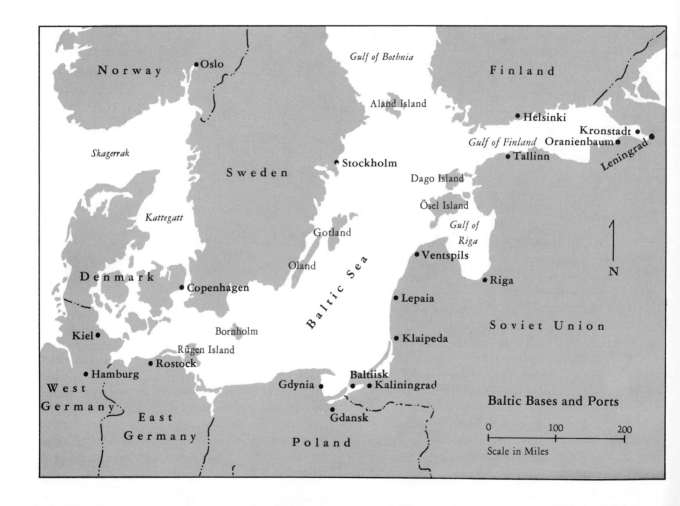

Baltic Bases and Ports

Baltic Bases and Ports

Baltiisk (Pillau)

Town with naval and fishing port in what was formerly East Prussia. Situated on the 1,800-foot Pillau Channel, which connects the Frisches Haff with the Baltic Sea, it was an outport of Königsberg. Most of the town was destroyed during the Second World War, and the limited rebuilding that was done was for purely military purposes. It is the site of a fishery combine and the home port of a task group (two cruisers and several destroyers), a submarine brigade, a motor torpedo boat brigade, and a flotilla of the Border Patrol of the MVD. It is garrisoned by naval infantry. Headquarters of the commander-in-chief of the Baltic Fleet are in Baltiisk, and two air divisions are based nearby. A subsidiary of the Schichau shipyard that was located there is probably among the facilities that have been rebuilt.

Kaliningrad (Königsberg)

Naval port (formerly a commercial port also) on both sides of the Pregel River, some four miles above the river's confluence with the Frisches Haff. The Königsberger Canal, which is 26 miles long, 156 feet wide, and up to 26 feet deep, connects it to the Pillau Channel, via the Frisches Haff. The Schichau shipyard, built in 1931 and destroyed in 1945, where fishing vessels and warships up to about frigate size were con-

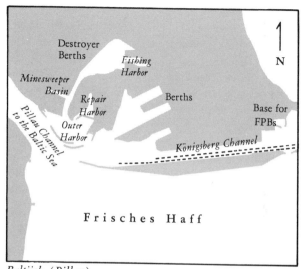

Baltiisk (Pillau)

structed, has probably been rebuilt. The five harbor basins cover a total area of 617 acres. There is a fishing harbor with fish-processing factories, and there are manufacturers of railway cars and lifting machinery, as well as a cellulose industry. Headquarters of the commander-in-chief of the Naval Air Force, Baltic, are in Kaliningrad, which is also a submarine base and the site of a submarine school. In winter, the port and the canal have to be kept open by icebreakers.

Klaipeda (Memel)

Sea and river port opposite the northern tip of the Kurische Nehrung, on the exit of the Kurisches Haff (Memel Channel) to the Baltic, at the mouth of the Memel River. The Lindenau shipyard, which was located there and was destroyed in 1945, has probably been rebuilt. There are facilities for building fishing and coastal vessels, and warships up to the size of minesweepers. According to reports, Klaipeda is becoming an important oil port at the head of an elaborate pipeline system: four basins to take ships of 25,000 tons, deadweight, and channels from 42 to 49 feet deep, were to be completed by 1965. Emergency base for warships.

Lepaia (Libau)

Commercial and naval port on a narrow sandspit between the Baltic and Lake Libau. It covers about 16 square miles. Both harbors are protected by large moles, and there is a repair yard (see page 228). The biggest Baltic Fleet submarine school is at Lepaia.

Ventspils (Windau)

Baltic port at the mouth of the 200-mile-long Venta River. Timber transshipment is the most important activity of its commercial harbor, but there are extensive facilities for grain storage. There are also engineering works, and a temporary warship base, used especially in the winter, since it is almost always ice-free.

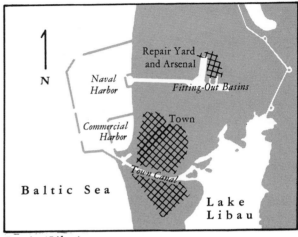

Lepaia (Libau)

Riga

Capital of the Latvian Soviet Republic, situated on the Dvina River, eight miles above its mouth in the Gulf of Riga. One of its four shipyards is large, and there is a commercial port. Its two miles of quays can accommodate ships that draw up to 26 feet. Its installations are in the process of being extended. The center of Soviet trade in the Baltic, its industries include metal and machinery, textiles, leather, sugar refineries, milling and fish combines. The light naval forces that are based at Riga move to the vicinity of Ventspils in the winter.

Tallinn (Revel)

Capital of the Estonian Soviet Republic, on the steep, rocky coast of the Gulf of Finland. Its commercial and naval ports are ice-free most of the time, or are kept open by icebreakers, and its industry is varied—shipbuilding, machinery, railway workshops and car construction, cotton, leather, cellulose, foodstuffs, and timber. There is an airfield nearby. A task group, consisting of three cruisers and 18 destroyers and frigates, is based at Tallinn, as are about 24 submarines and minesweeping units. The garrison includes a naval infantry and a pioneer brigade and an antiaircraft division. An air division is also based there.

Leningrad (Petrograd, St. Petersburg)

Built on the delta of the Neva River, at the eastern end of the Gulf of Finland, it has a population of over 3.5 million and is the second largest city of the Soviet Union. It lies in a key position for the transshipment of goods destined for the interior and is, consequently, the terminus of many rail routes. It is connected to the inland waterway network, via the Neva. The core of the city is on Zayachi Island, but its most important sections are on the left bank of the Neva, with the industrial sections to the south and west. Industries include shipbuilding (see page 228), electrical equipment, precision machinery, textiles, and chemicals. The commercial port is being dredged to about 60 feet, nearly three miles of

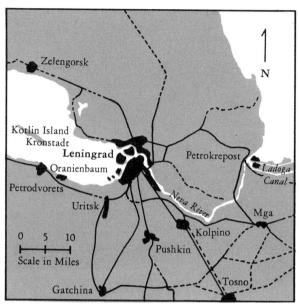

Leningrad and Environs

quays are being provided, and 33 new cranes and other facilities are being installed. A 15-mile channel connects the port to Kotlin Island. Although many naval schools are located there, Leningrad's importance lies mostly in its numerous shipyards, which form the main center of Soviet warship-building, and not in its naval base.

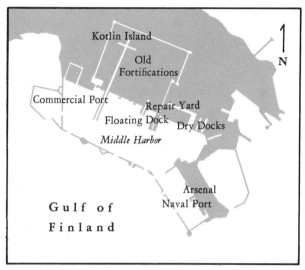

Kronstadt

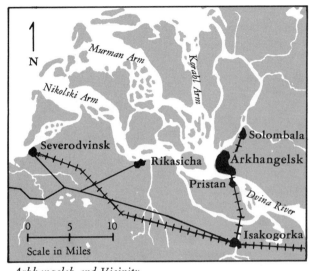

Arkhangelsk and Vicinity

Kronstadt

Important naval and commercial port on Kotlin Island, in the Gulf of Finland, to the west of Leningrad. Large repair yard and naval base at the eastern end of the island (see page 232).

Oranienbaum

Town on the Gulf of Finland, south of Kronstadt. It is a base for light naval forces.

Arctic Bases and Ports

Arkhangelsk

Provincial capital and port in the north of the Soviet Union. It is situated on the right bank of the Northern Dvina, 28 miles above its mouth, and has a population of over 300,000. In spite of being blocked by ice for up to 190 days per year and requiring the use of very efficient icebreakers to keep it open, this is a very

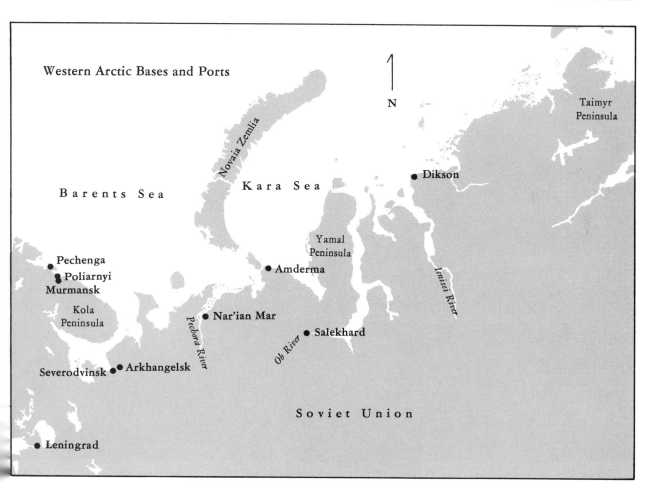

Western Arctic Bases and Ports

Taimyr
Peninsula

N

Novaia Zemlia

Kara Sea

Barents Sea

Dikson

Yamal
Peninsula

Pechenga

Poliarnyi
Murmansk

Amderma

Kola
Peninsula

Yenisei River

Nar'ian Mar

Pechora River

Salekhard

Ob River

Severodvinsk Arkhangelsk

Soviet Union

Leningrad

Ships take on lumber at the Arctic port of Arkhangelsk.

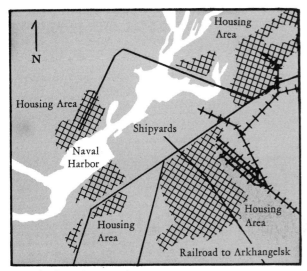

Rough plan of Severodvinsk

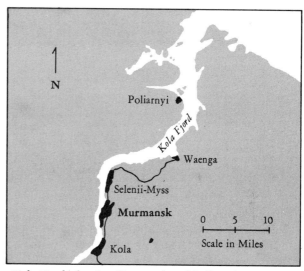

Kola Fjord, showing Murmansk and Poliarnyi

important port with rail and inland-waterway connections to the south. It has an extensive area of quays, and is the most important Soviet center for the timber industry, including exporting. There· is a repair yard there.

Severodvinsk (Molotovsk)

Town and port to the northwest of Arkhangelsk, with over 40,000 inhabitants. It was founded in 1938, and has grown very rapidly. It has an important shipbuilding yard, especially for warships, and a metal industry. A 28-mile branch railway track connects it to Arkhangelsk.

Murmansk

Port and naval base on the northwestern coast of the Kola Peninsula. Its population is over 200,000. Terminus of the 900-mile Leningrad-Murmansk Railway, it is ice-free throughout the year. A fishing fleet of about 500

Approaches to Dikson

vessels is based there, and its industry includes ship-building and repair, metal works, and foodstuffs. It is the main base of the Northern Fleet.

Poliarnyi (*Aleksandrovsk*)

North of Murmansk. Squadron and flying-boat base. Its well-protected harbor is almost always ice-free.

Pechenga (*Petsamo*)

Situated on the 9-mile-long Petsamo Fjord. A commercial center with port facilities.

Nar'ian-Mar

At the mouth of the Pechora River.

Amderma

On the Iugorski Peninsula, this port is used for supplying Novaia Zemlia.

Salekhard

At the mouth of the Ob River.

Dikson

Off the mouth of the Ienisei River.

Nordvik

On Khatanga Bay.

Tiksi

Southeast of the delta of the Lena River.

Ambarchik

Near the mouth of the Kolyma River.

Uelen

On the Bering Strait.

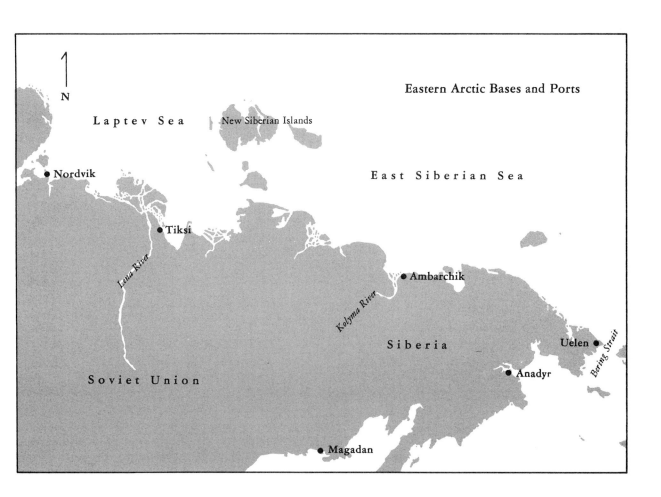

N

L a p t e v   S e a

New Siberian Islands

E a s t   S i b e r i a n   S e a

Eastern Arctic Bases and Ports

● Nordvik

● Tiksi

Lena River

● Ambarchik

Kolyma River

S i b e r i a

Uelen ●

Bering Strait

● Anadyr

S o v i e t   U n i o n

● Magadan

Pacific Bases and Ports

Vladivostok

With a population of some 300,000, this port, well situated on a bay at the southern end of the Muraiev Peninsula, is the largest one the Soviet Union has in the Pacific area. It is an important trade center and fishing port, and has extensive fish-processing plants. It was the original Pacific terminus of the Trans-Siberian Railway, which supports its shipbuilding and repair yard (see page 233) as well as the extensive installations for the 5th Fleet (see page 9), with arsenals, torpedo and mine depots, and so forth. Its submarine base can shelter 25 boats, and there is a school and operations room on the adjacent island of Russki.

Nakhodka

Port southeast of Vladivostok, to which it is connected by rail. It is a submarine base, and its harbor is in the process of being greatly developed for commercial purposes and for the expanding fishing industry. One floating dock for repairs.

Khabarovsk

With more than 300,000 inhabitants, this is the largest and most important city in the Soviet Far East. It is situated on the right bank of the Amur River which, at this point, is almost two miles wide, below the mouth of the Ussuri River. The Amur-Ussuri Railway, which crosses the Amur by the one and only bridge, passes through the city. Its industries include shipbuilding (see page 233), motor vehicle and aircraft construction, tractors and farm machinery, and oil refining. It has no naval base, but is a center for sea, rail, and air communications. It is ice-free only from July to the end of October.

Komsomolsk

Town in Khabarovsk district on the left bank of the Amur River, about 280 miles above its mouth. Its population exceeds 150,000, and its important industries are shipbuilding, steel, aircraft construction, and oil refining. It is on an extension of the Trans-Siberian Railway, and it is important as the largest shipbuilding center in the Far East, but not as a base. Only from July to the end of October, is it free of ice.

Sovetskaia Gavan (Imperatorhafen)

Port on the Pacific coast, with a population of about 40,000. Connected by rail to Komsomolsk, it has a commercial port which exports timber, and its repair yard has a floating dock. It is an important base for the Pacific Fleet, especially for destroyers, submarines, and MTBs. It is the site of a submarine school and a large coastal radio station.

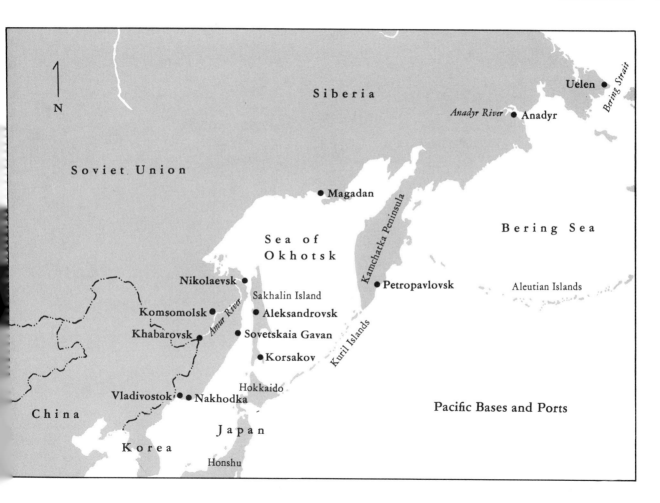

Shipping facilities line the waterfront at the Pacific port of Nakhodka.

Korsakov (Otomari)

At the southern tip of Sakhalin Island, this is a naval supply and destroyer base. There is a naval air station as well as a fighter airfield in the vicinity. Rails link the southern coast.

Aleksandrovsk-Sakhalinski

In the north of Sakhalin Island, on the Tatarski Strait. The naval port started in 1945 is still under construction. There is a shipbuilding and repair yard (see page 233).

Nikolaevsk

On the left bank of the Amur River, about 23 miles from its mouth, this capital of the Lower Amur district has a population of about 35,000. There is a center for fishing and processing salmon and, in the vicinity, a large source of iron ore. The harbor which is, on average, open for only 100 days per year—July to the end of October—is of little importance.

Magadan

Port, with about 60,000 inhabitants, on Nagayevo Bay, in the northern Sea of Okhotsk. Like Petropavlovsk and Nikolaevsk, it has road, but no rail, connections. The newly built naval base is usable during the summer months. There is one floating dock and a submarine base.

Petropavlovsk

Capital of Kamchatka, with a population of about 30,000. It is a commercial and fishing port, and a summer base with repair facilities for units of the Pacific Fleet. There are four naval air stations nearby. To the west, in Talinskaia Bay, a submarine base has been in existence since 1935. Naval facilities have recently been greatly expanded. It is ice-free from May to October.

Anadyr

Capital of the Chukotski District on the Anadyr River. It is a coaling depot, is important for Arctic shipping, and has an airfield, and a base for light naval forces.

Black Sea Bases and Ports

Odessa

Industrial city and commercial port, with a population of over 600,000, on the northwestern shore of the Black Sea. Its important industries include eight machinery works, five chemical works, a steel and rolling mill, and a large refinery. The harbor which, to the eastward, is protected by a mole, covers more than 247 acres and contains about five miles of quays. In spite of the mild climate, it is frozen over for more than three months of the year. There are three floating docks, and many large oil-storage tanks.

Nikolaev

Port and largest industrial and shipbuilding city on the Black Sea, with over 250,000 inhabitants. Its industry includes shipbuilding, railways, agricultural machinery, textiles, leather, and foodstuffs. There are grain elevators, and about two miles of quays. It is important as a shipbuilding center, not as a base.

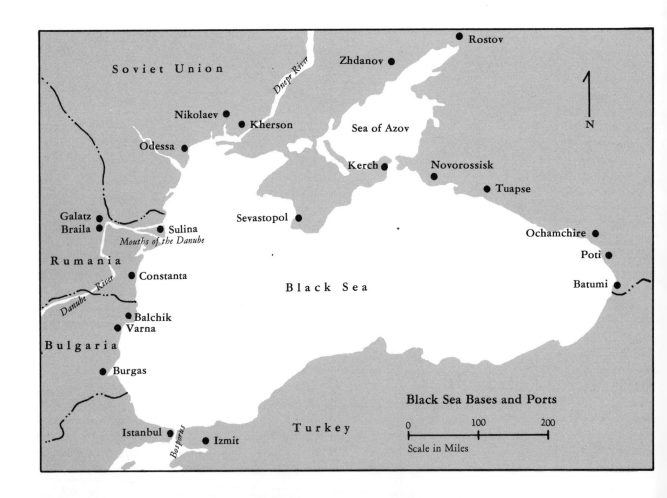

Black Sea Bases and Ports

Kherson

District capital in the Ukrainian Soviet Republic, with more than 100,000 inhabitants. It lies about 19 miles from the mouth of the Dnepr River, and has port and shipyard facilities. It is a center for grain transshipment, and its industries are agricultural machinery and foodstuffs. From December to early March, it is icebound.

Sevastopol

Fortress and naval and commercial port, with about 150,000 inhabitants. Its extensive harbor facilities include three shipyards (see page 235), a naval arsenal for mines and torpedoes, and capacious storage installations. It is the main base for the Black Sea Fleet. The motor torpedo boat and submarine base at Balaklava lies eight miles to the southeast.

Zhdanov (Mariupol)

Port and industrial city on the Sea of Azov, with a population of over 250,000. Its industries include smelting and rolling mills, and electrical equipment. It now handles the transshipment of grain, ore, and coal, but when a 2.4-mile tanker pier and extensive bunkering arrangements, now under construction, have been completed, it will handle oil, also. The channel is to be dredged to 50 feet. There is a repair yard with a floating dock.

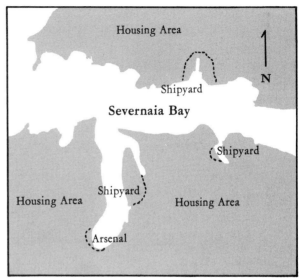

Sevastopol

Rostov

Port, with about 510,000 inhabitants, situated on the north bank of the Don River, about 28 miles above its mouth. A rail and important industrial center—machinery, metal works, textiles, timber, paper, and chemicals. Since the opening of the Volga-Don Canal, this well-built port has become an important transshipment point between inland and coastal shipping.

A view of the deep-water quays at the Black Sea port of Novorossisk.

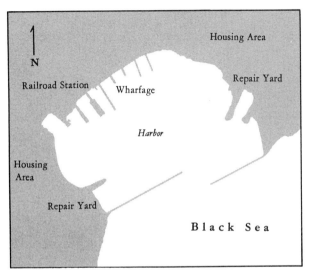

Novorossisk

Novorossisk

Port on the northeastern shore of the Black Sea, with a population of more than 100,000. Its industries are cement, leather goods, and metal works. The commercial port is especially important for the export of cement and wheat. Its quay and loading facilities, already extensive, are being increased—two miles of quays, loading gantries, and a rail connection. There are ship-repair workshops. It is a base for light naval forces.

Tuapse

Commercial and naval port on the east coast of the Black Sea. Its population exceeds 40,000. It is the terminal of an oil pipeline from Maikop, and cereal and oil exports are handled. The harbor, which has berths for light naval forces, is protected by moles. A naval arsenal and a repair yard are among its facilities.

Ochamchire

Small commercial port and submarine base on the eastern shore of the Black Sea, about 75 miles north of Batumi.

Poti

Commercial port on the Black Sea, at the mouth of the Rion River, about midway between Ochamchire and Batumi. Its population exceeds 60,000, and it is important for the export of manganese. The naval section of the port has a repair yard and two floating docks.

Batumi

Capital of the Adzhar Soviet Republic, it is in the farthest southeast corner of the Black Sea, near the Turkish border, and has a population of nearly 100,000. It is the starting point of the Trans-Caucasian Railway, and the terminal of the oil pipeline from Baku. Its very modern harbor specializes in oil transshipment. It has a base for light naval forces, and a naval arsenal.

Opposite: A large fishing vessel nears completion at Nikolaev.

CHAPTER 9

Shipbuilding Industry

There are about 500 shipyards in the Soviet Union, but many of them are situated far inland on the large rivers, and few of them have the capacity to build even medium-sized vessels. The chief center for building large and medium-sized vessels is, as it always has been, Leningrad, where there are six big shipyards and from 28 to 30 launching ways. All told, there are probably about 100 launching ways in the Soviet Union, but only 12 to 15 of them can handle ships longer than 200 meters.

Most shipyards, especially the big ones, date from Tsarist times, but their present-day efficiency far surpasses what it was in the past. Damage to their industrial structure and lack of skilled labor forced them to close immediately after the Bolshevik Revolution, and it took years to repair them, make good the shortcomings, and approach their former efficiency. In the years between the wars, it often happened that a yard, lacking basic technical and administrative facilities, was suddenly swamped with orders, and its installations had to be hastily rebuilt. These circumstances were repeated shortly before the outbreak of war in 1939, and again before the German attack on the Soviet Union in the summer of 1941. It was during this period that the Soviets began to step up the building of warships. After the German attack, the yards engaged in such construction had to close, either because they lacked material and labor, or because they had been damaged, if not completely destroyed. When the Germans retreated, the yards were restored to use as quickly as possible.

After the end of the war, the Soviets used prisoners of war and internees to reorganize most of their shipyards. They also had the benefit of all the material that either fell into their hands through their occupation of eastern Germany, or was acquired as reparations from the western occupation zones. In the latter category were the installations of Blohm and Voss, of Hamburg, and of the Naval Dockyard at Wilhelmshaven. All this booty enabled the Soviet yards to make remarkable technical progress. It took several years to make all the organizational and other changes necessary if the new methods were to be converted into increased capacity. Some yards were converted to the construction of prefabricated sections or parts, and almost all of them made the changeover from riveting to electric welding, theretofore an unusual practice in shipbuilding.

Certain shortcomings resulted from the layout of permanent installations and could be overcome only by improving and extending transportation arrangements, providing appropriate workshops, and ensuring a reliable supply of materials. By 1951, the reconstruction of the yards was virtually complete and a start could be made on the intensive program of shipbuilding that is still in operation.

Most Soviet shipyards have unusually short water frontages, and because, in many cases, both subsoil and river bank are unsuitable foundations for building, their construction sheds, workshops, and stores are situated some distance from the water's edge. At the time the yards were built, there was an acute lack of space, which led to the selection of sites that would not otherwise have been considered for the purpose. These conditions are especially marked in Leningrad and on the Amur River, and the use of broadside slips, which need less extensive foundations than do stern-first slips, is widespread in the yards in those areas. Broadside launching has an advantage in that it does not create the bending forces that the stern-first method does, and is consequently safer. Furthermore, broadside slips can be used to haul up ships below a certain tonnage, thus saving dock space.

Many Soviet stern-first building ways have long extensions out into the water—another consequence of poor bank and subsoil conditions and the associated shallow water. The water off many Soviet shipyards, both on the sea and on rivers, is so shallow that it has to be dredged constantly.

The extremely cold weather encountered in certain regions of the Soviet Union, especially the Arctic and Baltic, necessitates the covering and heating of launching ways: not only would all hand work otherwise be impossible, but materials would be seriously damaged. Naturally, covering and heating the ways does not afford anywhere near complete protection, and it will be readily appreciated that the capacity of yards in areas with a severe climate is limited.

Scaffolding surrounds the 735-foot, fish-processing ship Vostok *during construction at Leningrad in 1968.*

Crane and transport facilities have a lot to do with the tempo of work in shipyards. On account of the subsoil conditions mentioned above, few permanent cranes were in use in Soviet yards before the war, and those that did exist were of low efficiency. In the years following the war, most of them were replaced by more efficient ones, and equipment that had been captured or acquired as reparations was also installed. Recently, traveling cranes, which not only are more efficient but require scarcely any foundations, have been coming into more and more use. Of course, only the large yards have been given these improvements.

Transportation arrangements within the yards developed along similar lines. It used to be that only a few large yards had concrete roadways for heavy transport. In most Russian yards, narrow-gauge railways using steam—rarely diesel—locomotives still predominate, and there is no system of regular maintenance. Tracks are realigned only as required, a method that not only increases wear and tear on them, but is most inefficient. Not all yards have rail connections with the state railways, the large ones at Leningrad, which are situated on an island, being cases in point.

Soviet shipyards either have their own generating stations for electric power or are connected to the local system, usually by means of a number of transformer stations. The greatly increased demand for electricity created by the adoption of electric welding is said to have been met without any significant difficulties. However, severe winter conditions that freeze up overhead lines and cable conduits do cause problems, especially for cranes and transportation and, in some cases, steam pipes have been laid in the conduits.

Construction of prefabricated sections, especially for submarines, has been increased since electric welding reached its present state of development. In the 1930s, when the Soviets first used prefabrication of sections (see Chapter 3, page 30, and Chapter 5, page 143), a number of adaptations and organizational changes, particularly in transportation and supply services, had to be made. Nevertheless, they are not, even now, employing the method the Germans were using to build submarines in 1944 and 1945. They are still building submarines in the conventional way, although some individual sections are completed inland and moved by water in floating docks to the assembling yards. Provided these deliveries are made on schedule, prefabrication does reduce somewhat the time required to build submarines and small warships. However, not only are there problems involved in keeping transportation moving during the long, cold winters but, in many cases, there is an immense distance between the shipyard and a fabricating plant, and that factor has an adverse effect on construction time and cost. Furthermore, the industries supplying components have never yet been able to keep pace with the shipbuilders.

Nevertheless, it would seem that the Soviet shipbuilding industry has, at least, fulfilled the demand for warships. According to general estimates, about 1.3 million tons of new warship construction have been completed since 1948 or 1949, corresponding to an annual output of around 100,000 tons. This means that most yards have been required to build warships only, and many orders for merchant and fishing vessels, just as urgently required as warships, have had to be placed with foreign shipyards, not only in satellite countries, but even in countries of the Western alliance. The annual capacity of the numerous yards on the rivers and inland waters of the Soviet Union has been estimated at 100,000 tons of tugs and self-propelled barges and more than 500,000 tons of barges.

Repair yards seem to be less efficient than building yards. Apparently, it is not unusual for ships to be under repair for a whole year, while others have to wait for their turn. The Five-Year Plan that ended in 1960 called for the number of repair yards to be doubled, but it is not known whether that goal was met.

A Soviet shipyard that employs more than 5,000 workers may be classified as major. Many yards, especially the big ones, have exhausted all possibilities of expansion because of space limitations. And it is very difficult for the Soviets to build new yards, because suitable land is often not available and the cost of making land suitable may be prohibitive.

It frequently happens that a ship cannot be completed by the yard in which she was built, because the water is too shallow, and she has to be moved to a fitting-out yard where there is deeper water. This applies especially to ships built in the Leningrad and Amur yards, and it often causes considerable delay in the completion of the ships.

In general, the strain on Soviet yards is relieved by a policy of having naval vessels built at home, while merchant vessels are commonly built abroad.

Very little is known about some Soviet shipyards, especially those in remote areas, but all available information on the most important ones is given below. Details of the yards in Europe can be regarded as fairly reliable.

Baltic

Kaliningrad (Königsberg)

Former German Friedrich-Schichau Shipyard. Reportedly, builds warships under 1,500 tons, tugs, and so forth. Mainly an arsenal and technical support base for the units stationed in Baltiisk (Pillau).

Klaipeda (Memel)

Former German Lindenau Shipyard. Reportedly builds minesweepers and smaller vessels.

Lepaia (Libau)

Situated about 2 miles northeast of the new town. Total area, about 32,000 square meters. Depths: in the basin, 9.5 to 11 meters, canal, 9 to 11 meters, off the docks, 9.5 meters. Two dry docks, 190 x 31 meters and 200 x 34 meters. One floating dock, 46 x 15 meters. Arsenal and training center for the submarine force. Builds minesweepers, landing craft, and tugs. Employees, 2,800.

Riga

Former Mülgraben Shipyard (until 1918 a subsidiary of the German Friedrich-Schichau Shipyard, operated again for the Schichau yard during the Second World War). Nine launching ways, rail connection. Reportedly, builds medium-sized merchant ships.

Collective I, Tallinn (Revel)

Former Peters Shipyard. Situated immediately to the northwest of Tallinn. Borders on the naval harbor to the west. Total area, about 20,000 square meters. Depth of water, 6 meters at the most. Rail connection. Builds ships' machinery. One stern-first launching way of 120 meters, and two of 65 and 75 meters each (can be used as hauling-up slips). Two floating docks, 52 x 18.8 meters and 61 x 17.7 meters, respectively. Today, probably only an arsenal and repair yard (some reports mention construction of small merchant ships and, recently, destroyers also).

Collective II, Tallinn (Revel)

Former Nobel and Lessner Shipyard. Dismantled after the end of the First World War and, after 1945, rebuilt by the Soviets on a large scale. Total area, about 120,000 square meters. Rail connection. Considerable possibility for expansion. Three 250-meter launching ways, and four of 130 meters each. Two dry docks, 130 x 42 meters. Builds destroyers, escort vessels, and submarines.

Sudomech, Leningrad

Former Neva Admiralty Dockyard. Next to the old Petersburg Metal Works, on an island between the Neva and Moika rivers. Area, about 150,000 square meters. Depth of water off the yard, 9.5 to 12 meters. No rail connections and no possibility of expansion. Ships' machinery and, possibly, boilers are built at the former Petersburg Metal Works (see page 230, under the Marti yard). Builds destroyers and below, special types of submarine and, reportedly, merchant ships of up to 25,000 grt. One stern-first launching way, 230 meters long, and three 130-meter ways. Fitting-out berths on the banks of the Neva, and, for smaller ships, on the lower Moika also. Employees, 8,000.

Zhdanov, Leningrad

Former Northern Shipyard, situated on the northern bend of the Neva River. Area, about 165,000 square meters. Water depth averages 9 to 10 meters, at the

An ore carrier built for export to Sweden lies alongside a fitting-out pier at the Ordzhonikidze Yard, Leningrad.

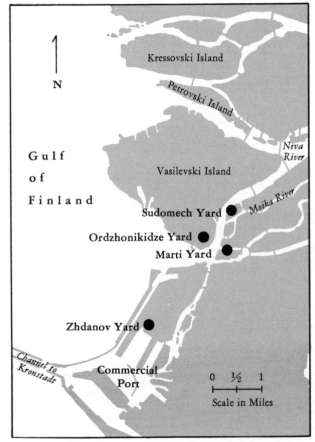

Leningrad Waterfront

fitting-out berth only 5 meters. Total water frontage, 370 meters. No rail connection and no possibility of expansion. Builds escort vessels and below, supply and merchant ships up to 10,000 grt, and, occasionally, submarines. Three (some sources say six) stern-first launching ways between 90 and 120 meters long. Apparently, only hulls are built here, and ships are completed by other yards. Employees, 6,000.

Nevski, Leningrad

Former Okhtenskoi Shipyard. On a peninsula in the Neva River, at the mouth of the Greater Okhta River. Depth of water, between 21 and 13 meters, considerably less in the fitting-out basin. Total water frontage, 675 meters. No rail connection and no possibility of expansion. Builds mainly river vessels, occasionally warships up to about 400 tons. Three stern-first launching ways between 50 and 65 meters long. Of little importance, since its installations are obsolescent. Employees, 5,000.

Marti, Leningrad

Formerly Putilov Shipyard. On Galernyi Island, immediately opposite the Ordzhonikidze yard. Divided into two parts. The yard itself lies to the west, while to the east, in the suburb of Kolomna and separated from the yard by the 35-meter-wide Proshka River, is the former Petersburg Metal Works, which is linked administratively with the Marti yard, but also works for Su-

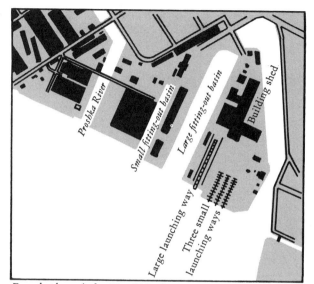

Rough plan of the Marti Yard, Leningrad

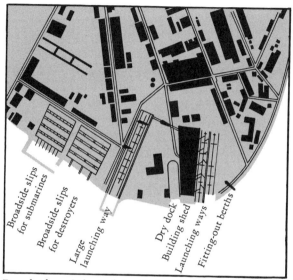

Rough plan of the Ordzhonikidze Yard, Leningrad

domech. Depth of water opposite the yard averages 10 meters. No rail connection and no possibility of expansion. Builds machinery and, possibly, boilers. Construction of destroyers and below, and merchant ships of up to 25,000 grt. One 220-meter-long launching way and three 130-meter ways. One large fitting-out basin, 500 x 70 meters, and one small basin, 250 x 45 meters. One floating dock, 110 x 25 meters. Employees, 12,000.

Ordzhonikidze, Leningrad

Former Baltic Shipyard and Engineering Works, St. Petersburg/Petrograd, situated at the mouth of the Neva River, on the southern tip of Vasilevski Island. About 300,000 square meters in area, with a water frontage of 1,000 meters. Depth of water opposite the launching ways, 10 meters on average, at the fitting-out berth, 8 meters. No possibility of expansion and no rail connection. Own machinery and boiler works. Builds cruisers, destroyers, submarines, large icebreakers, and merchant ships. Three stern-first slips—290 x 43 meters, 235 x 33 meters, and 200 x 30 meters—for the construction of the largest ships. Two groups of five broadside slips each, one for destroyers, the other for submarines: both groups are building slips and cannot be used as hauling-up slips. Three to four hulls can be built on each group, and must be launched in turn, as the hull nearest the water is completed. One dry dock, 130 x 20 meters, which can also be used for building. Employees, 20,000. There is a submarine section that works independently and co-ordinates submarine development; for this purpose, the yard is an external agency of the Atomic Institute of Leningrad University.

Kronstadt

Arsenal and repair yard situated at the eastern end of Kotlin Island. Total area, about 115,000 square meters. Depth of water: middle harbor, 7 to 11 meters, less alongside the quays; naval harbor, 10 to 11 meters, at the entrance 9 to 13 meters. Total water frontage, 2,400 meters. Three dry docks, 280 x 48 meters, 220 x 39 meters, and 200 x 35 meters. Reportedly, there is a former German floating dock for ships up to 40,000 tons. There is an oil pier in the naval harbor. Repairs naval and merchant ships, and fits out cruisers, destroyers, and submarines.

Izhorsk

A shipyard at Kolpino on the Izhora tributary of the Neva River, about 12 miles southeast of Leningrad, reportedly laid out in 1950 and probably still being developed. Builds destroyers and below.

Arctic

Krasnaia Kuznitza, Arkhangelsk-Solombala

Builds merchant ships and has repair facilities.

Shipyard 402, Severodvinsk (Molotovsk)

About 25 miles northwest of Arkhangelsk on the Dvinskaia Gulf. Built just before the outbreak of war. Rail connection. Among other installations, there are two 280-meter covered, heated launching ways. Probably has machinery and boiler works. Builds cruisers, destroyers, submarines, and, recently, large freighters.

Murmansk

Builds minesweepers and below, mainly engaged in repair work. Provides technical support for the fisheries fleets and bases for units of the Northern Fleet and for vessels of the Northern Sea Route. Probably only an arsenal and repair yard. Still being developed.

Pacific

Vladivostok

Repairs and builds merchant and fishing vessels. Four dry docks.

Voroshilov, Vladivostok

May be the yard described above under Vladivostok. Repairs and builds small ships. Four dry docks, two floating docks. Rail connection.

Nakhodka

Small yard to the southeast of Vladivostok. Builds merchant ships. One floating dock.

Sovetskaia Gavan

Yard began in 1945 and is, reportedly, still under construction. Rail connection. One floating dock. Builds destroyers and below.

Aleksandrovsk

Shipyard, started in 1945 and probably not yet completed, is said to be due for expansion into a large yard. Reported to be building destroyers and submarines.

Khabarovsk

About 435 miles south of the mouth of the Amur River. Builds small warships, freighters, and tankers.

Komsomolsk

On the Amur River, about 280 miles above its mouth. Rail connection. Builds cruisers and below, and, possibly, machinery and boilers. Because of the bar at the mouth of the river, large ships have to be sent to Nikolaev or Vladivostok for completion.

Black Sea

Odessa

Engaged mainly in repair of merchant ships. Builds small vessels.

I. I. Nosenko (formerly Marti) Shipyard, Nikolaev

Largest shipyard in the Soviet Union. Divided into the South Yard and the North Yard. Could be extended, has rail connection, and includes machinery and boiler works. Extensive workshops produce components for building and fitting out. Launching ways: one of 260 meters, two of 230 meters, two of 130 meters, three of 90 meters (for submarines), three broadside slips (can be used as hauling-out slips) of 70 meters each. One floating dock for ships up to 40,000 tons. Large war and merchant ships are built in the North Yard, destroyers and below in the South Yard.

Cargo ships line a building way at Kherson, in the first Soviet use of continuous-assembly ship construction.

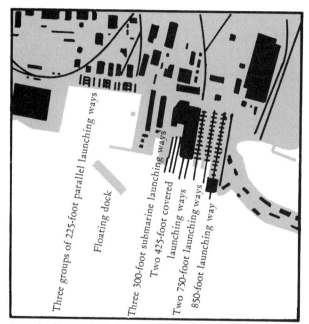

Three groups of 225-foot parallel launching ways

Floating dock

Three 300-foot submarine launching ways

Two 425-foot covered launching ways

Two 750-foot launching ways

850-foot launching way

Rough plan of the I. I. Nosenko Yard, Nikolaev

Nosenko, Kherson

Above the town, on the left bank of the Dnepr River, near where it enters the Black Sea. Reportedly, builds tankers and merchant ships up to 20,000 grt, and floating docks.

Sevastopol

Situated on an inlet of Severnaya Bay. Rail connection. Reportedly, three dry docks and five smaller launching ways. Small ships can be built, but repair work is principal task.

Tuapse, Taganrog, and Zhdanov (Mariupol)

New shipyards at these three ports will build standard freighters and tankers of 4,000, 8,000, and 12,000 tons deadweight. Together, they employ 45,000 men.

Novorossisk

Does repair work only.

Inland

It is estimated that there are 86 river and other inland yards building motor torpedo boats, landing craft, and other small naval vessels, but the only ones known are:

Krasnaia Sormovo, Gorki (Volga)

Builds small submarines, prefabricated sections for large submarines, and river vessels.

Kolomenski Kuibyshev, Kolomna (on the Oka River)

Builds small submarines and prefabricated sections for large submarines.

CHAPTER 10

Satellite Navies

The following Communist satellite states are signatories to the Treaty of Friendship and Mutual Assistance of 14 May 1955 (the Warsaw Pact): Albania, Bulgaria, Czechoslovakia, East Germany (the so-called German Democratic Republic), Poland, Rumania, and Hungary. However, since its break with Moscow, Albania may be considered to have withdrawn from the pact. The member states have set up a unified military command with headquarters in Warsaw. The commander-in-chief of the Warsaw Pact Forces is always a Soviet Marshal. The pact provides the "legal" justification for the Soviet Union to station its armed forces in the countries mentioned above.

Some Communist countries—Red China, for example,

—have been omitted from the following review of naval forces, either because they are so much at loggerheads with Moscow that, for the time being at any rate, they would be disinclined to provide military assistance to the Soviet Union, or because their maritime effectiveness is insignificant. Yugoslavia, on the other hand, has been included because the rift between her and the Soviet Union has recently been narrowed somewhat.

The satellite fleets are no more than tools for Moscow's power politics. Moscow can rely on them, however, only so long as it maintains unceasing surveillance over them and keeps them in a state of dependence on the Soviet Union. Measures taken by the authorities in Moscow have that single end in view.

237

Albania

General

During the first years after the war, the Navy was part of the People's Army (now at least 26,000 strong) and was subordinate to it. Then, with Soviet assistance, naval strength increased, but the present breach between Tirana and Moscow makes it unlikely that further Soviet reinforcement will be forthcoming. Red China, with which Albania has lately been in sympathy, might provide some warships, but the probability is that, for some years to come, the Albanian Navy will remain in a state of stagnation. Its present strength is about 2,000 men.

Naval Forces

The Albanian fleet is believed to consist of:

4 submarines (Soviet W class)
4 submarine chasers (Soviet *Kronstadt* class)
2 minesweepers (Soviet T-43 class)
6 minesweepers (Soviet T-301 class)
12 fast patrol boats (Soviet P-4 class)
1 depot ship (Soviet *Atrek* class)
1 oiler (Soviet *Khobi* class).

Naval Air Force

No details available.

Naval Infantry

No details available.

Schools and Training

No details available.

Ports and Bases

Apart from Durazzo, there are no harbors of importance; there are only open anchorages off Valona, Lesh (Alessio), and Sarandë. With Soviet assistance, a naval base, consisting of berths, four submarine shelters, and defensive installations, was built on Saseno Island, in the Gulf of Valona. The shelters were intended solely for Soviet submarines and, until June 1961, from 8 to 12 were based there.

Shipbuilding Industry

No yards for new construction, and only limited repair facilities.

Merchant Marine

A few coasters only.

Bulgaria

General

The peace treaty concluded on 10 February 1946 between the Allies and Bulgaria established limits for Bulgaria's armed forces: 35,000 men in the Army, including the Border Patrol; 18,000 men and 300 aircraft in the Air Force, and 4,500 men in the Navy.

Under the protection of the Soviet Union, Bulgaria has set up a People's Army that far exceeds that limit and whose organization, weapons, and training follow the Soviet pattern. There is conscription from 18 to 50 years of age with a two-year period of active service. The Navy consists of seagoing units manned by 2,700 men, a number of coast defense battalions (Naval Infantry), and an air squadron.

Naval Forces

Most of the ships are of Soviet origin, and, at this writing, there may be:

2 frigates—the *Druzki* and the *Smeli* (Soviet *Riga* class, acquired in 1957 or 1958)
2 submarines (Soviet W class, transferred in 1958)
1 minelayer
2 minesweepers (Soviet T-43 class)
4 minesweepers (Soviet T-301 class)
2 submarine chasers (Soviet *Kronstadt* class)
6 submarine chasers (Soviet SO-I class)
16 landing craft
24 small minesweeping launches
8 fast patrol boats (Soviet P-4 class)
50 small patrol craft
1 training vessel.

Naval Air Force

One air squadron, equipped with Soviet aircraft, including helicopters that are probably used for mine-sweeping duties, is allocated to the Navy. No information is available regarding the strength of the squadron.

Naval Infantry

A number of coast defense battalions patterned on the Soviet naval infantry. Total strength is not known.

Ports and Bases

Varna. Bulgaria's most important ice-free port above the mouth of the Provadiia River. A large commercial port protected by moles, it has a naval harbor, shipyards, and berths for naval vessels.

Burgas. The most important harbor in Bulgaria. Center of the Bulgarian fishing industry in the Black Sea, base for two motor torpedo boats flotillas and a coast defense flotilla. It may become a submarine base.

Kavaklar. Base for the landing-craft flotilla.

Shipbuilding Industry

The only important concern is the Georgi Dimitrov Shipyard in Varna. It builds tankers, concrete lighters, fishing vessels, and other craft for use on rivers; and tankers, freighters, and passenger ships up to 4,000 grt for the Black Sea and Sea of Azov. May, in the future, be licensed to build Soviet warships, e.g., escort vessels, minesweepers, and small submarines. Employs about 5,000 men.

Merchant Marine

The merchant fleet is of little importance: at the end of 1966, it comprised 63 ships of 236,550 tons gross. A ten-year program, started in 1959, foresees the construction of 400,000 grt of freighters, 200,000 grt of tankers, and 100,000 grt of river craft (including combined Danube-seagoing vessels, harbor vessels, and so forth). Ten per cent of the total is to be built in Bulgarian yards. Orders for freighters and tankers, totaling 150,000 grt and 80,000 grt, respectively, have been placed with Polish and Soviet-zone shipyards.

Czechoslovakia

Czechoslovakia has no coastline and therefore does not maintain a navy. It has just a few armed motor launches on the Danube. Although the Danube flows for only a short distance through her territory, Czechoslovakia, with a reported 500,000, or more, grt of river shipping, plays an important part in the river traffic. Among her shipyards, the one in Komarno is the most efficient and builds vessels of up to about 2,000 dwt.

East Germany

General

The Navy is part of the National People's Army, whose strength stands at more than 200,000 men. East German forces began building up soon after 1945, when the so-called Kasernierte Volkspolizei (KVP) was established. This disguised re-armament was "legalized" in 1956.

East German naval forces, known since 1960 as the People's Navy, comprise more than 300 vessels and nearly 200,000 men.

Naval Forces

Composition is estimated to be:

4 frigates—the *Ernst Thälmann,* the *Karl Liebknecht,* the *Friedrich Engels,* and the *Karl Marx* (Soviet *Riga* class acquired in 1957 or 1958)
12 guided-missile patrol boats (Soviet *Osa* class)
50 fast patrol boats (Soviet P-6 class and *Iltis*-class torpedo boats)
12 minesweepers and minelayers (*Krake* and *Habicht* classes)
12 submarine chasers (Soviet SO-I class)
8 or more submarine chasers (*Hai* class)
65 coast defense vessels (*Sperber, Tümmler,* and *Del'fin* classes)
6 landing ships (*Robbe* class)
12 landing vessels (*Labo* class)
80 (approx.) auxiliaries.

Vessels of the *Iltis, Krake, Habicht, Schwalbe, Hai, Sperber, Tümmler, Del'fin, Labo,* and *Robbe* classes were built in East Germany.

Three Krake-*class minesweepers of the East German Navy arrive on a visit to Leningrad in 1969.*

An East German P-6 fast patrol boat passes in review.

Organization

The Navy is divided into three flotillas:

1st Flotilla with five squadrons in Peenemünde (minesweepers, minelayers, submarine chasers, and supply ships).

4th Flotilla with three squadrons in Warnemünde (minesweepers, minelayers, small minesweepers, and supply ships).

6th Flotilla in Sassnitz, comprising one coast defense brigade and 12 squadrons (frigates, guided-missile patrol boats, torpedo boats, landing ships).

Naval Air Force

So far, it is known only that a naval air group has been or will be formed. Nothing is known of its strength or the type of aircraft involved, although it is certain that only Soviet types will be used. Close co-operation between surface forces and five different types of Soviet helicopters has recently been observed.

Naval Land Forces

Although Naval Infantry units do not appear to have been formed as yet, there are several cadres of naval pioneers, which include clearance divers. Two coastal rocket sections have been formed in recent years, and four battalions of the "coastal border brigade" are stationed on land.

Training and Schools

Officer candidates have to serve from one to two years as ratings in the People's Navy, during which time their suitability as officers is determined. They must not be over 23 years of age, must have completed 10 classes or have elementary school education, must have completed a course of vocational training or have proof of at least one year's activity in "Socialist Production." If accepted as officer candidates, they must agree to remain in the Navy or Armed Forces for at least 10 years. Training to be an officer takes four years and is counted as part of the compulsory service. Thus, the candidate is promoted to the lowest commissioned rank after five or six years of total service. As in all Communist countries, emphasis is placed on political instruction during the training of officers, petty officers, and junior ratings.

Almost all flag and senior officers of the People's Navy must complete a one- or two-year course at a Soviet training establishment (usually in Kaliningrad/Königsberg), ending with an examination. It should be mentioned that part of the instruction, especially training in weapons and equipment, is given by Soviet instructors belonging to a unit permanently stationed in the Soviet zone. Pre-military training and instruction of youths (and girls—a feature of Communist regimes) is the responsibility of the Organization for Sport and Technical Skills (Gesellschaft für Sport und Technik—GST). This organization is supported by the state and is comparable to the Soviet DOSAAF (see page 15). The fact that, since 1956, it has been subject to supervision by the Defense Ministry makes further comment on its role superfluous. The *Seesport* section of GST has 12 training vessels.

Ports and Bases

Rostock. The most important port in East Germany, situated on the left bank of the Warnow River, at a point where it is 1,640 feet wide. In recent years, a considerable amount of money has been spent on extending the port: in particular, the channel to the open sea, which is about 22 miles long and 260 feet wide, has been dredged to a minimum of 44 feet. Expansion plans include East and West moles, 2,132 and 1,575 feet long, respectively, and a basin for an oil terminal, 1,608 feet long and 512 feet wide, for ships up to 22,000 dwt. Preparations are also under way for three new basins, each 1,968 feet long and 722 feet wide, on the east bank of the river. The construction of a base for 20 minesweepers is supposed to have started in 1962. Rostock is the home of the Neptun Shipyard and of a large fish co-operative.

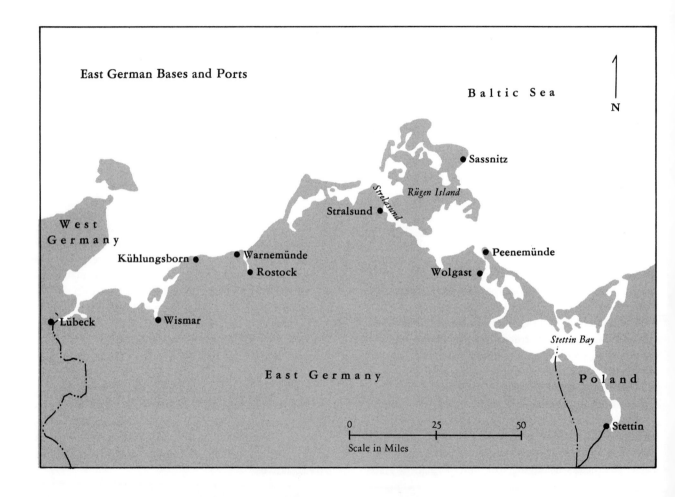

East German Bases and Ports

Baltic Sea

N

Sassnitz

Rügen Island

Stralsund

Strelasund

Peenemünde

Wolgast

West Germany

Kühlungsborn

Warnemünde

Rostock

Lübeck

Wismar

East Germany

Stettin Bay

Poland

Stettin

0   25   50

Scale in Miles

Warnemünde. An outer port of Rostock and a seaside resort. It is a supply base and port for Soviet-zone naval forces, and the home of the Warnow Shipyard.

Wismar. Situated at the southern end of the Wismar Gulf, is the largest Soviet-zone port for the transshipment of potash. Its extensive harbor has three sections and its channel to the open sea is navigable by ships of up to about 12,000 dwt. Construction of an oil terminal basin is apparently under consideration. Wismar is the home of the Matthias-Thesen Shipyard.

Stralsund. Situated on the Strelasund, it is the site of a newly built People's Shipyard, is a naval base and a grain-transshipment and fishing port. It is accessible only to ships of under 2,500 dwt.

Wolgast. Situated about four miles above the mouth of the Peene River, this port is the home of both the main ordnance depot of the People's Navy and of the Peene Shipyard.

Peenemünde. Site of the former Luftwaffe's research and experimental establishment. It has been greatly extended as a naval base.

Sassnitz. This port on the north coast of Rügen Island, is the terminus of the Berlin-Stralsund-Sassnitz railway and of the train ferry to Trelleborg, Sweden. Its harbor is protected by moles and has docks for the train ferries. It is also used by naval forces.

It is said that a base to accommodate 10 submarines and to provide logistic and repair facilities is to be built on Rügen Island, and that the shelters will be blasted out of the chalk cliffs.

Shipbuilding Industry

There are 54 shipbuilding and repair yards in East Germany and they are engaged as follows:

5 in the construction and repair of seagoing vessels,

27 in the construction and repair of inland-waterways vessels,

8 in the construction and repair of fishing vessels, and

14 in the construction and repair of small craft.

Most shipyards are People's Enterprises (Volkseigene Betriebe): only a few of the least significant ones are still in private hands. The most important yards are:

Matthias-Thesen, Wismar. Builds ships up to about 5,000 dwt, mostly freighters and special-purpose ships, and boilers. Five launching ways (2 more are planned), 2 docks. About 9,000 employees.

Neptun, Rostock. Builds ships up to 7,000 dwt, mostly freighters, passenger, and special-purpose ships. Five launching ways. One hauling-up slip is planned. About 3,000 employees.

Warnow, Warnemünde. Construction of freighters and special-purpose ships up to 10,000 dwt. Four launching ways, 2 hauling-up slips planned. Three docks for ships of 10,000, 18,000, and 40,000 dwt, respectively, are in the process of construction. About 10,000 employees.

Volkswerft (People's Shipyard), Stralsund. Reputed to be the largest shipyard in Europe for the mass production of fishing vessels. (Construction time is 37 days —even less for a drifter.) Five launching ways and 2 more, each 558 feet long, under construction. A dock for ships up to 12,000 dwt is also being built. About 6,000 employees.

Peene, Wolgast. Engaged almost entirely in the construction of warships and auxiliaries (minesweepers, submarine chasers, coastal patrol launches, depot ships, supply ships, and so forth), and turbines. Four launching ways, 1 hauling-up slip for ships of up to 1,200 dwt, another 328-foot-long hauling-up facility is planned, 1 dock, another construction dock 426 feet long is either planned or already under construction. About 3,000 employees.

Fürstenberg, Fürstenberg. Builds fishing vessels and craft for inland waterways; will build minor naval vessels, also (coastal patrol launches and small submarine chasers). Three launching ways, 2 more planned. About 1,200 employees.

Köpenick (formerly Engelbrecht), near Berlin. Builds craft for inland waterways and minor naval craft. Four launching ways. About 800 employees.

Oderberg, Eberswalde. Builds vessels for inland waterways. Has 3 hauling-up slips, and about 700 employees.

Rosslau, near Dresden. Builds ships for inland waterways, small freighters, special-purpose vessels, and warships. Four hauling-up slips, 3 more planned. About 2,500 employees.

Übigau, Dresden. Builds craft for inland waterways, occasionally small passenger vessels and special-purpose ships. Three hauling-up slips. About 1,500 employees.

There are also the Ernst Thälmann Shipyard at Brandenburg/Havel, and the Edgar André Shipyard at Magdeburg.

In 1956 the East German shipbuilding industry employed more than 40,000 men, and between 1945 and 1958, it built more than 2,600 ships and craft of all kinds, totaling 600,000 grt, but only a small number of them were for East German use. The majority of them were delivered to the Soviet Union and to the satellite states.

Merchant Marine

All seagoing and inland shipping is controlled by the Ministry of Transport's Chief Administration for Shipping, and most of the ships are state property. Seagoing ships are operated by the German People's Shipping Line (VEB Deutsche Seereederei), the inland traffic by the German People's Inland Shipping Line (VEB Deutsche Binnenreederei). Private shippers are not allowed to make their own freight contracts: they may only subcontract from the state lines.

At mid-1966, East Germany had a seagoing merchant fleet of 274 vessels, totaling 591,106 tons gross.

Hungary

Like Czechoslovakia, Hungary has no access to the open sea and, consequently, has no navy. On the Danube, however, she has a river flotilla of 25 armed vessels, which are under Army command, and are deeply involved in river traffic. Apart from her numerous river craft, she has a number of freighters that sail regularly from the Danube to ports on the Black Sea. Several shipyards build river vessels, the best known being the Ghiurghiu Dej yard in Budapest, which also builds coastal motor vessels.

Poland

General

The ambitious naval program upon which Poland had embarked before the outbreak of the war in 1939, was energetically resumed after the war, when the German territory on the far side of the Oder River came under Poland and increased her Baltic coastline from a bare 31 miles in 1939 to nearly 310 miles in 1945. Much rebuilding had to be done in order to make Polish ports and shipyards usable again, and her maritime development since the war shows how successfully it was accomplished. The Polish People's Army follows faithfully along Soviet lines. There is universal liability for military service from 18 until 50 years of age, the period of active service in the Navy being three years. In 1965 the strength of the Navy stood at about 20,000 men. Until 1956, all high-ranking positions were occupied by Soviet officers of Polish origin. In most years, a large number of men volunteer for the Navy, but only 2,000 to 3,000 are accepted. The Polish Navy is reputed to be better trained than any other satellite navy.

Naval Forces

2 destroyers—the *Grom* (ex-*Smetlivyi*) and the *Wicher* (ex-*Skoryi*) (Soviet *Skoryi* class, acquired in 1957 or 1958)

1 old destroyer—the *Blyscawicza* (British-built)

5 submarines (Soviet W class, acquired in 1962 or 1963)

6 old submarines (Soviet M-V class)

1 old submarine (Netherlands-built)

12 minesweepers (Polish-built)

12 minesweepers (Polish-built T-43 class)

4 old minesweepers

12 guided-missile fast patrol boats (Soviet *Osa* class)

20 fast patrol boats (Soviet P-6 class)

10 submarine chasers (including 8 Soviet *Kronstadt* class)

38 patrol boats

26 landing vessels (including several Polish-built landing ships of the *Polnochnyi* class)

50 auxiliaries.

Naval Air Force

Four squadrons with 40 MIG-17 jet fighters, some helicopters, a number of training and communications aircraft. Manpower stands at about 2,500 men. Personnel belong to the Navy and wear naval uniform, but are administered by the Air Force. Operational bases are at Gdansk (Danzig), Gdynia (Gdingen), and Jastarnia (Heisternest).

Naval Land Forces

There are a number of Naval Infantry and coastal artillery units with a strength of about 6,500 men, but nothing is known of their organization.

Training and Schools

Training centers are reputed to have an annual capacity of 3,500 men, and to have 500 Soviet officers and petty officers on their instructional staffs. A large proportion of Polish naval personnel attend Soviet training establishments (so far, about 4,500 men).

Ports and Bases

Gdynia. From 1935 to 1945, Gotenhafen. Until 1925 an insignificant fishing village, it became a city in 1926, and now has about 140,000 inhabitants. Being the only satisfactory port in the former Polish Corridor, it was developed into a large commercial port and naval base: the harbor covers a total of more than 2,470 acres, with

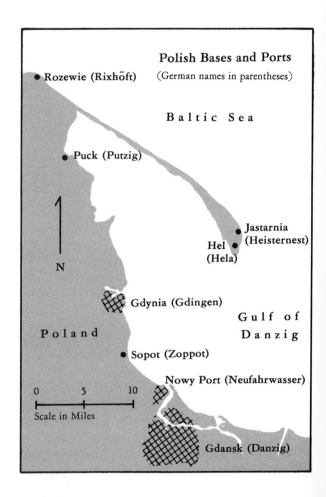

Polish Bases and Ports
(German names in parentheses)

Rozewie (Rixhöft)

Baltic Sea

Puck (Putzig)

Jastarnia (Heisternest)

Hel (Hela)

N

Gdynia (Gdingen)

Gulf of Danzig

Poland

Sopot (Zoppot)

Nowy Port (Neufahrwasser)

0   5   10
Scale in Miles

Gdansk (Danzig)

moles 2.4 miles long, and 7.5 miles of quays, the deepest water being almost 40 feet. A transshipment port, particularly for coal from Upper Silesia, it is also the main base of the Polish Navy and has dockyard and logistic facilities.

Gdansk. Heavily damaged during the war but now fully operational, this is an important transshipment port. It handles 50 per cent of Poland's seaborne trade, and is the site of big shipyards. Since 1 January 1950, the commercial ports of Gdynia and Gdansk have been under combined administration. Fleet base, naval garrison.

Szczecin (Stettin). An important transshipment port with a very efficient shipbuilding industry. Apparently, there are no naval establishments there.

Elblag (Elbing). The site of the Schichau Shipyard, which, although only slightly damaged during the war, has discontinued building ships and builds propulsion machinery only (supplies the shipyards of Szczecin and Gdansk).

Hel (Hela). A base for light naval forces.

Jastarnia. The site of logistic facilities.

Shipbuilding Industry

The former German shipyards that were taken over by Poland have been rebuilt and considerably enlarged, and today are considered to be very efficient (up to 1960, they had built about one million grt). Merchant ships and fishing vessels are built for Poland's own use, for the Soviet Union, and for almost all the states of the European eastern bloc. So far, warships have been built for the Polish Navy only. The following shipyards are known:

Gdanska (formerly Schichau, Danzig), Gdansk. Builds large merchant ships.

Adolf Warski (formerly Vulcan, Stettin), Szczecin. Builds large merchant ships. The yard is to be enlarged during the next 10 years, in order to bring its capacity up to 150,000 dwt per year.

Polocna (formerly Danziger), Gdansk. Builds large merchant ships up to about 10,000 dwt, and prefabricated fishing vessels.

Paris Commune, Gdynia. Developed from the former German naval dockyard, it builds small ships of up to 1,550 dwt, fishing vessels, and minor naval craft (minesweepers, patrol boats). A large expansion was begun in 1961 and, among other facilities, a dry dock, 787 feet long and 197 feet wide, is being built to enable the yard to build ships of up to 65,000 dwt.

Remontawa, Gdynia. Builds small vessels.

Rybacka, Puck (Putzig). Builds small vessels.

Weichsel, Modlin. Builds river craft.

Merchant Marine

With considerable encouragement from the state, the Polish merchant fleet has been greatly expanded since

1945. Nevertheless, it took longer than expected to reach the goal of 560,000 grt set for 1956. The total of about 1,040,000 grt, comprising 390 ships, reached in mid-1966 greatly exceeded the prewar figure of something over 100,000 grt. It seems unlikely that the new goal of 4.5 million dwt by 1980 will be achieved, because Polish shipyards have been so heavily engaged in building ships to the order of the Soviet Union (between 1958 and 1965 alone, 100 ships of 720,000 dwt) that they have scarcely any capacity left for Poland's own requirements.

The fishing fleet also has been greatly expanded and, in 1961, it included 3 fish carriers, 68 trawlers, 67 drifters, etc., 2 fish factory ships, and 549 inshore fishing boats. All ships are state property and are administered by three state shipping lines.

Rumania

General

A peace treaty concluded in 1947 required Rumania to limit her armed forces, and maximum tonnage allowed the Navy was 15,000, maximum manpower, 5,000. These treaty obligations have been ignored, and the Rumanian People's Army has been building up steadily since 1948. In organization, armament, and training, it is patterned entirely on the Soviet model.

Naval Forces

  4 minesweepers
  3 submarine chasers (Soviet *Kronstadt* class)
22 minesweepers (Soviet T-301 class)
  4 guided-missile fast patrol boats (Soviet *Osa* class)
  8 fast patrol boats (Soviet P-4 class)

A report that the Soviet cruiser *Kerch* (ex-Italian *Emanuele Filiberto Duco d'Aosta*) had been transferred to the Rumanian Navy has proved to be incorrect.

Naval Air Force

No information available.

Naval Land Forces

There are coast defense troops and naval infantry but nothing is known of their strength or organization.

Training and Schools

No details available.

Ports and Bases

Constanta. This, the principal port, handles overseas trade, is the terminal point of the Ploesti pipeline, and is the fleet's main base.

Sulina. Situated at the central mouth of the Danube, this port is of secondary importance, but is being extended as a joint Soviet-Rumanian submarine base: the channel is being dredged to about 50 feet, and a submarine repair yard, protected logistic bunkers, a torpedo depot, and oil tanks are being built. When the project has been completed, the port will be closed to merchant shipping.

Shipbuilding Industry

There are 5 large shipyards with about 34,000 employees, and 20 small yards for the construction of river craft and fishing vessels. The most important are the yards at Sulina, which build motor freighters up to 2,200 grt. Other yards are at:

Constanta. Has the capacity to build vessels up to about 4,000 grt. Freighters of 1,200 and 500 grt are in series production.

Galatz. Engaged in the series production of standard freighters of 9,850 grt. Between 1938 and 1945, built warships, including 1 minelayer and 2 submarines.

Sfântu Gheorghe. Builds coastal vessels of 1,200 and 500 grt.

Braila. Standard 18,000-dwt tankers are to be built here. Below Braila and Galatz, the Danube has been dredged to about 40 feet, to make it navigable by large vessels, which have to go to Constanta to be fitted out.

Merchant Marine

There are 25 seagoing vessels, totaling about 80,000 grt. Other vessels, besides standard tankers of up to 18,000 dwt, are to be built.

Yugoslavia

General

The People's Army of Yugoslavia consists of the Army, Navy, and Air Force. There is universal liability for military service between the ages of 20 and 50, the active-service period being two years. The commander-in-chief of the Armed Forces is the President of Yugoslavia. The strength of the Navy is 27,000 men.

Naval Forces

1 destroyer—the *Split*

2 destroyers—the *Kotor* (ex-British *Kempenfelt*) and the *Pula* (ex-British *Wager*)

2 frigates—the *Durmitor* (ex-Italian *Ariete*) and the *Ucka* (ex-Italian *Balestra*)

2 frigates—the *Biokovo* (ex-Italian *Alieso*) and the *Triglav* (ex-Italian *Indomito*)

4 submarines—(*Sutjeska* class, built at the Uljanik Yard, Pula)

1 old submarine—the *Sava* (ex-Italian *Nautilo*)

7 guided-missile fast patrol boats (Soviet *Osa* class)

6 fast patrol boats (Soviet *Shershen* class)

1 minelayer

90 motor torpedo boats

3 patrol vessels

16 submarine chasers

34 small minesweeping boats

A number of small landing and miscellaneous craft.

Yugoslav and Albanian Bases and Ports

0   50   100
Scale in Miles

Trieste
Rijeka
Kraljevica
Pula
Zadar
Sibenik
Split
Kardeljevo
Dubrovnik
Kotor
Lesh
Tirana
Durazzo
Valona
Sarandë

Adriatic Sea

Yugoslavia

Italy

Albania

Strait of Otranto

N

Naval Air Force
   Existence and details not known.
Naval Land Forces
   Existence and details not known.
Training and Schools
   No details are known.

Ports and Bases
   Pula. From 1919 to 1945, the Italian town of Pola. Formerly the main base of the Austro-Hungarian Navy. Situated at the tip of the Istrian Peninsula. About 40,000 inhabitants. Shipbuilding yard and naval arsenal.
   Rijeka. From 1919 to 1945, the Italian city of Fiume. Situated at the mouth of the Recina River, it is the most important port in Yugoslavia. Over 70,000 inhabitants. Installations include shipyards, engineering works, and oil refineries. The small port of Kraljevica is nearby.
   Zadar. From 1920 to 1945, the Italian town of Zara. Port on a narrow tongue of land on the Dalmatian coast. About 25,000 inhabitants.
   Sibenik (Italian, Sebenico). At the mouth of the Kerka River. About 25,000 inhabitants. Handles a large volume of exports.
   Split (Italian, Spalato). Second largest port in Yugoslavia. About 80,000 inhabitants. Shipbuilding and many other industries.
   Dubrovnik (Italian, Ragusa). Situated on a peninsula in southern Yugoslavia. About 20,000 inhabitants.

Guided-missile patrol boats of the Komar *class, a type operated by many of the satellite navies.*

Shipbuilding Industry

Shipyards in Yugoslavia are:

Uljanik, Pula. Developed from the old Austrian naval yard, which operated under Italian direction from 1920. Builds ships up to about 20,000 dwt and diesel engines.

3rd May, Rijeka. Formerly the Danubius Vereinigte Schiffbau und Maschinenfabrik, and under Italian direction between 1920 and 1945. Builds vessels of up to 35,000 tons.

Split, Split. Formerly connected with the French Chantiers de la Loire, Nantes. Builds small vessels.

Titovo, Kraljevica. Formerly connected with the British Yarrow Shipyard. Builds ships up to 4,000 dwt.

Merchant Marine

At mid-1966, the Yugoslav merchant fleet consisted of 353 ships, totaling 990,846 grt. In 1959 it carried about 53 per cent of all Yugoslavia's foreign trade.

Details and Profiles of Soviet Warships

Many classes of Soviet warships are known in the West by names given them by NATO. In this appendix, such classes are identified by an asterisk.

It has not been possible to use the same scale for all the profiles. Because of their size, helicopter carriers and cruisers have had to be drawn to a scale of 1:1250. In order to allow important details to be seen clearly, patrol boats, submarine chasers, and minesweepers have been drawn on the larger scale of 1:500. The scale for all other ships is 1:1000. Dimensions are given in feet.

The drawings are based on photographs, and the most important of the variations that often exist between ships in the same class are illustrated.

Helicopter Carriers: *Moskva* Class

2 ships: *Moskva* and *Leningrad*. A third is said to be under construction. Laid down between 1963 and 1964, completed between 1967 and 1968. Builders: Marti Yard, Nikolaev. Displacement: 15,000 tons standard, 18,000 tons deep load. Dimensions: length, 672.5; beam, 88.5; draft, 22.9. Machinery: steam propulsion for 29 to 30 kts. speed. Armament: 15 to 20 helicopters (Kamov-25K); 2 twin launchers for Goa surface-to-air missiles, 1 twin launcher for antisubmarine missiles; 2 12-barreled antisubmarine-rocket launchers; 4 57-mm. AA in twin mounts.

General: The Western World had no inkling that a Soviet helicopter carrier was under construction, and was surprised when the *Moskva* made her appearance in 1968. According to the latest information, the first two ships of this class were laid down to fill an order from the Indonesian Navy, but when Moscow broke with Djakarta, they were not delivered. That may well be the case, because in 1963 or 1964 there was a rumor that Indonesia, which has one *Sverdlov*-class cruiser, was trying to buy a second and wanted her to be converted to an aircraft carrier. The *Leningrad* was first seen on 21 April 1969, when she passed through the Bosporus en route to the Mediterranean.

It was assumed that these ships would be equipped with vertical take-off and landing planes but, so far, only Kamov-25K antisubmarine helicopters have been identified positively. They have one hangar deck, one lift, and a noteworthy array of modern electronics. Improved versions of this class may be under construction or planned.

Moskva Class

1:1250

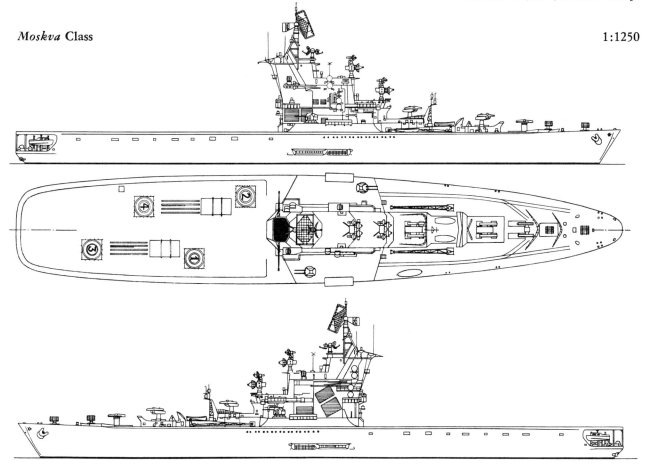

Moskva, 1969

Cruisers: *Kirov* Class

2 ships: *Kirov* and *Slava* (ex-*Molotov*). Laid down, 1935 and 1936; launched, 1936 and 1939. Completed, 1938 and 1944. Builders: Marti Yard, Leningrad, and Marti Yard, Nikolaev. Displacement: 8,800 tons standard, 11,500 tons deep load. Dimensions: length, 627; beam, 59.1; draft, 20. Machinery: geared steam turbines (with diesels for cruising), 6 boilers, 2 shafts, 110,000 SHP for 35 kts. Radius of action: 3,500 miles at 19 kts. Complement: 750. Armament: 9 7.1-inch guns in triple turrets, 6 3.9-inch AA in single mounts, 10 to 18 37-mm. AA in twin mounts; possibly, 60 to 90 mines.

General: The design of these ships was begun in 1933 or 1934. Six of them were completed: the two mentioned above, the *Voroshilov,* the *Maxim Gorki,* the *Petropavlovsk* (ex-*Kalinin*), and the *Kaganovich.* The *Voroshilov* has apparently been struck off the active list and may have been broken up; the *Maxim Gorki* was decommissioned sometime ago and her armament may have been removed; and the *Kaganovich* is reported to have been handed over to Communist China about 1957. The Ansaldo Yard, of Genoa, designed the class and supervised its construction. Originally, the ships had a catapult between the funnels, and 6 21-inch torpedo tubes in triple mounts. The class is divided into two groups: the *Kirov* and the *Voroshilov* have a heavy quadrupod mast above the bridge, while the *Maxim Gorki* has a control tower with a light tripod mast behind it. Formerly, all ships had the main mast abaft the after funnel, but this was changed after 1945. In 1954 or 1955 the *Kirov* underwent partial modernization (new light AA armament, fire-control equipment, radar). More recently, a high deckhouse (probably for classrooms) has been fitted aft. The *Slava* has also been modernized to some extent. The two vessels still serving are approaching the end of their active lives, and are probably now used only for training purposes.

Kirov **Class**

1:1250

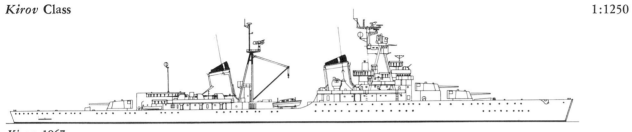

Kirov, 1967

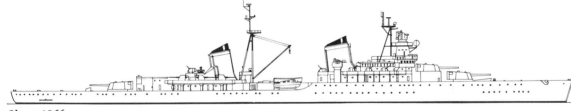

Slava, 1966

Cruisers: *Chapaev* Class

3 ships: *Zhelezniakov, Komsomolets* (ex-*Chkalov*), and *Kuibyshev*. Laid down, 1938–40; launched, 1941; completed, 1948–51. Builders: Ordzhonikidze Yard, Leningrad (*Kuibyshev*); Marti Yard, Nikolaev. Displacement: 11,500 tons standard, 15,000 tons deep load. Dimensions: length, 659; beam, 64; draft, 23.4. Machinery: geared steam turbines (with diesels for cruising), 6 boilers, 2 shafts, 113,000 SHP for 35 kts. Radius: 4,500 miles at 20 kts. Complement: 850. Armament: 12 5.9-inch guns in triple turrets, 8 3.9-inch AA in twin mounts, 24 to 28 37-mm. AA in twin mounts; possibly, 100 to 200 mines.

General: A prewar design started in 1937 or 1938. Twelve ships were planned, but only 6 were laid down, and 5 of them did not enter service until some considerable time after the end of the war. The sixth ship, the *Ordzhonikidze,* was demolished on the slip. The *Frunze* was taken out of service in 1961 or 1962, and the *Chapaev* (ex-*Ordzhonikidze*) in 1965 or 1966. The original design included torpedo tubes and catapults but they were never fitted. In 1957 or 1958 the ships were partially modernized: one important improvement was the type of radar, including a Uda-Yagi aerial on the after AA gun deck, with which they were fitted. The *Chkalov* was renamed the *Komsomolets* in 1961. The class is now used only for training.

Cruisers: *Sverdlov* Class

13 ships: *Sverdlov, Admiral Lazarev, Admiral Nakhimov, Admiral Seniavin, Admiral Ushakov, Aleksandr Nevski, Aleksandr Suvorov, Dmitri Donskoi, Kuzma Minin, Dmitri Pozharski, Mikhail Kutusov, Oktiabr'skaia Revoliutsiia* (ex-*Molotovsk*), and *Murmansk* (ex-*Zhdanov*). Laid down, 1948–53; launched 1951–54; completed, 1952–58. Nearly all built in Leningrad (Ordzhonikidze Yard) or Nikolaev (Marti Yard); 1 or 2 ships may have been built in the Navy Yard, Severodvinsk. Displacement: 14,450 tons standard, 19,000 tons deep load. Dimensions: length, 689; beam, 70; draft, 24.7. Machinery: geared steam turbines, 6 to 9 boilers, 2 shafts, 150,000 SHP for 34 kts. Radius: 8,000 miles at 20 kts. Complement: 1,050. Armament: 12 5.9-inch guns in triple turrets, 12 3.9-inch AA in twin turrets, 21 37-mm. AA in twin mounts; possibly, 200 mines.

General: Postwar development based on the *Chapaev* class. Only some of the lessons learned from wartime experience were applied. The fire-control systems and some of the armament (stabilized AA mounts) are based on German practice. Twenty-four ships were planned; 20 were begun; 17 were launched; and 14 entered service. The remaining 6 hulls, some of which were still on the slips, were broken up between 1953 and 1956. All were originally intended to displace 12,800 tons

Chapaev Class

1:1250

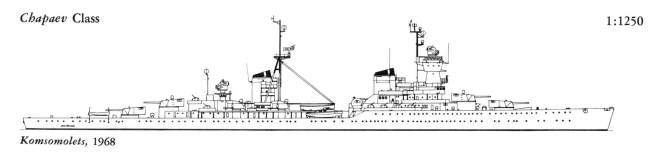

Komsomolets, 1968

Sverdlov Class

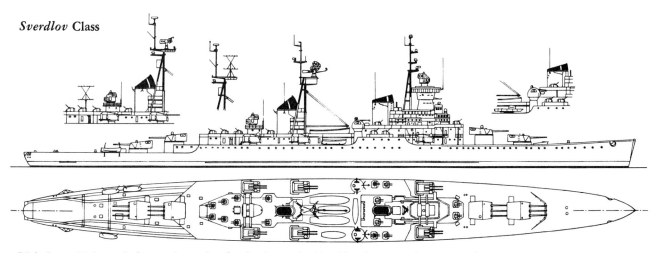

Right Inset: High AA platform and torpedo tubes fitted on early ships. They have since been removed.

standard and 17,000 tons deep load, but subsequent alterations and additions resulted in an increase of nearly 2,000 tons. The thirteenth ship of the class, the *Dzerzhinski,* was converted to a guided-missile cruiser in 1961 or 1962 (*see Dzerzhinski*), and the fourteenth ship, the *Ordzhonikidze,* was sold to Indonesia in October 1962 and renamed the *Irian.* The *Admiral Nakhimov* is supposed to have been equipped with a missile system (for Strela missiles), the after 5.9-inch turret having been removed, but this has not yet been confirmed. The AA platform on the forward funnel of the *Sverdlov,* the *Murmansk,* the *Dzerzhinski,* and the former *Ordzhonikidze* is significantly higher than it is on the others.

The 10 21-inch torpedo tubes in two quintuple mounts that were fitted between the funnels of the earlier ships of the class were removed soon after they were fitted.

Radar equipment has been changed several times. Since 1956, most of the ships have had a Uda-Yagi aerial on the mainmast; some, including the *Sverdlov,* were subsequently fitted with a Head Net-1, also on the mainmast, the Uda-Yagi aerial being moved to the after AA platform. In recent years some ships have carried a Big Net aerial on the mainmast, but no Uda-Yagi aerial. The *Molotovsk* was renamed the *Oktiabr'skaia Revoliutsiia* in 1957, and the *Zhdanov* became the *Murmansk* in 1964.

Guided-Missile Cruiser: *Dzerzhinski* Class

1 ship: *Dzerzhinski.* For building and technical data, *see Sverdlov* class. Armament: 9 5.9-inch guns in triple turrets, 1 twin launcher for Guideline surface-to-air missiles, 12 3.9-inch AA in twin mounts, 16 37-mm. AA in twin mounts; 200 mines.

General: This ship was completed as a *Sverdlov*-class cruiser and converted to a guided-missile cruiser in 1961 or 1962. The after 5.9-inch turret was replaced by a magazine and twin launcher for Guideline surface-to-air missiles. A blast deflector, situated forward of the launchers, extends across almost the whole width of the ship. The after director has been removed and, in its place, a cylindrical superstructure carrying missile-guidance radar has been fitted. On the mainmast there is a Big Net aerial, and above that a Head Net-2. Abaft the forward funnel, there is a large air-search radar, which can be used only on the beam. Light AA armament has been reduced by 50 per cent. The missile system looks as though it consists, basically, of equipment intended for use in a fixed installation ashore. Apparently, trials have not been entirely satisfactory and no other ships of the *Sverdlov* class have been converted.

Dzerzhinski Class

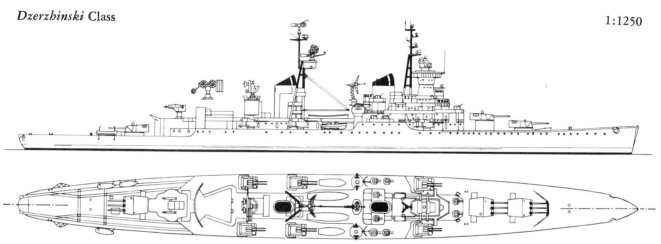

Dzerzhinski, after conversion

Guided-Missile Cruisers: *Kynda* Class*

4 ships: *Variag, Groznyi, Admiral Fokin* (ex-*Grom?*), and *Admiral Golovko.* First ship laid down June 1960, launched April 1961, and completed June 1962. Second ship launched November 1961, and fitted out in August 1962. The other 2 ships were launched in 1962, but not completed until early 1965. Builders: Zhdanov Yard, Leningrad. Displacement: 4,800 tons standard, 6,000 tons deep load. Dimensions: length, 486; beam, 50.9; draft, 15.9. Machinery: geared steam turbines, 4 boilers, 2 shafts, 2 rudders, 85,000 to 100,000 SHP for 35 kts. Complement: 390. Armament: 2 quadruple launchers for Shaddock surface-to-surface missiles, 1 twin launcher for Goa surface-to-air missiles, 4 3-inch, dual-purpose guns in twin mounts, 6 antisubmarine-torpedo tubes in triple mounts, 2 12-barreled antisubmarine-rocket launchers. Equipment for a helicopter.

General: The comprehensive armament of these ships enables them to operate independently over a wide area. Two magazines, one below the bridge and one abaft the after funnel, can each carry 4 Shaddock missiles, while the outfit of Goa missiles probably totals 30. There is a helicopter flight deck aft. The funnel tops have been altered since the ships were built, and the after funnel has been fitted with vanes. Recent reports indicate that these cruisers are undergoing some reconstruction aimed at improving their stability.

Guided-Missile Cruisers: *Kresta* Class*

5 ships: the name of one may be *Krasnii Kavkaz.* Began building in 1964, first ship completed at the end of 1966 or in the spring of 1967. Builders: Zhdanov Yard, Leningrad. Displacement: over 6,000 tons standard, 7,000 tons or more, deep load. Dimensions: length, 492; beam, 59.1; draft, not known. Machinery: gas turbines (probably with diesels for cruising). Speed; 34–35 kts. Armament: 2 twin launchers for Shaddock surface-to-surface missiles, 2 twin launchers for Goa surface-to-air missiles, 4 57-mm. AA in twin mounts, 6 antisubmarine-torpedo tubes in triple mounts, 2 12-barreled antisubmarine-rocket launchers (forward) and 2 6-barreled antisubmarine-rocket launchers (aft). Equipment for a helicopter.

General: This, the latest type of Soviet guided-missile cruiser, incorporates the weapon system of the *Kynda*-class cruisers and the propulsion system of the *Kashin*-class destroyers. It is the first Soviet warship to have a helicopter hangar. The double funnel, with a radar mast protruding between the uptakes, is similar to the "macks" of modern U.S. warships. Shaddock launchers are situated alongside the bridge and the magazine is forward. Series production is likely.

Kynda Class

1:1000

Kresta Class

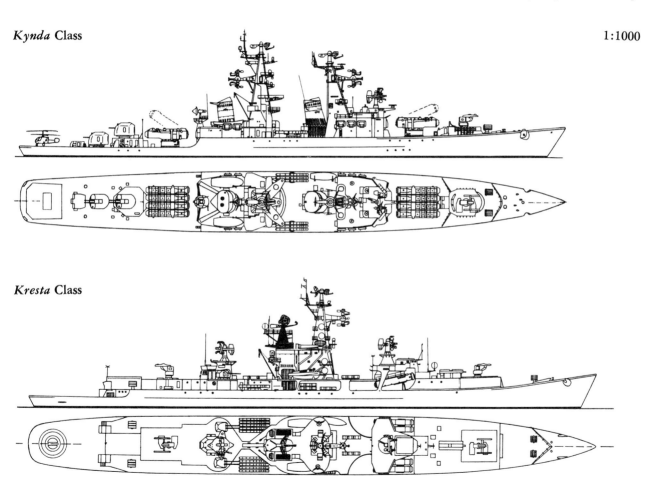

Destroyers: *Skoryi* Class

50 ships, including the Modified *Skoryi* class: *Bespokoi-nyi, Bessmennyi, Bessmertnyi, Besstrashnyi, Bessumnyi, Beznervnyi, Bezukoriznennyi, Bezuprechnyi, Blagorod-nyi, Bystryi, Obrazovannyi, Ochodzhivyi, Ognennyi, Osmyslennyi, Osnovatelnyi, Ostervenelyi, Ostorozhnyi, Ostroglaznyi, Otchaiannyi, Otvetsvennyi, Ozhestochen-nyi, Ozhivlennyi, Ozloblennyi, Serdityi, Sereznyi, Serioz-nyi, Smelyi, Smotriashchyi, Smyslennyi, Sokrushitel'nyi, Solidnyi, Sovershennyi, Sposobnyi, Statnyi, Stepennyi, Stoikyi, Stremitel'nyi, Surovyi, Svobodnyi, Vashnyi, Vdumchivyi, Vedushchii, Vernyi, Vidnyi, Vikhrevoi, Vnezapnyi, Volevoi, Vozbuzhdennyi, Vrazumitel'nyi, Vyderzhannyi.* Built between 1949 and 1953, completed between 1952 and 1956. Builders: Zhdanov Yard, Leningrad, and other yards in Nikolaev, Komsomolsk, and Severodvinsk. Displacement: 2,300 tons standard, 3,100 tons deep load. Dimensions: length, 394; beam, 39.4; draft, 15. Machinery: geared steam turbines, 4 boilers, 2 shafts, 70,000 SHP for 36 kts. Radius of action: 4,000 miles at 15 kts. Complement: 260. Armament: 4 5.1-inch guns in twin turrets, 1 3.3-inch AA twin turret, 8 37-mm. AA in twin mounts, 10 21-inch torpedo tubes in quintuple mounts, 4 depth-charge throwers; possibly, 80 mines.

General: These destroyers are a postwar development based on the *Otlichnyi* class which, although designed before the war, was not completed until after it. The *Skoryi* design did not incorporate wartime experience to any great extent, and when the class entered service it really represented a stage of development that had been reached in 1939–40. Although the forecastle is somewhat longer than it is in previous designs, seakeeping qualities leave something to be desired. At first, only a limited amount of navigational radar was fitted. A total of 73 ships have been built. Early versions had 7 37-mm. single AA guns, but about 1953 these began being replaced by 8 37-mm. twin mounts. Originally, there were minor differences in the masts. Some of the ships, but it is not known how many, were rebuilt between 1958 and 1961 (*see* Modified *Skoryi* class). Several of these destroyers have been sold abroad.

Destroyers: Modified *Skoryi* Class

There are 50 *Skoryi*s in service, but how many have been modified is not known. For building and technical data, *see Skoryi* class. Rebuilt between 1958 and 1961. Armament: 4 5.1-inch guns in twin turrets, 5 single 57-mm. AA, 5 21-inch torpedo tubes in a quintuple mount, 2 16-barreled antisubmarine-rocket launchers; possibly, 80 mines.

General: Modification has probably been confined to those ships whose condition justified the work, and the

Skoryi Class

1:1000

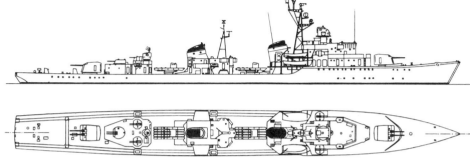

Modified *Skoryi* **Class**

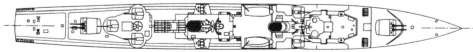

number involved is probably not great. The forward torpedo tubes have been removed and the superstructure deck between the funnels has been enclosed. Modern 57-mm. AA guns have replaced the older 3.3-inch and 37-mm. weapons, directors are mounted on either side of the after funnel and improved antisubmarine weapons have been fitted. The improved and more extensive radar equipment that has been added required alterations to the masts. The funnels now have high cowls.

Destroyers: *Tallinn* Class*

1 ship: *Nastoichivyi* (ex-*Neustrashimyi*). Probably laid down in 1953, completed in 1955. Built in a Baltic yard. Displacement: 3,200 tons standard, 4,300 tons deep load. Dimensions: length, 436; beam, 44.3; draft, 15.9. Machinery: geared steam turbines, 4 boilers, 2 shafts, 100,000 SHP for 38 to 40 kts. Radius: 6,000 miles at 15 kts. Complement: 340. Armament: 4 5.1-inch, dual-purpose guns in twin turrets, 16 47-mm. AA in quadruple mounts, 10 21-inch torpedo tubes in quintuple mounts, 2 16-barreled antisubmarine-rocket launchers; possibly, 60 mines.

General: Designed back in 1949, she is the prototype for a large, fast destroyer, and is the first Soviet destroyer to be built with a flush deck in order to improve seakeeping qualities. The hull is extensively welded. Main machinery is operated by remote control, and the boilers are in one compartment. The main armament and directors are fully stabilized. Due to her high freeboard, she lacks stability and, in spite of her flush deck, did not prove satisfactory in her seakeeping qualities. Consequently, the design was not put into series production. Her original AA armament consisted of 6 37-mm. twin mounts, and depth charges only were carried. Since 1960, a Uda-Yagi aerial has been installed amidships. The layout of the mine rails is noteworthy: due to lack of space they cross abaft the after funnel.

Tallinn Class

1:1000

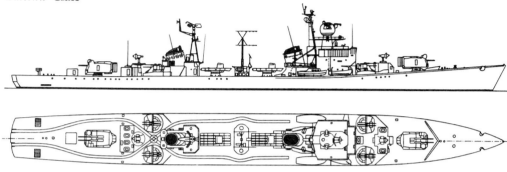

Kotlin Class

Kotlin Class with
helicopter platform

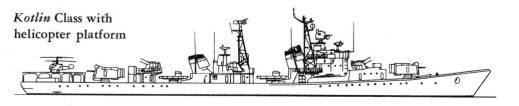

Destroyers: *Kotlin* Class/Modified *Kotlin* Class*

19 ships: the following names are known—*Besslednyi, Byvalyi, Blestiashchii, Spravedlivyi, Svetlyi, Burlivyi, Naporistyi, Vdokhnovennyi, Vozmushchennyi, Plamennyi.* Began building in 1954, the last ship being completed in 1958. Builders: various yards in Leningrad and Nikolaev. Displacement: 2,850 tons standard, 3,885 tons deep load. Dimensions: length, 418.3; beam, 42.4; draft, 15. Machinery: geared steam turbines, 4 boilers, 2 shafts, 80,000 SHP for 36 kts. Complement: 285. Armament: 4 5.1-inch, dual-purpose guns in twin turrets, 16 47-mm. AA in quadruple mounts, 10 21-inch torpedo tubes in quintuple mounts, 6 depth-charge throwers; possibly, 80 mines. Ships of the modified *Kotlin* class have only 5 torpedo tubes and 2 16-barreled antisubmarine-rocket launchers; no depth-charge throwers. Several ships carry a helicopter.

General: Based on experience gained from the *Tallinn*, this is a successful design that has turned out to be very seaworthy. Lighter-weight machinery enabled the overall dimensions to be kept smaller than those of the *Tallinn.* Modified *Kotlin*s have had the after group of torpedo tubes replaced by a deckhouse (apparently, an area for the maintenance and preparation of torpedoes); also, the mainmast and antisubmarine-rocket launchers forward of the bridge have been changed: these modifications were also made in the original *Kotlin*s. Origi-nally, a Head Net-1 was fitted on the mainmast; now, all ships carry Head Net-2. From 4 to 6 hulls that had not been completed were converted to guided-missile destroyers in 1957 or 1958 (*see Kildin* class). In 1961 or 1962, one vessel was given a surface-to-air missile launcher (*see Kotlin-Sam* class).

Guided-Missile Destroyers: *Kotlin-Sam* Class*

5 ships: names not known. For building and technical data, *see Kotlin* class. Rebuilt 1961–62 and 1966–67. Armament: 2 5.1-inch dual-purpose guns in twin mount forward, 1 twin launcher for Goa surface-to-air missiles, 4 (later 12) 47-mm. AA in quadruple mounts. No antisubmarine armament.

General: The first two ships of the *Kotlin* class to be converted have a Goa surface-to-air weapon system in place of their after 5.1-inch twin mounts. Their 47-mm. quadruple AA mounts forward of the radar tower were replaced some time after the conversion.

The next three conversions, designated *Kotlin-Sam IIs,* differ slightly from the first two. They have twin launchers for Goa missiles, 2 5.1-inch AA in a twin mount, 4 57-mm. AA in a quadruple mount, 5 torpedo tubes in a quintuple mount, and 2 12-barreled antisubmarine-rocket launchers.

Modified *Kotlin* Class

1:1000

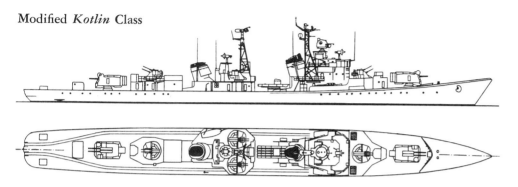

***Kotlin-Sam* Class**

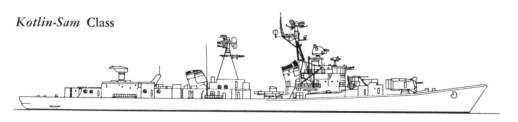

Kotlin-Sam II

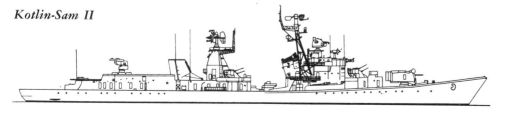

Guided-Missile Destroyers: *Kildin* Class*

4 ships: only names known are *Bedovyi* and *Neulovimyi*. Laid down after 1952, began rebuilding 1957–58, completed in 1959 or 1960. Builders: Zhdanov Yard, Leningrad, and Marti Yard, Nikolaev. Displacement: 3,000 tons standard, 4,000 tons deep load. Dimensions, machinery, SHP, and speed, as *Kotlin* class. Complement: 300. Armament: 1 single launcher for Strela surface-to-surface missiles, 16 57-mm. AA in quadruple mounts, 6 antisubmarine-torpedo tubes in triple mounts, 2 16-barreled antisubmarine-rocket launchers.

General: These ships were laid down as *Kotlin*-class destroyers and completed as guided-missile ships. A magazine for a maximum of 6 Strela missiles and a single launcher were fitted aft. The prototype, *Kildin-I*, retained the *Kotlin*-type funnel and Wasphead director. The *Kildin-II* and *Kildin-III* are further variations that can be distinguished from one another only by their funnel tops.

Guided-Missile Destroyers: *Krupnyi* Class*

8 ships: the following names are not confirmed—*Boikii, Gordyi, Gnevnyi, Gremiashchii, Besstrashnyi, Besposhchadnyi, Upornyi,* and *Zorkii*. Laid down from 1958 onwards, completed between 1961 and about 1963. Builders: Zhdanov Yard, Leningrad, and other yards in Nikolaev and, possibly, though not likely, in Komsomolsk. Displacement: 3,650 tons standard, 4,560 tons deep load. Dimensions: length, 456; beam, 49; draft, 18.1. Machinery: geared steam turbines, 4 boilers, 2 shafts, 80,000 SHP for 34 kts. Armament: 2 single launchers for Strela surface-to-surface missiles, 16 57-mm. AA in quadruple mounts, 6 antisubmarine-torpedo tubes in triple mounts, 2 16-barreled antisubmarine-rocket launchers. Equipment for a helicopter.

General: These destroyers were developed from the *Kildin* class, but have 2 missile launchers, instead of one. The first sighting was made in the Black Sea in June 1961, when the vessel concerned was in transit and her launchers were in watertight coverings. A few weeks later, another *Krupnyi*-class vessel appeared at the traditional Fleet Review on the Neva River at Leningrad, and this time the launchers were visible. Maximum missile outfit is 16, 8 being carried in each magazine. It was planned that 12 ships would be built but, after the tenth, construction was halted in favor of the *Kynda*-class cruisers. Normal electronic equipment is Head Net-3 on the foremast instead of all-round search radar on the mainmast, but there are variations, one of which is a Head Net-4 on the after mast, and another is two Head Net-3s on the foremast. Presumably, the variations are experimental installations.

Kildin Class

1:1000

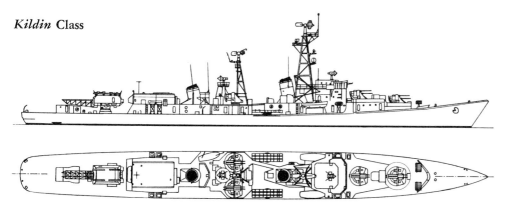

Krupnyi Class

2   1   4   3   Antenna arrangement: either 1 + 2
or 1 + 4
or 3 + 2

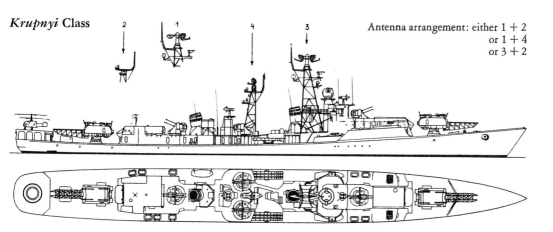

Guided-Missile Destroyers: *Kashin* Class*

10 ships: only names known are *Provornyi, Soobrazi-tel'nyi, Slavnyi, Steregushchii, Otlikhnyi, Provedennyi,* and *Obraztsovyi.* Built between 1962 and 1964 or 1965. Builders: yards in Leningrad built 2, and yards in Nikolaev built 2. May go into series production. Displacement: 4,300 tons standard, 5,200 tons deep load. Dimensions: length, 476; beam, 50.9; draft, 19. Machinery: 4 sets gas turbines (probably with diesels for cruising), 2 shafts, 100,000 SHP for 35 kts. Complement: not known. Armament: 2 twin launchers for Goa surface-to-air missiles, 4 3-inch dual-purpose guns in twin mounts, 5 antisubmarine-torpedo tubes in a quintuple mount, 2 12-barreled antisubmarine-rocket launchers (forward) and 2 6-barreled antisubmarine-rocket launchers (aft); possibly, mines. Equipment for a helicopter.

General: The first series-produced class of destroyer to have surface-to-air missiles as main armament and, at the same time, the first major Soviet warship fitted with gas-turbine main propulsion machinery. The 4 funnels are sited in two athwartships pairs. Outfit of Goa missiles is estimated to be 60. Helicopter flight deck is marked out aft. First sighted in 1964. Originally, the forward funnels were 10 feet lower than they are now, and the after ones were three feet lower. One vessel has a lower mainmast carrying a Big Net aerial, and a new version has a Big Net radar on its quadrupod mainmast.

Guided-Missile Destroyers: *Kanin* Class*

2 ships: names not known. For building and technical data, *see Krupnyi* class. Armament: 1 twin launcher for Goa surface-to-air missiles, 8 57-mm. AA in quadruple mounts, 10 antisubmarine-torpedo tubes in quintuple mounts, 3 12-barreled antisubmarine-rocket launchers.

General: These are *Krupnyi*-class destroyers that were converted in 1967 or 1968: their surface-to-surface guided-missile systems were replaced by Goa launchers and their helicopter platforms were enlarged.

Kashin Class

1:1000

Modified *Kashin*

Kanin Class

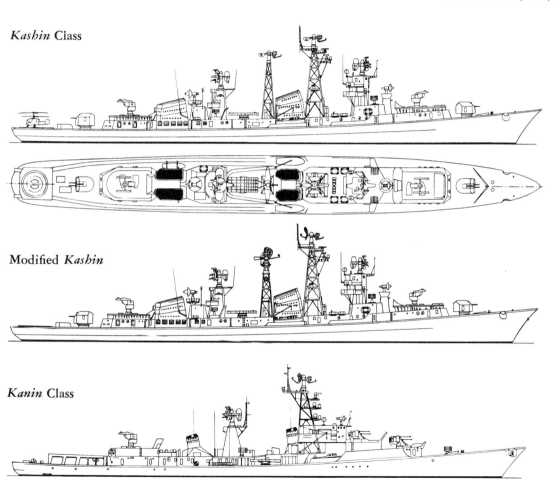

Frigates: *Kola* Class*

10 ships: published names—*Doblestnyi, Dostoinyi, Drushnyi, Zharkii, Zherskii, Zhguchii, Zhivuchii,* and *Zhostkii*—are doubtful. All built in Baltic yards between 1950 or 1951 and 1957 (first vessel completed 1953 or 1954). Displacement: 1,500 tons standard, 2,000 tons deep load. Dimensions: length, 321; beam, 33; draft, 11.2. Machinery: geared steam turbines, 2 boilers, 2 shafts, 24,000 to 30,000 SHP giving 28 to 31 kts. Complement: 190. Armament: 4 3.9-inch guns in single mounts, 4 37-mm. AA in twin mounts, 3 21-inch torpedo tubes in a triple mount, 4 depth-charge throwers; possibly, 30 mines.

General: Successor to the prewar *Iastreb* class. The original, simple, range-finder cupola above the bridge was replaced by a Wasphead director. Apparently designed for duty in coastal waters where conditions are unfavorable (Arctic, North Pacific). Armament is not effective for present-day operations. It is not known whether the ships have been modernized.

Frigates: *Riga* Class*

50 ships: the following names are known—*Buivol, Byk, Shakal, Gepard, Hiena, Leopard, Lev, Lisa, Medved, Pantera, Tigr, Volk, Komsomolets Litvyi,* and *Komsomolets*

Ukrainyi. Began building 1952 or 1953, the first vessels being completed in 1955, the last in 1958. Builders: various yards in the Baltic, the Black Sea, and Siberia. Displacement: 1,200 tons standard, 1,600 tons deep load. Dimensions: length, 299; beam, 31.2; draft, 11.4. Machinery: geared steam turbines, 2 boilers, 2 shafts, 25,000 SHP. Speed: 28 kts. Complement: 150. Armament: 3 3.9-inch guns in single mounts, 4 37-mm. AA in twin mounts, 3 21-inch torpedo tubes in a triple mount, 4 depth-charge throwers (on several of the vessels, 2 5- or 16-barreled antisubmarine-rocket launchers have replaced depth-charge throwers); possibly, 50 mines.

General: Successor to and improvement on the *Kola* class. Has been put into series production and 80 ships built. In comparison with the *Kola* class, over-all dimensions and speed have been reduced, resulting in a very simple and seaworthy design capable of carrying out a variety of tasks. The simple tripod is similar to that of the *Kola* class. On most of the ships, modern antisubmarine weapons have either replaced the depth-charge throwers or have been added to the armament. The new weapons are mounted forward of the bridge on either side of the enlarged gun deck. Modernized units have improved electronic equipment and a higher smokestack assembly. A number of *Riga* frigates have been transferred to other countries and, since 1955, Red China has built 4 of them at the Watun Yard in Shanghai.

Kola Class
Inset: Original fire-control director.

1:1000

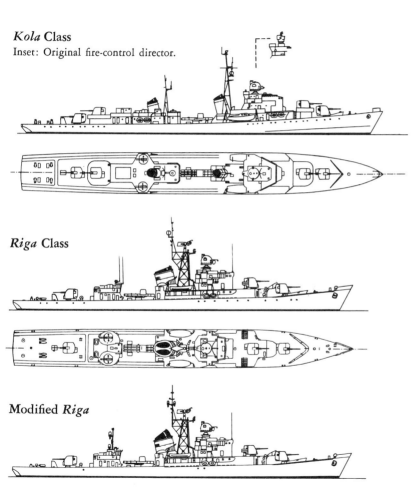

Riga Class

Modified **Riga**

Frigates: *Petya* Class*

35 ships: only name known is *Protivnika*. Began building in 1960, and the first was completed in 1961.
Builders: yards in Nikolaev and Kaliningrad. Displacement: 1,050 tons standard, 1,200 tons deep load. Dimensions: length, 262; beam, 32; draft, 9.8. Machinery:
2 sets gas turbines, 10,000 SHP giving 30 kts; 2 diesels,
4,000 BHP for cruising; 2 shafts. Complement: not
known. Armament: 4 3-inch, dual-purpose guns in twin
mounts, 5 short, antisubmarine-torpedo tubes in a quintuple mount, 4 16-barreled antisubmarine-rocket launchers. Equipped for minelaying. Modernized units, *Petya-
IIs*, have a somewhat different radar array (Head Net-
4), 10 antisubmarine-torpedo tubes in quintuple
mounts, 2 12-barreled antisubmarine-rocket launchers.

General: At first, there were problems with this class,
and that may be why it was fitted with a forecastle
bulwark to increase freeboard and improve seakeeping
qualities. Two uptakes are enclosed in a single casing.
Diesel exhausts are situated in the hull, abreast the
torpedo tubes. The class is intended mainly for antisubmarine operations in restricted waters, e.g., the Baltic,
where air attack could be expected.

Frigates: *Mirka* Class*

22 ships: only names known are *Gangutets* and *Tuman*.
Began building in 1964, the first completed in 1965.
Builders: yards in Leningrad and Kaliningrad. Series
building possible. Displacement: 1,050 tons standard,
1,200 tons deep load. Dimensions: length, 262; beam,
29.5; draft, 9.1. Machinery and speed, similar to *Petya*
class. Complement: not known. Armament: 4 3-inch,
dual-purpose guns in twin mounts, 5 short antisubmarine-torpedo tubes in a quintuple mount, 4 12-barreled
antisubmarine-rocket launchers. Not equipped for minelaying.

General: Successor to the *Petya* class and of improved
design. The gas turbines are situated right aft beneath a
raised upper deck. Exhaust gases escape through vents in
the transom stern, and two air intakes project from the
raised deck immediately above the gas turbines.

1:1000

Petya Class
Petya-I

Petya-II

Mirka Class

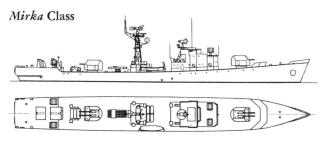

Attack Submarines: W Class*

145 boats, including those converted to radar picket submarines: names not known. Began building in 1950, the first was completed in 1952, the last in 1959. Builders: not known. Displacement: 1,030 tons, surfaced; 1,300 tons, submerged. Dimensions: length, 246; beam, 23.9; draft, 14.4. Machinery: diesel-electric, 2 shafts; 2 diesels, 4,000 BHP for 17 kts., surfaced; 2 electric motors, 2,500 HP for 15 kts., submerged. Radius: 13,000 miles at cruising speed. Complement: 60. Armament: 6 21-inch torpedo tubes (4 bow, 2 stern), 18 torpedoes carried. Diving depth: 460 feet.

General: This first postwar Soviet submarine is still the standard boat of the Soviet submarine fleet. The design, which was begun in 1944, was considerably influenced by German submarine development (particularly Type XXI). Numerically, a very large class; 276 boats are believed to have been built, but it may be that some of the earliest boats of this class have already been broken up. As they were not seen until 1956, it has been suggested that their introduction into operational service was delayed by difficulties. Suitable for medium-range, oceangoing operations, these submarines carry stores for sixty days. They probably do not carry reloads for the stern torpedo tubes. The outfit of 18 torpedoes can be replaced by 40 mines, which would be discharged through the torpedo tubes.

Various versions of this design have been produced and the principal differences among them are as follows:

W-I—no after extension of the conning tower; a twin 25-mm. AA mount forward of the conning tower.

W-II—conning tower similar to that of the W-I, but it is extended aft and has a mount for either a single 3.9-inch gun or a twin 25-mm. AA mount on the after superstructure.

W-III—conning tower similar to that of the W-II, but no AA armament.

W-IV—similar to W-III but has a snorkel and a twin 25-mm. AA mount forward of the tower.

W-V—at present, the standard version of the W class —as W-IV but no mount.

W-V(A)—immediately forward of the conning tower, there is a hatch for the embarkation and disembarkation of frogmen.

Most boats of the class have a sonar dome above the bow. Two of the boats, the *Severianka* and the *Slavyanka,* have been converted for hydrographic research, and a number of them have been sold to other navies. Between 1956 and 1964, Communist China built 21 of this class in her own yards.

Besides the 145 boats referred to at the beginning of this section, there are approximately 12 W-class submarines that have been converted to guided-missile submarines (*see* W Class/Single Cylinder, W Class/Twin Cylinder, and W Class/Long Bin).

W Class

1:1000

W-I

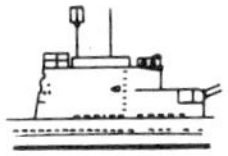

W-II

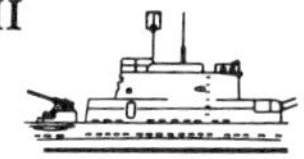

W-III

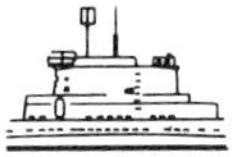

W-IV

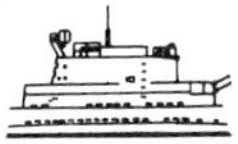

W-V

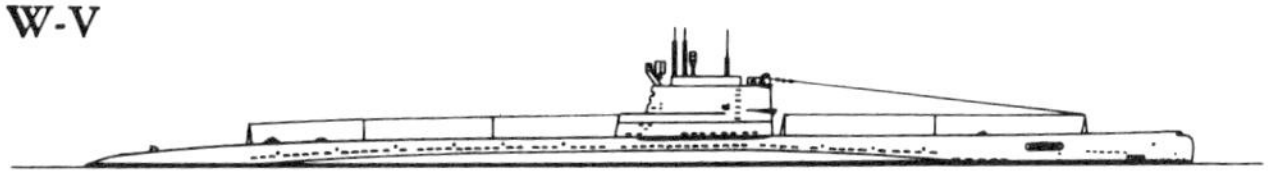

W-V(A)

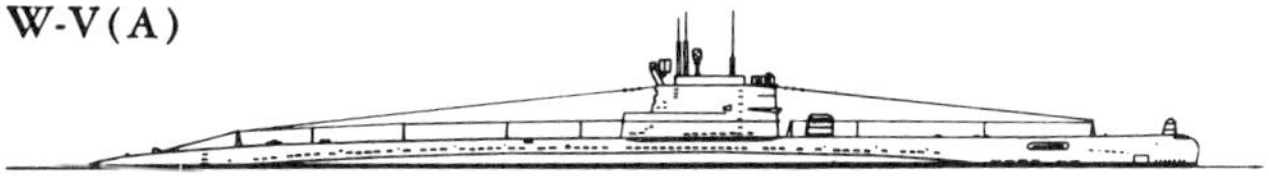

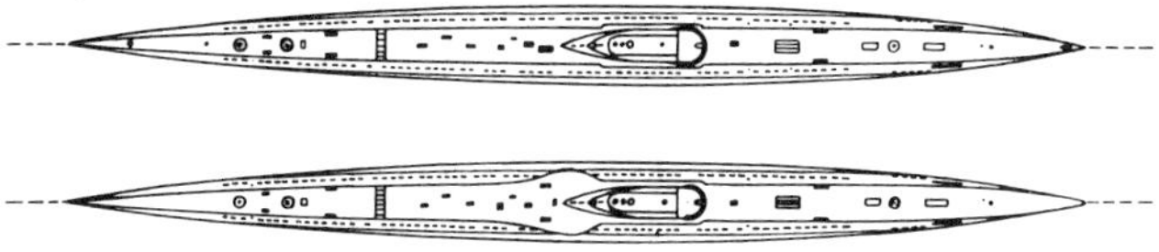

Lower plan view: Note how deck curves abaft the conning tower to accommodate gun crew.

Radar Picket Submarines: W Class/Canvas Bag*

Number not known: no names known. For building dates and technical data, *see* W class. Rebuilt in 1963 or 1964.

General: A modification of the W class, these boats have a large radar antenna above the rebuilt conning tower. Armament apparently unchanged.

Attack Submarines: Z Class*

25 boats: names not known. Began building in 1951, the first was completed in 1954, the last in 1960. Builders: Sudomech Yard, Leningrad, built 18, and Navy Yard, Severodvinsk. Displacement: 1,950 tons, surfaced; 2,200 tons, submerged. Dimensions: length, 295.2; beam, 25.9; draft, 19. Machinery: diesel-electric, 2 shafts; diesels, 10,000 BHP for 18 kts., surfaced; electric motors, 3,500 HP for 16 kts., submerged. Radius: 20,000 to 26,000 miles at cruising speed. Complement: 70. Armament: 10 21-inch torpedo tubes (6 bow, 4 stern), 24 torpedoes, or 4 torpedoes and 40 mines. Maximum depth: 460 feet.

General: When first introduced, this oceangoing class appears to have given the Soviets considerable difficulty. The intention seems to have been to equip it with a Walther propulsion system, and the first boats were so fitted. However, either because it was not satisfactory or because the Soviet engineers had not perfected it, the Walther system was replaced by an efficient diesel-electric system which may incorporate, for the first time, a considerable amount of the experience gained from the German Type XXI submarine. The propulsion problem caused a lengthy delay in the completion of this class because only two yards were involved in its construction. As in the case of the W class, the original design of the Z class allowed for gun armament to be carried. A later decision not to carry guns resulted in changes to the shape of the conning tower. Thus:

Z-I had two superimposed 25-mm. AA mounts on the after part of the conning tower.

Z-II had the AA mounts replaced for a time by a 3.9-inch gun mounted forward of the conning tower.

Z-III had no gun armament.

Z-IIIA had a conning tower that was somewhat higher than those of the previous versions.

Z-IV, the present standard version, is recognizable by the tower abaft the conning position.

Some boats have a sonar dome above the bow. It is believed that at least one has been converted to a submarine oiler, and at least three to radar picket submarines (these may be identical to W Class/Canvas Bag).

Besides the 25 attack submarines, 10 Z-class boats have been converted to ballistic-missile submarines (*see* Z-V class).

W Class/Canvas Bag

1:1000

Z Class

Z-I

Z-II

Z-III

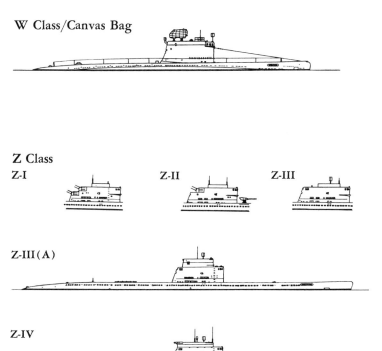

Z-III(A)

Z-IV

Attack Submarines: Q Class*

15 boats: names not known. Began building in 1955, the first was completed in 1958, the last in 1962. Builders: Sudomech Yard, Leningrad; some may have been built elsewhere. Displacement: 650 tons, surfaced; 740 tons, submerged. Dimensions: length, 183.7; beam, 18.1; draft, 13.1. Machinery: diesel-electric, 2 shafts; diesels, 3,000 BHP for 18 kts., surfaced. Radius: 7,000 miles. Complement: 40. Armament: 4 21-inch bow torpedo tubes, 8 to 10 torpedoes carried. Diving depth: 460 feet.

General: The Soviet designation for this, the third postwar class of submarines, is Type 615A. It was designed to replace the obsolescent SC class for operations in restricted waters. These submarines were intended to have a Walther system driving a third shaft, which would permit short bursts of 20-knot speed. It seems, however, that this plan was abandoned after trials with the first of the class. Apparently, the Walther system did not prove satisfactory and, at the same time, nuclear propulsion was becoming more important as the system of the future. The two factors led to a fundamental change being made in the propulsion installation, resulting in considerable delays before the class became operational. The early boats had a twin 25-mm. AA mount installed forward of the conning tower, but it was soon removed.

Attack Submarines: F Class*

40 boats: only names known are *Pskovskii Komsomolets, Jaroslavskii Komsomolets,* and *Vladimirskii Komsomolets.* Began building in 1956 and ceased in 1962; first boat completed in 1958, the last in 1963. Builders: probably, all built by the Sudomech Yard, Leningrad. Displacement: 1,960 tons, surfaced; 2,300 tons, submerged. Dimensions: length, 299; beam, 26.9; draft, 19. Machinery: diesel-electric; 2 shafts; 2 diesels, 10,000 BHP giving 18 kts., surfaced; 2 electric motors, 4,000 HP giving 17 kts., submerged. Radius of action: 20,000 miles at cruising speed. Complement: 70. Armament: 8 21-inch torpedo tubes (6 bow, 2 stern), 20 torpedoes carried. Maximum depth: 750 feet.

General: Developed from the Z class, with emphasis on deep-diving capability. First seen in 1958. Yearly output was 6 to 8 boats; the 18th was launched in April 1961. At the beginning of 1963, there were 34 of these boats in commission. The class was intended for long-range operations, and patrol endurance is estimated to be three months. A new snorkel is expected to enable this class to attain a higher snorkeling speed than hitherto. The bulbous bow with its sonar dome is worthy of note.

Q Class

F Class

Attack Submarines: R Class*

15 boats: names not known. Began building in 1959; the first was completed in 1961, the last in 1963. Builders: not known. Displacement: 1,100 tons, surfaced; 1,600 tons, submerged. Dimensions: length, 266.4; beam, 23.9; draft, 14.7. Machinery: diesel-electric, 2 shafts; 2 diesels, 4,000 BHP for 18.5 kts., surfaced; 2 electric motors, 2,500 HP for 15 kts., submerged. Radius: 13,000 miles at cruising speed. Complement: 65. Armament: 6 21-inch bow torpedo tubes.

General: These are hunter-killer submarines, whose design appears to be based on that of the W class. The elliptical tube projecting from the conning tower seems to be in three sections and telescopic: it surrounds the snorkel and its purpose may be to protect the latter when it is in the raised position and the boat is moving at high speed.

Attack Submarines, Nuclear-Powered: N Class*

15 boats: the following names are known—*Leninskii Komsomol, Cheliabinskaia Komsomolka.* Began building in 1960; the first in class completed in 1961 or 1962. Builders: not known. Displacement: 3,500 tons, surfaced; 4,000 tons, submerged. Dimensions: length, approx. 384; beam, 33(?); draft, 23(?). Machinery: 2 shafts, 1(?) nuclear reactor, and 2 geared steam turbines; 35,000(?) SHP for 25 kts., surfaced, or 30 kts., submerged. Complement: 88. Armament: 6 bow torpedo tubes.

General: These oceangoing, hunter-killer submarines have whale-shaped hulls. The *Leninskii Komsomol* made news in the summer of 1962 by navigating to the North Pole. Reported to have a very noisy propulsion system. Pressure-water reactors. Improved versions may already be in existence.

Submarines Under Construction: 5 new types

As of mid-1968, some 30 submarines were under construction in various yards. They are reported to be of 5 different types, one of which is the 300-foot, nuclear-powered class that was building at the Krasnaia Sormovo Yard at Gorki in 1967; and another is the new Y class* ballistic-missile boat that will carry from 12 to 16 launchers, similar to the SSBNs of the U.S. Navy. No other details are available.

R Class 1:1000

N Class

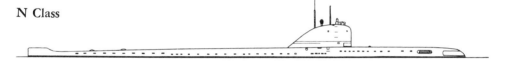

Guided-Missile Submarines: W Class/Single Cylinder and W Class/Twin Cylinder*

6 boats: no names are known. For building and technical data, *see* W class. The one and only single-cylinder version began rebuilding in 1956, and the twin-cylinder ones in 1958 or 1959. Armament: abaft the tower, they have either a single or a twin launcher for Shaddock surface-to-surface missiles. Probably only 4 21-inch twin torpedo tubes.

General: Quite obviously, the missile-equipped submarines were patterned after the American boats *Tunny* (SS-282) and *Barbero* (SSG-317). One, and probably only one, W-class boat carried on her superstructure a cylindrical container/launcher which could be elevated to 20–25 degrees for launching the missile stowed inside. Intensive trials began in 1956, and the version that followed them has twin launchers mounted on a common ramp immediately abaft the conning tower. Both launchers project over the sides to some extent. Missiles are launched over the stern. Covers at both ends of the containers have to be removed before launch, in order to permit the gases to disperse aft. Blast deflectors in front of and to the side of the containers also serve as protection from the sea. This version has not been put into series production, probably because the containers reduce submerged speed and almost certainly cause cavitation, which would increase the possibility of detection.

A submarine of this type appeared at the Fleet Reviews at Sevastopol in 1967 and 1968.

Guided-Missile Submarines: W Class/Long Bin*

6 boats: no names known. Began rebuilding in 1961 or 1962. Displacement: 1,250 tons, surfaced; 1,700 tons, submerged. Dimensions: length, 270.6; beam, 27.8; draft, 14.1. Machinery: diesel-electric, 2 shafts; 2 diesels, 4,000 SHP for 17 kts., surfaced; 2 electric motors, 2,500 HP for 15 kts., submerged. Radius of action: as for the W class. Armament: 4 single launchers in two pairs for the Shaddock surface-to-surface missile system; 6 21-inch torpedo tubes, as on the basic W class.

General: In 1961 or 1962, Soviet ship designers began adopting new ways of making use of W-class submarines. This design shows that considerable effort was made to diminish the possibility of detection by the enemy by reducing, or even eliminating, the drag caused by the external launchers. To this end, a 21-foot-long section was built into the midships portion, and on it was installed a long tower that slopes aft and has rounded edges. Inside the tower, there are 2 pairs of forward-firing launchers, each elevated about 14 degrees, and arranged so that the after pair fires over the forward pair.

W Class/Single Cylinder

W Class/Twin Cylinder

W Class/Long Bin

Guided-Missile Submarines: J Class*

8 boats: names not known. Began building in 1960, first vessel launched in 1962 and completed 1963, the second in 1966. Builders: not known. Displacement: 1,800 tons, surfaced; approx. 2,500 tons, submerged. Dimensions: length, 278.8; beam, 33; draft, 15. Machinery: diesel-electric, 2 shafts; 2 diesels, 4,000 BHP for 19 kts., surfaced; 2 electric motors, 2,000 HP for 15 kts., submerged. Radius of action: 15,000 miles at cruising speed. Complement: 70. Armament: 2 twin launchers for Shaddock surface-to-surface missiles, 4 21-inch bow torpedo tubes.

General: The small number of boats in this, the last class of conventional submarine, tends to indicate that it was developed as an experimental class for the nuclear-powered, E-class, guided-missile submarines, which were designed to have a similar Shaddock installation. Forward and aft of the conning tower, there are twin Shaddock launchers, both of which are faired into the pressure hull. Both pairs of launchers can be elevated to about 30 degrees and they fire forwards, the after pair firing over the conning tower. The forward part of the tower opens up so that the missile-guidance radar inside it can be used. A distinguishing feature of this class is its high freeboard.

Guided-Missile Submarines, Nuclear-Powered: E Class*

25 boats: only name known is *Frunze*. The prototype design, E-I, began building in 1961 and the first boat was completed in 1963; E-II version began building in 1964. There are 5 E-Is and 20 E-IIs. Builders: Navy Yard, Komsomolsk.

	E-I	E-II
Displacement:	4,600 tons, surfaced	5,000 tons, surfaced
	5,000 tons, submerged	5,600 tons, submerged
Length:	377 feet	394 feet
Beam:	33 feet	33 feet
Draft:	28 feet	30 feet

Machinery: 2 shafts, 1(?) nuclear reactor, 2 geared steam turbines, number of boilers not known; 35,000 SHP for 20 to 22 kts. surfaced/submerged speed. Complement: 92. Armament: E-I, 3 twin launchers, E-II, 4 twin launchers for Shaddock surface-to-surface missiles. Possibly, 6 torpedo tubes.

General: A development of the J class, but with nuclear propulsion. It is believed that when experience had been gained from the E-I boats, the E-II design was developed and put into series production. Missiles are in launching tubes, as in the J class. The conning tower is relatively small and its forward section opens to enable a missile-guidance radar to be used. The entire E class is thought to be stationed in the Pacific.

J Class

1:1000

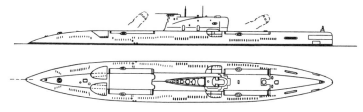

E Class
E-I

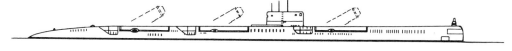

E-II

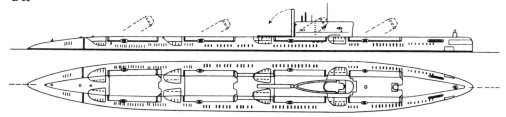

Ballistic-Missile Submarines: Z-V Class*

10 boats: names not known. For building dates, *see* Z class. Six of the boats began rebuilding in 1958, the last 4 in 1961. All were rebuilt at the Zhdanov Yard, Leningrad. Displacement: 2,100 tons, surfaced; 2,600 tons, submerged. Dimensions, machinery, speed, and radius, as for the Z class. Complement: 85. Armament: 2 vertical launchers for a ballistic-missile system (Sark or Serb), 6 21-inch bow torpedo tubes. Maximum depth: 460 feet.

General: In the course of their conversion, these submarines received an enlarged conning tower, in which the 2 vertical launching tubes are housed. Some boats of the class have a sonar dome.

Ballistic-Missile Submarines: G Class*

30 boats: names not known. Began building in 1958, the first was completed in 1960, the last in 1962. Builders: the Navy yards in Severodvinsk and Komsomolsk. Displacement: 2,700 tons, surfaced; 3,200 tons, submerged. Dimensions: length, 328; beam, 27.8; draft, 21.3. Machinery: diesel-electric, 3 shafts; 3 diesels, 6,000 BHP for 17.6 kts., surfaced; 3 electric motors, 6,000 HP for 17 kts., submerged. Radius: 22,700 miles at cruising speed. Complement: 86. Armament: 3 vertical ballistic-missile launchers (Sark or Serb), 10 21-inch torpedo tubes (6 bow, 4 stern). Modernized units, G-IIs, have 3 launchers probably for Sawfly missiles. Maximum depth: 750 feet.

General: The first Soviet submarines to be designed specifically for the task of carrying ballistic missiles. The launching tubes are carried in the very long conning tower. Sonar dome above the bow.

Ballistic-Missile Submarines, Nuclear-Powered: H Class*

13 boats: one may be named *Krasnogvardeets*. Began building in 1959 or 1960, the first being completed in 1963. Builders: not known. Displacement: 3,700 tons, surfaced; 4,100 tons, submerged. Dimensions: length, 360.8; beam, 33; draft, 26.2. Machinery: 2 shafts, 1 (?) nuclear reactor, 2 geared steam turbines, number of boilers not known; 35,000 SHP for 25 kts., surface speed, 30 kts., submerged. Complement: 90. Armament: H-Is have 3 vertical launchers for Sark or Serb ballistic missiles, and converted boats, H-IIs, have 3 launchers, probably for Sawfly missiles. 6 bow torpedo tubes.

General: A development of the G class, but with nuclear propulsion. The hull and conning tower are similar to those of the G class, but the planes project above the waterline. The propellers may be mounted in tandem on a single shaft.

Z–V Class

G Class

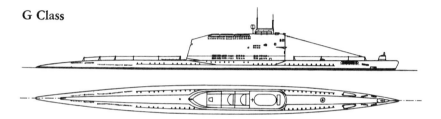

H Class

Fast Patrol Boats: P-4 Class

Number of boats not known: no names known. All built between 1952 and 1958. Displacement: 45 tons standard. Dimensions: length, 82; beam, 16.7; draft, 4.9. Machinery: diesels for 40 to 42 kts. Armament: 2 single torpedo tubes, 2 12.7-mm. AA machine guns in twin mount.

General: The small size of these aluminum-hulled planing boats restricts their employment to inshore waters. Only a few are now in commission, as many have been transferred to other countries.

Fast Patrol Boats: P-6 Class

Number of boats not known: no names known. Built between 1953 and 1960. Builders: not known. Displacement: 65 tons standard. Dimensions: length, 85.3; beam, 14.7; draft, 5.5. Machinery: 4 diesels, 4 shafts, 5,000 BHP for 42 to 45 kts. Complement: approx. 20. Armament: 2 21-inch single torpedo tubes; 2 twin 25-mm. AA. Some of the boats have depth charges.

General: Successor to the P-4 class. About 400 of these uncomplicated, wooden-hulled, rugged boats were built in less than 7 years. Either to save space or to give the helmsman in his enclosed steering position a better view, the early versions had their 25-mm. AA guns sited asymmetrically. Later boats have this armament on the centerline. They do not all carry the same radar equipment, but most of them have a flattish radome of fairly large diameter. Many of the class have been transferred to other countries. Some of those that East Germany has were built under licence in her own yards.

The MO-VI class of fast submarine chasers and the *Osa* class of guided-missile fast patrol boats were developed from the P-6 class. (*See* MO-VI and *Osa* classes.)

Fast Patrol Boats: P-8 and P-10 Classes

Number of boats not known: no names known. Built between 1955 and 1960. Builders: not known. Displacement: 90 tons standard. Dimensions: length, about 91.8; beam, 21.3; draft, 5.5. Machinery: gas turbines. Speed: 45–50 kts. Armament: 2 21-inch torpedo tubes; 4 25-mm. AA in twin mounts; possibly, a number of mines.

General: Developed from the P-6 class for trials with gas-turbine propulsion. The P-8 class was equipped with hydrofoils. Uptake is behind the bridge. Probably only a small number of each class was built.

Fast Patrol Boats: *Shershen* Class*

25 to 50 or more boats: no names known. Built since 1962. Builders: not known. Displacement: about 150 tons standard. Dimensions: length, about 131.2; beam, 22.9; draft, 6.5. Machinery: diesels. Speed: 41 kts. Arma-

1:500

P-4 Class

P-6 Class

**P-8 and
P-10 Classes**

Shershen **Class**

ment: 4 21-inch single torpedo tubes; 4 30-mm. AA in twin mounts.

General: The Soviet Navy's first large torpedo boats. They may have been designed as a counter to the West German *Jaguar* class. At first, not all the boats were fitted with an AA director. Some boats of this class have gone to other countries.

Fast Patrol Boats, Hydrofoils: *Pchela* Class*

25 or more boats: no names known. Began building in 1964 or 1965. Builders: not known. Displacement: 50 to 60 tons standard, 75 tons deep load. Dimensions: length, 88.5; beam, 20; draft, 5.5. Machinery: 1 diesel, 6,000 HP for 50 kts. Armament: 1 23-mm. twin mount.

General: This class, also designated as P-12, may be used as fast submarine chasers in coastal areas.

Guided-Missile Fast Patrol Boats: *Komar* Class*

42 boats: names not known. Built between 1959 and 1961. Builders: not known. Displacement: 75 tons standard. Dimensions: length, 85.3; beam, 19.7; draft 4.9. Machinery: 3 diesels, 3 shafts, 5,000 BHP. Speed: 40 kts. Armament: 2 single launchers for Styx surface-to-surface missiles, 2 25-mm. AA in twin mount.

General: These modified P-6-class boats have their launchers fixed in the forward firing position. Upper deck is extended sideways abeam the launchers to protect them from the sea. Some of these boats have been transferred to other countries.

Guided-Missile Fast Patrol Boats: *Osa* Class*

110 boats: only names known are *Brestskii Komsomolets, Tambovskii Komsomolets,* and *Kirovskii Komsomolets.* Built since 1960. Builders: not known. Displacement: 160 tons standard, 200 tons deep load. Dimensions: length, 131.5; beam 26.2; draft, 6.5. Machinery: 3 diesels, 3 shafts, 4,800 BHP for 35 kts. Armament: 4 launchers for Styx surface-to-surface missiles, 4 30-mm. AA in twin mounts.

General: These boats, built of steel, were introduced at the same time as the *Komar* class, and were first seen in 1961. There are 2 launchers on either side of the upper deck, and the after one fires over the forward one. Target acquisition and tracking radar has a 60-degree arc either side of dead ahead. There are two versions, the second of which has the after 30-mm. AA gun mounted higher and the after launchers farther forward than the first version does. Between the launchers there is a raised platform for an AA director, which was fitted to some of the boats after their completion. There is also an AA director on a raised platform aft. The radar array varies from boat to boat. Many of this class have been transferred to other countries.

Komar Class

1:500

Osa Class
Osa-I

Osa-II

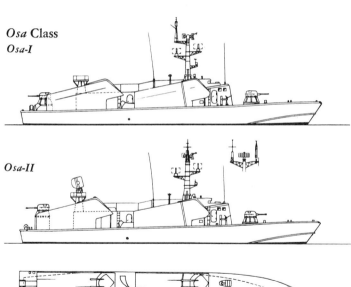

Submarine Chasers: *Kronstadt* Class*

100 ships, including *Libau*-class communications vessels: names not known. Built between 1948 and 1956. Builders: not known. Displacement: 300 tons standard, 350 tons deep load. Dimensions: length, 183.7; beam, 21.3; draft, 7.3. Machinery: 2 diesels, 2 shafts. Speed: 23 to 25 kts. Complement: 40. Armament: 1 single 3.3-inch gun, 2 single 37-mm. AA, 6 12.7-mm. AA machine guns in twin mounts, 2 depth-charge throwers, and depth-charge racks or mine rails.

General: These ships were developed from the wartime *Artillerist* class, and more than 200 of them have been built. The spacious after part permits either antisubmarine armament or mining rails to be carried. Originally, the mast had a searchlight platform. The armament is outdated and is probably being replaced by more modern types; 2 5-barreled antisubmarine-rocket launchers have been fitted forward. The *Libau*-class communications vessels have the same hull and may, in fact, be converted *Kronstadt*s (*see Libau* class). A number of *Kronstadt*s have gone to other countries, and some have been built in Chinese yards.

Fast Submarine Chasers: SO-I Class

90 ships: names not known. Built between 1956 and 1960. Builders: not known. Displacement: 215 tons standard, 250 tons deep load. Dimensions: length, 147.6; beam, 21.3; draft, 6.5. Machinery: 3 diesels, 3 shafts, 3,500 BHP for 24 kts. Complement: 40. Armament: 4 25-mm. AA in twin mounts, 4 5-barreled antisubmarine-rocket launchers, 2 depth-charge racks, outfit about 24 charges, mine rails. Modernized ships have 2 single antisubmarine-torpedo tubes and only 2 25-mm. AA (forward).

General: These steel ships carry 4 groups of antisubmarine-rocket launchers on the forecastle. Since about 1965, the armament has been modified: the after 25-mm. twin mount has been replaced by 2 single antisubmarine-torpedo tubes. A considerable number of SO-Is have gone to other countries.

Submarine Chasers: *Poti* Class*

80 ships: no names known. Built since 1961. Builders: not known. Displacement: 350 tons standard, 380 tons deep load. Dimensions: length, 200.1; beam, 27.8; draft, 9.8. Machinery: gas turbines and cruising diesels. Speed: 28 to 30 kts. Complement: 50. Armament: 2 57-mm. AA in twin mount, 2 to 4 single antisubmarine-torpedo tubes, 2 12-barreled antisubmarine-rocket launchers.

General: New class, whose prototype was built in 1961, and which has many similarities, including the layout of the gas-turbine installation, to the *Mirka*-class frigates. Probably in series production.

1:500

Kronstadt Class

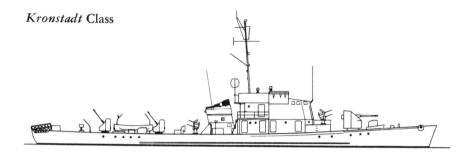

SO-I Class

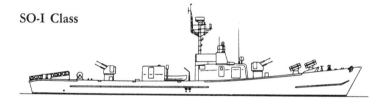

Poti Class

Fast Submarine Chasers: MO-VI Class

Number not known: no names known. Built between 1956 and 1960. Builders: not known. Technical data, as for P-6 class. Armament: 4 25-mm. AA in twin mounts; up to 24 depth charges.

General: These modified P-6-class boats can be used in a variety of roles, for example, as minelayers, on commando raids, for patrol and surveillance.

Fast Submarine Chasers: *Stenka* Class*

3 to 5 ships: names not known. Began building in 1967. Builders: not known. Displacement: 210 tons standard. Dimensions: length, 131; beam, 23; draft, 6.5. Machinery: 3 diesels for 10,000 HP. Speed: 40 kts. Armament: 4 30-mm. AA in twin mounts, 4 antisubmarine-torpedo tubes in single mounts, and 2 depth-charge racks, aft.

General: This is a new class of fast submarine chasers.

Communications Vessels: *Libau* Class*

Number of ships not known: no names known. Probably converted *Kronstadt*s rebuilt between 1956 and 1960. Builders: not known. Displacement: 300 tons standard. For dimensions and machinery, *see Kronstadt* class. Armament: none, but could carry 4 25-mm. AA.

General: There are, apparently, only a few ships in this class. The fact that they have the same hull as the *Kronstadt* class indicates that they have, at least, been developed from the latter, if, indeed, they are not conversions. They have a larger bridge than their forerunners have, and the original funnel has been removed. There are diesel exhausts on the after side of the bridge, a long deckhouse aft, and many whip aerials. Forward and aft, there are fittings for 25-mm. twin AA mounts, but they have not been installed.

Radar Picket Ships: T-43-AGR Class

Number of ships not known: no names known. Rebuilt in 1963 or 1964. Builders: not known. For technical data, *see* T-43-class minesweepers. Armament: 4 37-mm. AA in twin mounts, 2 25-mm. AA in twin mount.

General: Converted to radar picket ships from the T-43 class. A Big Net air surveillance radar has been fitted to a broad, quadrupod, lattice mast that contains two electronic compartments. The after AA armament has been removed and only the 25-mm. AA twin mount remains.

MO-VI Class

Stenka **Class**

1:500

Libau **Class**

T-43-AGR Class

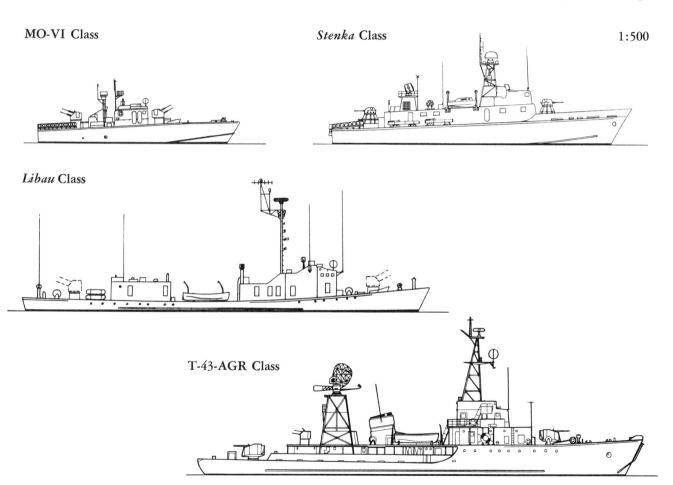

Minesweepers: T-301 Class

36 ships: names not known. Built between 1944 and 1955 or 1956. Builders: not known. Displacement: 130 tons standard, 150 tons deep load. Dimensions: length, 124.6; beam, 14.7; draft, 4.9. Machinery: 2 diesels, 2 shafts, 480 BHP. Speed: 10 kts. Complement: 30. Armament: 2 37-mm. AA in single mounts, 4 12.7-mm. AA machine guns in twin mounts.

General: More than 200 of these uncomplicated, rugged, steel ships were built and, although they began building in 1944, only minor alterations and additions—funnel, minesweeping equipment—have been made since. Some of the older ones have been broken up: others serve as survey vessels, harbor tenders, and so on. Many of this class have been sold to other countries.

Minesweepers: T-43 Class

130 ships, including Modified T-43 minesweepers and T-43-AGR radar picket ships: names not known. Built between 1948 and 1957. Builders: not known. Displacement: 500 tons standard, 600 tons deep load. Dimensions: length, 196.8; beam, 27.8; draft, 7.3. Machinery: 2 diesels, 2 shafts. Speed: 18 kts. Armament: 4 37-mm. twin AA, 4 12.7-mm. AA machine guns in twin mounts (or, since 1958 or 1959, 4 25-mm. twin AA). For a while, some ships had 8 25-mm. AA in twin mounts. In about 1958 they began carrying 2 depth-charge throwers.

General: Altogether, about 175 of these steel vessels, successors to the prewar *Fugas* class, have been built. There have been two versions of the design: the first had a simple pole mast, and the second, a tripod mast and several 25-mm. AA in place of the machine guns. Bridge and gun arrangements in the second version varied from those of the first. Vessels built according to the first version have probably been modified to the design of the second version. Other differences have also been seen: for example, several vessels have no AA machine guns or 25-mm. armament in front of the bridge. Both Poland and Red China built some T-43s under licence in their own shipyards.

Minesweepers: Modified T-43 Class

Number of ships not known: no names known. Rebuilding began in 1963 or 1964. Builders: not known. For technical data, *see* T-43 class. Armament: 4 57-mm. AA in twin mounts, 4 25-mm. AA in twin mounts; no antisubmarine armament.

General: Probably only a few of the T-43-class minesweepers have been modernized. During their modernization, they received up-to-date armament, improved electronic equipment, and a new bridge. The funnel was moved forward somewhat and, subsequently, a forecastle bulwark was fitted. These vessels now look quite similar to T-58s.

1:500

T-301 Class

T-43 Class

Modified T-43 Class

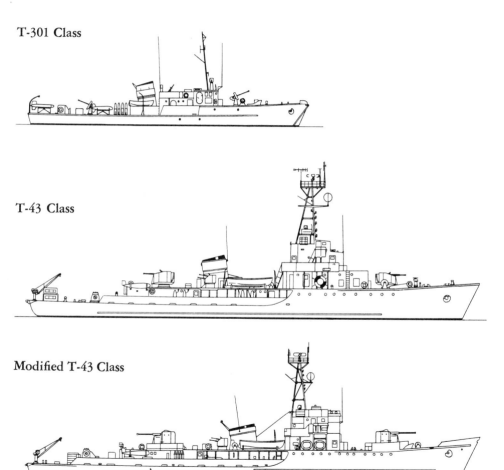

Minesweepers: T-58 Class

20 ships: only names known are *Komsomolets Estonii, Komsomolets Latviia, Primorskii Komsomolets,* and *Komsomolets Bielorussii.* Built between 1958 and 1960. Builders: not known. Displacement: 600 tons standard, 700 tons deep load. Dimensions: length, 229.6; beam, 31.2; draft, 7.3. Machinery: 2 diesels, 2 shafts. Speed: 18 kts. Armament: 4 57-mm. AA in twin mounts; probably, 2 5-barreled antisubmarine-rocket launchers.

General: These fleet minesweepers are larger and carry more modern armament than their predecessors, the T-43 class. Some of them have had an AA director fitted above the bridge, and 10 have been converted to submarine rescue ships (*see Valdai* class).

Minesweepers: *Sasha* Class*

50 ships: names not known. Built between 1957 and 1960. Builders: not known. Displacement: 180 tons standard, 250 tons deep load. Dimensions: length, 147; beam, 18.1; draft, 7.3. Machinery: 2 diesels, 2 shafts. Speed: 15 kts. Armament: 1 57-mm. AA, 4 25-mm. AA in twin mounts.

General: These steel ships are the only flush-decked minesweepers in the Soviet Navy. The spacious sweep deck occupies almost half the ship's length, and the 25-mm. twin AA mounts are close together on the superstructure, between the bridge and the funnel.

Minesweepers: *Vanya* Class*

48 ships: names not known. Began building in 1963. Builders: not known. Displacement: 250 tons standard, 300 tons deep load. Dimensions: length, 146.9; beam, 19.7; draft, 6.8. Machinery: diesels. Speed: 15 kts. Armament: 2 30-mm. AA in twin mounts; no antisubmarine armament.

General: The only class of wooden minesweepers in the Soviet Navy. Intended for inshore operations, replacing the T-301 and *Sasha* classes. Noticeably high freeboard, no funnel, two davits aft for minesweeping equipment. Quadrupod lattice mast above the bridge.

Minesweepers: *Iurka* Class*

35 ships: names not known. Began building in 1963. Builders: not known. Displacement: 550 tons deep load. Dimensions: length, 164; beam, 27.8; draft, 6.5. Machinery: diesels. Speed: 15 kts. Armament: 4 30-mm. AA in twin mounts; no antisubmarine armament.

General: Steel-built and significantly smaller than their predecessors, the T-58 class, these ships are intended for oceangoing duties. They have very high freeboard and a funnel that, from the side, appears very narrow, similar to that of *Kynda*-class cruisers. The quadrupod lattice mast carries numerous antennas, including an antiaircraft gunnery radar. There are two minesweeping davits right aft.

T-58 Class

1:500

Sasha Class

Vanya Class

Iurka Class

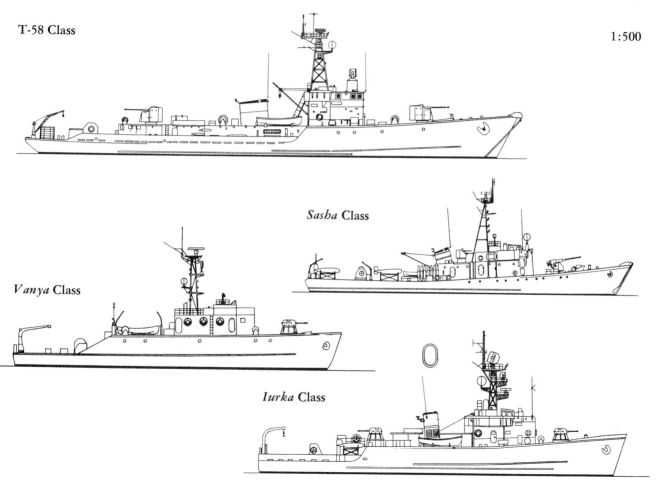

Landing Ships: MP-2 Class

16 ships: no names known. Built between 1956 and 1960. Builders: not known. Displacement: 750 tons standard. Dimensions: length, 183.7; beam, 22.9; draft, 7.3. Machinery: probably, diesels, 1,200 BHP for 16 kts. Armament: 6 25-mm. AA in twin mounts.

General: The first Soviet landing ship. Has bow doors and ramps, and can carry 4 armored cars or 200 infantrymen. Two of the twin mounts are on the forecastle.

Landing Ships: MP-4 Class

28 ships: no names known. Probably rebuilt in 1956 or 1957. Builders: not known. Displacement: 800 tons standard. Dimensions: length, 180.4; beam, 22.9; draft, 9.1. Machinery: probably, steam. Speed: not known. Armament: 6 25-mm. AA in twin mounts.

General: Originally built for use in coastal waters, converted to landing ships in 1956 or 1957, when bow doors and ramps were fitted. Two of the AA mounts are close together on the forecastle.

Landing Ships: MP-6 Class

10 ships: no names known. Rebuilt 1958 to 1961. Builders: not known. Displacement: 2,000 tons standard. Dimensions: length, 246; beam, 36; draft, 13.1. Machinery: diesels. Speed: 10 kts. No armament. A quadruple 47-mm. AA can be fitted.

General: These attack cargo ships or attack transports are converted *Bira*-class freighters. They have 2 tripod masts forward, a raised platform that may be intended for the AA mount, bow doors and ramps. Their carrying capacity is 6 to 10 tanks.

Landing Ships: MP-8 Class

18 ships: only name known is *Bira.* Built between 1958 and 1961. Builders: not known. Displacement: 800 tons standard. Dimensions: length, 246; beam, 33; draft, 7.3. Machinery: diesels. Speed: 15 kts. Armament: 4 57-mm. AA in twin mounts.

General: Apparently, a development of the MP-2 class, but larger. Bow doors and ramps, and a carrying capacity of 5 heavy armored cars, 10 amphibious vehicles, or 350 tons of freight.

Landing Ships: MP-10 Class

40 ships: no names known. Probably built between 1962 and 1965. Builders: not known. Displacement: 425 tons deep load. Dimensions: length, 157.4; beam, 19.7; draft, 6.5. Machinery: diesels. Speed: 10 kts. No armament.

General: These shallow-draft, flat-bottomed vessels are probably based on the *Marinefährprähme,* or prams, built by the Germans during the Second World War. They have bow doors.

MP-2 Class

1:1000

MP-4 Class

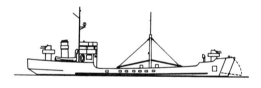

MP-6 Class

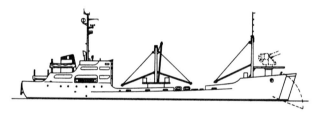

MP-8 Class

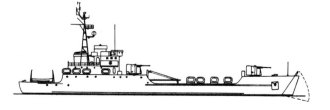

MP-10 Class

Landing Ships: *Polnochnyi* Class*

40 ships: no names known. Built since 1963. Builders: Polish yards. Displacement: 1,000 tons standard. Dimensions: length, 229.6; beam, 33; draft, 7.3. Machinery: diesels, 4,000 BHP for 15 kts. Armament: 2 30-mm. AA in twin mounts, 2 18-barreled rocket launchers.

General: These ships, which have bow doors and ramps, are in service with the Polish, as well as the Soviet, Navy. The first units had no AA guns, no fire-control director, and a tripod, instead of a lattice, mast.

Landing Ships: *Alligator* Class*

7 ships: only name known is *Voronezhskii Komsomolets.* Built since 1966. Builders: not known. Displacement: 4,000 tons standard, 6,800 tons deep load. Dimensions: length, 344.4; beam, not known; draft, not known. Machinery: diesels. Speed: 15 kts (some sources say, 22 kts). Armament: 2 57-mm. AA in twin mounts.

General: The first large landing ships to enter service with the Soviet Navy. First seen in 1967. They have bow doors, bow and stern ramps, and 3 cranes for heavy freight on the upper deck, which can also be used as a vehicle park. Thought to be in series production.

Landing Ships: *Vydra* Class*

20 ships: no names known. Began building in 1967. Builders: not known. Displacement: 300 tons standard, 500 tons deep load. Dimensions: length, 164; beam, 26; draft, 7. Machinery: 2 diesels. No armament.

General: A new class of landing ship.

Landing Ships: SMB-I Class

Number of ships not known: no names known. Builders: not known. Displacement: 200 tons standard, 400 tons deep load. Dimensions: length, 164; beam, 23; draft, 6.5. Machinery: 2 diesels for 400 HP. Speed: 10 kts. No armament.

General: These new landing ships are improved versions of the MP-10 class.

Landing Craft: T-4 Class

Number of craft not known: no names known. Began building in 1965 or 1966. Builders: not known. Displacement: 22 tons standard, 35 tons deep load. Dimensions: length, 65.6; beam, 16.4. Machinery: probably, diesels, for 11 kts. No armament.

General: Comparable to the British and American LCMs of World War II, these small landing craft have a bow ramp, wheel aft, and can carry one tank.

1:1000

Polnochnyi Class

Modified *Polnochnyi*

Alligator Class

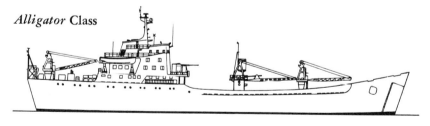

SMB-I Class

Depot Ships: *Atrek* Class

6 ships: the following names are known—*Atrek, Amburan, Ararat, Ayat,* and *Bakhmut.* Built between 1953 and 1956. Builders: Neptun Yard, Rostock, East Germany. Displacement: 3,500 tons standard, 6,700 tons deep load. Dimensions: length, 335.9; beam, 47.2; draft, 19.7. Machinery: expansion and exhaust turbines, 2 boilers, 1 shaft, 2,450 HP for 15 kts. Radius: 3,500 miles at 13 kts. No armament.

General: These ships belonged to the 14-ship *Kolomna* class of freighters until they were converted to depot ships. The conversions were made between 1955 and 1958, and they are now used as submarine tenders and supply ships.

Depot Ships: *Tovda* Class

4 ships: *Tovda, Smolensk, Inza, Vytegra.* Built between 1954 and 1958. Builders: Gdanska Shipyard, Gdansk, Poland. Rebuilt between 1958 and 1960. Where conversions were made is not known. Displacement: 3,000 tons standard, 4,000 tons deep load. Dimensions: length, 285.4; beam, 40; draft, 17.7. Machinery: 2 diesels, 1 shaft, 4,000 BHP for 16 kts. Radius: 7,000 miles at 16 kts. Armament: 6 57-mm. AA in twin mounts.

General: These ships, whose civilian designation is *Soldek* class, were built as Class B-30 coal-burning, coal carriers with reciprocating steam machinery. When they were converted to depot ships in the Soviet Union, they were fitted with an additional funnel forward, and 2 57-mm. twin AA mounts on the deckhouse between the funnels. Forward of the bridge, there is a hold for torpedoes and other stores, and on either side of the hatchway, there is a crane. Some ships have a straight-topped funnel.

1:1000

Atrek **Class**

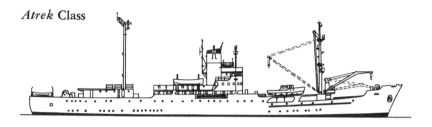

Tovda **Class**

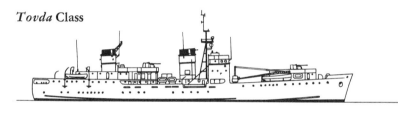

Don Class

Don-I

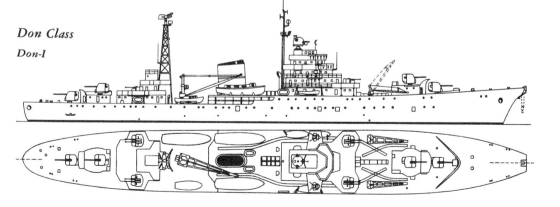

Depot Ships: *Don* Class*

6 ships: *Viktor Kotelnikov, Fedor Vidiaev, Nicolai Stolbov, Vasili Veresovoi, Mahomet Gadzhiev, Dmitri Galkin.* Built between 1958 and 1961. Builders: various Baltic and Black Sea yards. Displacement: 6,100 tons standard, about 10,000 tons deep load. Dimensions: length, 443; beam, 54.1; draft, 18.1. Machinery: 4 diesels, 2 shafts, 8,000 BHP for 20 kts. Complement: 300. Armament: 4 single 3.9-inch guns, 8 57-mm. AA in twin mounts; some have no 3.9-inch guns, but 8 57-mm. AA in twin mounts and equipment for helicopters.

General: The Soviet Navy's first large ship built as a supply ship. Noteworthy features are the 100-ton-capacity lifting equipment at the bow, which permits repairs to be made to submarine rudders and screws, and the long forecastle. Forward of the bridge, there are hatches and two cranes that can be stowed flat on the deck. The hold may be for the stowage of submarine torpedoes. Trolleys running on the tracks that lead from the hatches to the funnel are used to transport torpedoes. There are two versions of the class, *Don-I* and *Don-II:* the latter has no 3.9-inch guns and no Wasphead radar, but does have a helicopter platform aft.

Depot Ships: *Ugra* Class*

3 ships: only names known are *Ivan Kucherenko* and *Tobol.* Built since 1963 or 1964. Builders: probably, Black Sea yards. Displacement: 6,000 tons standard, 9,000 tons deep load. Dimensions: length, 419.9; beam, 52.5; draft, 19.7. Machinery: 2 diesels, 2 shafts, 7,000 BHP for 17 kts. Armament: 8 57-mm. AA in twin mounts; equipment for helicopters.

General: This development of the *Don* class was first seen in 1964. The ships have torpedo magazines forward of the bridge. A freight lift and a helicopter platform are situated aft. Forward of the helicopter platform there are two twin 57-mm. AA mounts on an elevated platform.

Missile Supply Ships: *Lama* Class*

3 ships: names not known. Built since 1963. Builders: Black Sea yards (?). Displacement: 5,000 tons standard, 7,000 tons deep load. Dimensions: length, 370; beam, 59.1; draft, 19. Machinery: 2 diesels, 2 shafts, 5,000 BHP for 15 kts. Armament: 8 57-mm. AA in quadruple mounts.

General: These ships, whose large missile magazine is forward of the bridge, were first seen in 1964. Their equipment includes an elevator and 2 heavy cranes. There are two versions of the class, with differing anti-aircraft fire-control equipment.

1:1000

Don-II

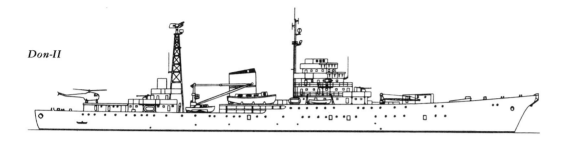

Ugra Class

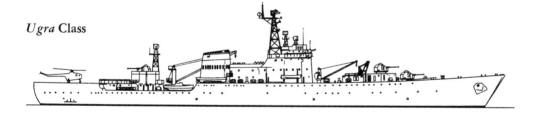

Lama Class

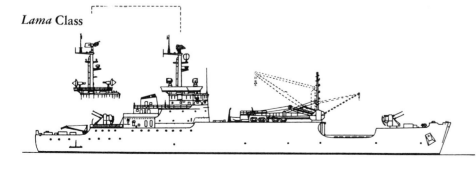

Repair Ships: *Dnepr* Class*

5 ships: names not known. Built between 1957 and 1964. Builders: probably, Black Sea yards. Displacement: 3,000 tons standard, 4,200 tons deep load. Dimensions: length, 328; beam, 45.6; draft, 14.4. Machinery: diesels. Speed: 12 kts. No armament.

General: General-purpose depot ships with comprehensive workshops, test equipment, and stores of spare parts. Lifting equipment forward. Converted ships, *Dnepr-II*s, have flush decks and different installations forward.

Repair Ships: *Oskol* Class*

4 or more ships: names not known. Built since 1964. Builders: probably, Polish yards. Displacement: 2,500 tons standard. Dimensions: length, 278.8; beam, 37.7; draft, 14.7. Machinery: diesels. Speed: 16 kts. Armament: 2 57-mm. AA forward, and 4 25-mm. AA in twin mounts aft; equipment for helicopters.

General: Apparently built in large numbers in Polish yards, these ships are of freighter design and have their machinery and bridge aft. A large deckhouse on the forecastle may serve as a helicopter platform.

Submarine Rescue Ships: *Valdai* Class

10 ships: only names known are *Valdai* and *Gidrolog*. For technical and building data, *see* T-58 class. Converted in Leningrad in 1960 or 1961. No armament; no minesweeping gear.

General: These ten T-58s were converted to submarine rescue ships during construction. Their extensive equipment includes a submarine rescue chamber, for which a crane is mounted on the port side.

Minelayers: *Alesha Class*

1 or 2 ships: only name known is *Alesha*. Builders: not known. Displacement: 3,600 tons standard, 4,300 tons deep load. Dimensions: length, 321; beam, 46; draft, 14.7. Machinery: 4 diesels for 8,000 HP. Speed: 20 kts. Complement: 150. Armament: 4 57-mm. AA in quadruple mount; probably, mines.

General: This new type of ship has been in service since 1965.

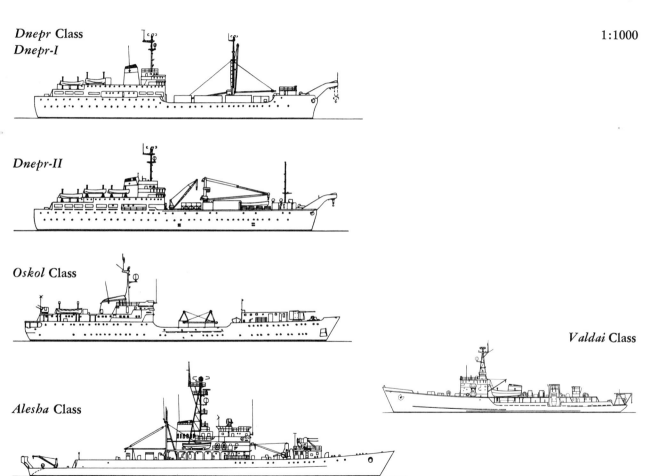

Dnepr Class
Dnepr-I

1:1000

Dnepr-II

Oskol Class

Valdai Class

Alesha Class

Fleet Oilers: *Khobi* Class*

29 ships: only names known are—*Orsha, Lovat', Zhelon,* and *Sosna.* Built between 1956 and 1959. Displacement: 800 tons standard. Dimensions: length, 219.8; beam, 33; draft, 14.7. Machinery: diesels. Speed: 12 kts. No armament.

General: These coastal motor tankers are the standard oilers of the Soviet Navy, and there are many of them in the merchant marine as well.

Fleet Oilers: *Nercha* Class

Number of ships not known: only names published are *Nercha* and *Nara.* Built between 1953 and 1955. Displacement: 1,100 tons standard. Dimensions: length, 229.6; beam, 33; draft, 14.1. Machinery: diesels. Speed: 12 kts. No armament.

General: Coastal tankers that are used by the merchant marine also.

Fleet Oilers: *Iakhroma* Class

Number of ships not known: only name known is *Iakhroma.* Built between 1955 and 1956. Displacement: 1,200 tons standard. Dimensions: length, 229.6; beam, 33; draft, 14.1. Machinery: diesels. Speed: 12 kts. No armament.

General: This class of coastal tankers is also in service with the merchant marine.

Fleet Oilers: *Vodolei* Class*

Number of ships not known: no names known. Built between 1956 and 1960. Displacement: 2,100 tons standard. Dimensions: length, 269; beam, 39.4; draft, 14.1. Machinery: diesels. Speed: 12 kts. No armament.

General: Coastal tankers used by the merchant marine.

Fleet Oilers: *Pevk* Class*

3 ships: *Olekma, Poliarnik,* and *Zolotoi Rog.* Date of building, not known. Builders: yards in Finland. Measurement: 3,300 tons gross. Dimensions: length, 400.2; beam, 59.1. Machinery: probably, diesels. Speed: 16 kts. No armament.

General: Comparable to the American AOG.

Supply Ships: *Uda* Class*

4 or more ships: only names known are *Terek, Dunai, Chechsna,* and *Svir.* Built between 1962 and 1964. Builders: not known. Displacement: 3,500 tons standard, 6,500 tons deep load. Dimensions: length, 394; beam, 49.2; draft, 19.7. Machinery: diesels. Speed: 17 kts. Armament: 6 25-mm. AA in twin mounts.

General: These ships are of tanker construction with machinery aft, but the bridge is forward. The version designated *Uda-I* has a simple pole mainmast, but the *Uda-II* has a bipod mainmast. Used as oceangoing tankers supplying submarines with oil and other stores.

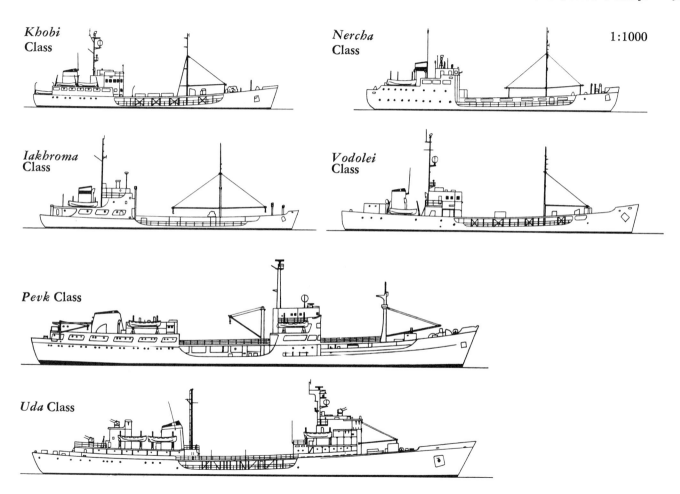

Khobi Class

Nercha Class

1:1000

Iakhroma Class

Vodolei Class

Pevk Class

Uda Class

Salvage Ships: *Pamir* Class

4 ships: *Pamir, Agatan, Aldan,* and *Arban.* Built between 1959 and 1960. Builders: A. B. Gävle Varvet (Sweden). Displacement: 1,500 tons standard. Dimensions: length, 255.9; beam, 41; draft, 13.1. Machinery: 2 diesels, 2 shafts, 4,200 BHP for 16 kts. No armament.

General: These vessels can be used as tugs. They have powerful pumping and fire-fighting equipment on board.

Salvage Ships: *Prut* Class*

6 ships: names not known. Built between 1960 and 1961. Builders: probably, Black Sea yards. Displacement: 2,560 tons standard, 3,500 tons deep load. Dimensions: length, 285.4; beam, 42.6; draft, 14.1. Machinery: diesels. Speed: 15 kts. No armament.

General: These vessels carry extensive fire-fighting equipment and can be used for submarine rescue, for towing, and can serve as amphibious transports for Naval Infantry.

Surveying Ships: *Samara* Class

10 ships: the following names are known—*Samara, Azimut, Gradus, Globus, Gorizont, Rumb, Vostok, Tropik, Pamiat Merkuria,* and *Zenit.* Built between 1962 and 1964. Displacement: 1,000 tons standard. Dimensions: length, 180.4; beam, 33; draft, 11.4. Machinery: diesels. Speed: 16 kts. No armament.

General: Long forecastle with a crane. Can be used also as tenders and salvage vessels.

Fleet Tugs: *Orel* Class

Number of ships not known: only names known are *Orel* and *Strogii.* Built between 1958 and 1960. Displacement: 1,000 tons standard. Dimensions: length, 203.4; beam, 39.4; draft, 16.4. Machinery: diesels. Speed: 13 kts. No armament.

General: Oceangoing tugs, also in service with the merchant marine.

Fleet Tugs: *Okhtenshiy* Class

8 or more ships: only name known is *Okhtenshiy.* Built between 1959 and 1961. Displacement: 950 tons standard. Dimensions: length, 164; beam, 36; draft, 13.1. Machinery: diesels. Speed: 13 kts. No armament.

General: Oceangoing tugs of the same design as the merchant marine's *Sil'nyi* class.

Pamir Class

1:1000

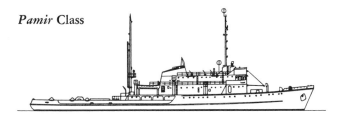

Prut Class

Samara Class

Orel Class

Okhtenshiy Class

Icebreakers: *Peresvet* Class

1 ship: *Peresvet.* Laid down in 1938, launched on 15 July 1939, completed in 1940. Builders: Schichau Yard, Danzig. Rebuilt between 1951 and 1956. Displacement: 5,200 tons standard, 6,300 tons deep load. Dimensions: length, 295.2; beam, 68.8; draft, 22.9. Machinery: triple expansion, 4 boilers, 3 shafts (1 bow, 2 stern), 9,000 IHP for 15 kts. Complement: 370. No armament.

General: This is the German ship *Castor,* which was sunk by a mine off Warnemünde on 15 March 1945, raised by the Soviets in 1951, and refitted. The *Peresvet* has been in service since 1956, and is stationed in the Baltic.

Icebreakers: *Kapitan Belousov* Class

3 ships: *Kapitan Belousov, Kapitan Melekhov,* and *Kapitan Voronin.* Laid down in 1952, launched between 1954 and 1956, completed between 1955 and 1957. Builders: Wärtsilä-Koncernen A/B, Sandvikens Skeppsdocka, Helsinki. Displacement: 4,415 tons standard. Dimensions: length, 278.8; beam, 63.6; draft, 20.3. Machinery: diesel electric with 6 diesel motors, 4 shafts (2 aft, 2 forward), 10,500 BHP for 16.5 kts. Complement: 117. No armament.

General: Successor to and improvement over the Finnish icebreaker *Voima.* Has no helicopter platform.

Icebreaker Tender: *Purga* Class*

1 ship: name may be *Purga.* Built between 1956 and 1958. Builder: not known. Displacement: 2,250 tons standard, 3,000 tons deep load. Dimensions: length, about 295; beam, about 44; draft, about 14. Machinery: diesels, 6,500 BHP for 18 kts. Complement: 200. Armament: 4 single 3.9-inch guns, 8 37-mm. AA in twin mounts.

General: First seen in 1959, this ship has the hull of an icebreaker, and may have been laid down as a *Kapitan Belousov*-class icebreaker, but completed as a special tender for service in the Arctic.

Icebreakers: *Moskva* Class

4 ships: *Moskva, Leningrad, Kiev,* and *Murmansk.* Laid down between 1958 and 1963, launched between 1959 and 1965, completed between 1960 and 1966. Two more ships under construction. Builders: Wärtsilä-Koncernen A/B, Sandvikens Skeppsdocka, Helsinki. Displacement: 12,840 tons standard, 15,360 tons deep load. Dimensions: length, 400.2; beam, 80.3; draft, 34.4. Machinery: diesel electric with 8 diesel motors, 3 shafts (all aft), 22,000 BHP for 18 kts. Complement: 100. No armament. Equipment for helicopters.

General: These are the largest diesel icebreakers in the world. They are equipped with a helicopter platform and hangar aft.

Peresvet Class

1:1000

Kapitan Belousov Class

Purga Class

Moskva Class

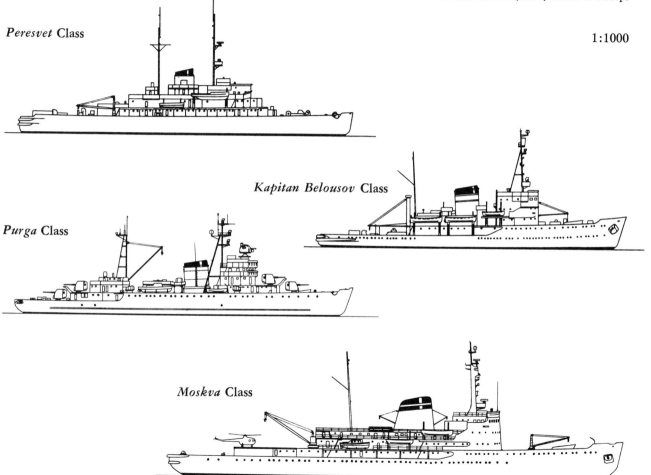

Icebreakers: *Dobrynia Nikitich* Class

5 ships: *Dobrynia Nikitich, Vyoga, Iuri Lisiansky, Vasili Poliarkov,* and *Vladimir Rusanov.* Built between 1961 and 1964. Displacement: 2,500 tons standard. Dimensions: length, 223; beam, 59.1; draft, 18.1. Machinery: diesels. Speed: 13 kts. No armament.

General: Six sister ships are in service with civil authorities and are designated *Ledokol* I–VI.

Icebreaker, Nuclear-Powered: *Lenin* Class

1 ship: *Lenin.* Laid down in 1956, launched on 5 December 1957, completed on 15 September 1959. Builders: Ordzhonikidze Yard, Leningrad. Displacement: 16,000 tons standard. Dimensions: length, 443; beam, 88.5; draft, 29.5. Machinery: 3 nuclear reactors and 4 steam turbines, 3 shafts (no bow shaft), 44,000 SHP for 18 kts. Complement: 230. No armament. Equipment for 2 helicopters.

General: Tubular mast forward, the after mast is a bipod, both of whose legs act as exhaust uptakes. She has a large helicopter hangar. Used on the Northern Sea Route.

Icebreakers, Nuclear-Powered: *Arktika* Class

1 ship under construction: *Arktika.* 1 planned. Builders: Ordzhonikidze Yard, Leningrad. Completion: 1972 (estimated). Displacement: 25,000 tons standard. Dimensions: length, 524.9; beam, 82; draft, 28.8. Machinery: 2 nuclear reactors, and steam turbines. Speed: 15 kts. No armament. Equipment for 4 helicopters.

General: This will be the largest icebreaker in the world and is, supposedly, for use on the Northern Sea Route. The profile of her, opposite, is based on an official Soviet drawing.

1:1000

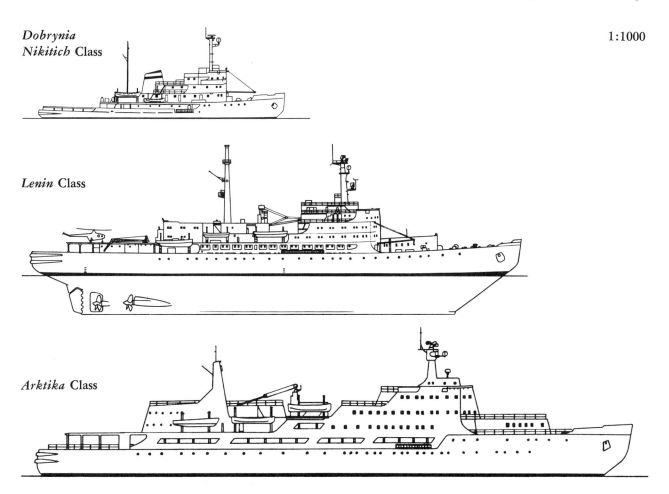

Dobrynia Nikitich Class

Lenin Class

Arktika Class

Missile-Range Instrumentation Ships:

Chukotka Class

4 ships: *Sibir, Suchan, Sakhalin,* and *Chukotka*. All launched between 1957 and 1959, and in service since 1959. Displacement: 4,000 tons standard, 5,000 tons deep load. Dimensions: length, 354.9; beam, 55.7; draft, 21.9. Machinery: triple expansion, 3,300 to 4,000 IHP for 15 kts. No armament.

General: These ships were formerly *Donbas*-class freighters. Only the *Sibir* and the *Suchan* have bubble-like domes forward, but all have a Big Net radar antenna on the after bipod mast, and a helicopter deck aft.

Missile-Range Instrumentation Ships:

Chazhma Class

2 ships: *Chazhma* and *Chumikan*. Built between 1953 and 1957. Builders: not known. Converted between 1962 and 1963. Displacement: 5,300 tons standard. Dimensions: length, 354.9; beam, 55.7; draft, 20.3. Machinery: diesels. Speed: 15 kts. No armament. Equipment for helicopters.

General: These ships were built as *Donbas*-class freighters. They have comprehensive electronic equipment, including a large radome above the bridge, and their helicopter platform is aft. They are in service in the Pacific.

Missile-Range Instrumentation Ships:

Astronaut Vladimir Komarov Class

1 ship: *Astronaut Vladimir Komarov;* another ship may be under construction. Built 1965–66. Builders: Leningrad yards. Measurement: 11,089 tons gross. Displacement: 8,000 tons standard. Dimensions: length, 459.3; beam, 65.6. Machinery: probably, diesels. Speed: 16 kts. No armament.

General: First seen in the Baltic in the summer of 1967, when she was probably in transit to the Pacific. She has a large radome fore and aft, and a smaller one on the long, tall superstructure.

Chukotka Class

1:1000

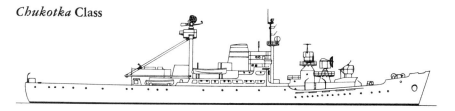

Chazhma Class

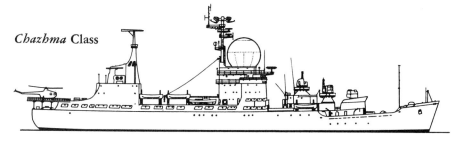

Astronaut Vladimir Komarov Class

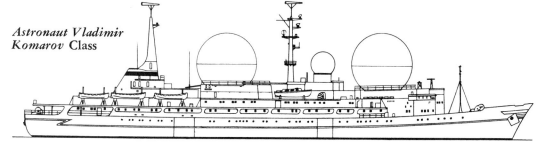

Opposite: A Tupolev-24 Blinder bomber carries a Kitchen air-to-surface missile under its fuselage.

Types of Soviet Naval Aircraft

Soviet naval and military aircraft are identified by letters that denote the name of the principal designer and numbers that denote the type of craft. Uneven numbers are assigned to fighters, and even numbers to bombers and transports. The TU-95 bomber is, however, an exception to that rule. Designers whose aircraft are mentioned in this book are:

Georgi Beriev	BE
Sergei Il'yushin	IL
V. M. Miasishchev	MIA
Andrei N. Tupolev	TU
Oleg K. Antonov	AN
Nikolai Kamov	KA
Mikhail L. Mil	MI

Designations given by NATO identify Soviet aircraft more precisely than do those given by the Soviet Union. Two-syllable names are assigned to aircraft with jet engines, one-syllable names to aircraft with piston engines. The first letter of the name denotes aircraft type:

F–Fighter or fighter bomber, including reconnaissance versions

B–Bombers, including tanker and reconnaissance versions

C–Cargo

L–Liaison

M–Miscellaneous

H–Helicopter.

The national marking for Soviet aircraft is a red star outlined with white, and it is carried on the fuselage, wings, and vertical fin.

327

TU-4—NATO designation Bull

Maximum take-off weight: 61.3 tons. Length: 99 feet. Span: 141 feet. Range: 4,100 miles. Maximum altitude: 35,100 feet. Power plant: 4 Shvetsov-A-SH-90 engines, 2,320 HP each. Maximum speed: 330 mph. Crew: 12. Armament: 12 12.7-mm. machine guns; maximum bomb load, 9 tons.

General: Copied from the American B-29 and first produced in 1944 or 1945, this was the first Soviet strategic bomber. The Naval Air Forces probably used it mainly for minelaying. Few TU-4s are still in service.

TU-95—NATO designation Bear

Maximum take-off weight: 188 tons. Length: 150 feet. Span: 177 feet. Range: 7,140 miles. Maximum altitude: 42,650 feet. Power plant: 4 Kuznetsov-NK-12-M turboprops, 12,000 HP each. Speed: 480–500 mph. Crew: 8–10. Armament: 4 23-mm. guns; maximum bomb, or equivalent, load, 9 tons.

General: Developed between 1953 and 1954 and originally designated the TU-20, this long-range bomber first appeared in 1955. The Naval Air Forces operate the Bear-B version, which is equipped with a Kangaroo air-to-surface missile.

MIA-4—NATO designation Bison

Maximum take-off weight: 165 tons. Length: 162.4 feet. Span: 170.6 feet. Range: 5,900–7,140 miles. Maximum altitude: 36,000 feet. Power plant: 4 Mikulin-M-209 jets, 18,000 pounds of thrust each. Maximum speed: 560 mph. Crew: 8. Armament: 7 23-mm. guns; maximum bomb, or equivalent, load, 9.5 tons.

General: Developed between 1953 and 1954, this long-range, heavy bomber is equivalent to the American B-52. It was first seen in 1954, and between 1955 and 1959 was in series production. About 480 of these aircraft were built. The naval version has more navigational and radar equipment and greater range than the military one. It is used on long-range reconnaissance and, recently, in submarine detection, for which purpose it carries a sting-like device in the tail.

MIA-200—NATO designation Bounder

Maximum take-off weight: 145 tons. Length: 185.3 feet. Span: 83.6 feet. Range: 2,670–4,470 miles. Maximum altitude: 59,000 feet. Power plant: 4 Soloviev-D-15 jets, total thrust 111,760 pounds. Speed: Mach 1.5. Crew: 6. Armament: no guns; bomb, or equivalent, load, between 5 and 8.5 tons.

General: A heavy, supersonic, long-range bomber developed between 1959 and 1960. The naval version for long-range, maritime reconnaissance first appeared in 1967: equipped for in-flight refueling, it carries more navigation electronics than does the military version.

TU-4 Bull

MIA-4 Bison

1:1000

TU-95 Bear

MIA-200 Bounder

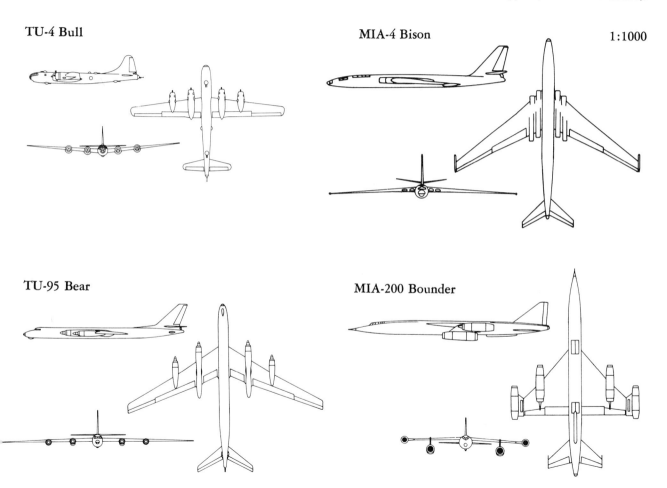

TU-14—NATO designation Bosun

Maximum take-off weight: 23.1 tons: Length: 78.7 feet. Span: 83.6 feet. Range: 2,980 miles. Maximum altitude: 42,650 feet. Power plant: 2 Klimov-VK-1 jets, 7,700 pounds of thrust each. Speed: 560 mph. Crew: 3. Armament: 4 23-mm. guns (2 nose, 2 tail); maximum bomb, or equivalent, load, 2.5 tons.

General: A medium reconnaissance and torpedo bomber, developed between 1948 and 1949, that has been used solely by the Naval Air Forces. About 480 aircraft were built, but since 1961 or 1962 Badger-B and Badger-C have been gradually replacing them.

IL-28—NATO designation Beagle

Maximum take-off weight: 19.9 tons. Length: 62.3 feet. Span: 67.9 feet. Range: 2,485 miles. Maximum altitude: 41,000 feet. Power plant: 2 Klimov-VK-1 jets, 5,940 pounds of thrust each. Speed: 540 mph. Crew: 3. Armament: 4 23-mm. guns (2 nose, 2 tail); 1.5 tons bombs, torpedoes, or mines.

General: This light attack bomber, developed at about the same time as the TU-14, was the first operational jet bomber in the Soviet Air Forces. It appeared in 1950, since when it has been built in large numbers.

TU-16—NATO designation Badger

Maximum take-off weight: 79.3 tons. Length: 121 feet. Span: 109.9 feet. Range: 4,240 miles. Maximum altitude: 37,730 feet. Power plant: 2 Mikulin-AM-3M jets, 19,140 pounds of thrust each. Maximum speed: 600 mph. Crew: 4–7. Armament: 2 23-mm. guns; 1 or 2 air-to-surface missiles.

General: About 2,000 of these medium strategic bombers, developed between 1954 and 1955 and first seen in 1954, have been built. The Navy operates the Badger-B and the Badger-C versions: Badger-B carries 2 Kennel missiles; Badger-C carries one Kipper missile and has a nose radome. A naval version was first seen in 1961. Comprehensive radar equipment permits the missiles to be launched even when the enemy has not been sighted visually.

TU-24—NATO designation Blinder

Maximum take-off weight: 67 tons. Length: 134.5 feet. Span: 90 feet. Range: 2,730 miles. Maximum altitude: 60,000 feet. Power plant: 2 Mikulin-M-209 jets, 19,800 pounds of thrust each; with afterburner, 24,970 pounds. Speed: Mach 2.1. Crew: 3. Armament: 2 23-mm. guns (tail); bomb, or equivalent load, 3 tons (2 torpedoes or missiles).

General: A supersonic medium bomber, developed between 1960 and 1961 and first seen in 1961. The naval version is probably equipped to carry the Kitchen air-to-surface missile.

TU-14 Bosun

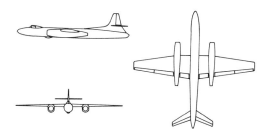

TU-16 Badger   1:750

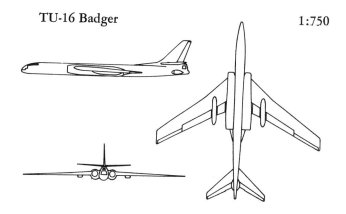

IL-28 Beagle

TU-24 Blinder

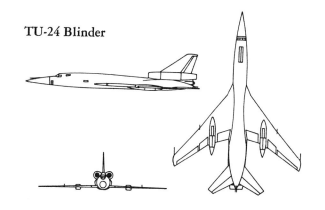

BE-6—NATO designation Madge

Maximum take-off weight: 23.4 tons. Length: 94.4 feet. Span: 100 feet. Range: 2,795 miles. Maximum altitude: 21,325 feet. Power plant: 2 Shvetsov-A-SH-73 engines, 2,000 HP each. Speed: 240 mph. Crew: 8. Armament: 1 20-mm. gun (nose) and 2 12.7-mm. machine guns (tail); bombs, mines, or depth charges.

General: Large numbers of this reconnaissance flying boat, developed in 1949 or 1950, have been built. It appears to be a copy of the Martin Marlin, and was first seen in 1954. In 1950 or 1951 an experimental version equipped with jet engines was identified and given the NATO designation Mail. Its trials were not satisfactory, and a completely new jet-powered flying boat, the BE-10, was developed. A few BE-6s are still in service.

BE-10—NATO designation Mallow

Maximum take-off weight: 44 tons. Length: 108.6 feet. Span: 80 feet. Range: 3,100–4,350 miles. Maximum altitude: 33,800 feet. Power plant: 2 Mikulin-AM-3M jets, 19,140 pounds of thrust each. Speed (with afterburner): 565 mph. Crew: 3–6. Armament: 2 23-mm. guns (tail); torpedoes, mines, or depth charges.

General: A reconnaissance and antisubmarine flying boat, developed between 1960 and 1961, and first seen in 1961. Comparable with the Martin Seamaster, and suitable for operations in the Arctic.

BE-12—NATO designation Mail

Maximum take-off weight: 29.5 tons. Length: 73.8 feet. Span: 108.2 feet. Range: 2,484 miles. Altitude: 40,000 feet. Power plant: 2 Ivshenko AI-20-D turbo prop engines, 8,000 HP. Speed: 280 mph. Armament: 2 23-mm. guns and antisubmarine weapons; maximum bomb, or equivalent, load, 10 tons.

General: This maritime-reconnaissance amphibian, whose Russian name is "Chaika," has a radome in its nose and MAD gear in its tail. It was developed in 1964 and began replacing the BE-6 in 1967.

BE-6 Madge

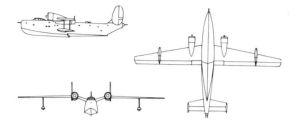

BE-12 Mail

1:750

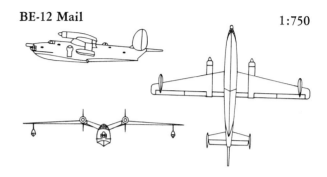

BE-10 Mallow

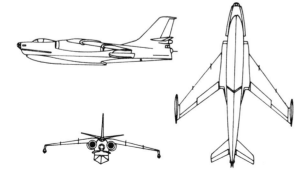

MI-1—NATO designation Hare

Maximum take-off weight: 4,950 pounds. Length: 39.7 feet. Rotor diameter: 45.9 feet. Range: 240 miles. Maximum altitude: 13,780 feet. Power plant: 1 Ivshenko-AI-26 W engine, 575 HP. Maximum speed: 120 mph. Crew: 1–2. No armament.

General: Developed between 1947 and 1948, in series production since 1949, and first seen in 1951, this helicopter can carry 3 or 4 passengers, and the Navy uses it for communications purposes. The naval version has longer undercarriage legs than does the military version. A version for civilian use has 4 inflatable floats and has been employed successfully in whaling operations.

KA-15—NATO designation Hen

Maximum take-off weight: 2,830 pounds: Length: 22.6 feet. Rotor diameter: 32.5 feet. Range: 275 miles. Maximum altitude: 10,760 feet. Power plant: 1 Ivshenko AI-14-R engine, 260 HP. Maximum speed: 96 mph. Crew: 2. No armament.

General: This helicopter was developed between 1955 and 1956. Some destroyers have a KA-15 embarked for communications purposes. Large numbers of these craft serve civilian uses, such as fishery protection.

KA-20—NATO designation Harp

Maximum take-off weight: 5,390 pounds. Length: 33.8 feet. Rotor diameter: 47.5 feet. Range: 370 miles. Maximum altitude: 16,000 feet. Power plant: 2 Isotov turbines, 1,000 HP each. Speed: 200 mph. Crew: 4. Armament: 2 37-mm. guns (nose), depth charges, 2 small air-to-surface missiles.

General: Developed between 1960 and 1961, this helicopter carries antisubmarine-detection equipment, has a radome under the nose, and 2 contra-rotating rotors.

KA-25K—NATO designation Hormone

Maximum take-off weight: 15,620 pounds. Length: 32 feet. Rotor diameter: 51.5 feet. Range: 250 miles. Maximum altitude: 11,500 feet. Power plant: 2 Glushenko turbines, 900 HP each. Speed: 140 mph. Armament: not known, but probably depth charges, antisubmarine torpedoes, and locator equipment.

General: This is the type of helicopter embarked on the *Moskva*-class helicopter carriers.

MI-1 Hare

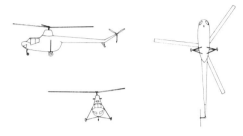

KA-20 Harp 1:500

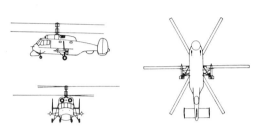

KA-15 Hen

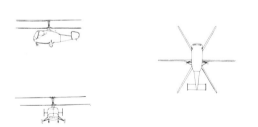

KA-25K Hormone

Notes

1. Hadeler. "Die sowjetische Kriegsmarine," *Nauticus,* 29, p. 48.

2. Rossi, *Zwei Jahre deutsch-sowjetisches Bündnis* (Cologne: Verlag für Politik und Wirtschaft, 1954), p. 100.

3. Meister, *Der Seekrieg in den osteuropäischen Gewässern 1941–45* (Munich: J. F. Lehmanns Verlag, 1958), p. 10.

4. *IMT,* 34, 697, and Brennecke, *Eismeer, Atlantik, Ostsee, Die Einsätze des Schweren Kreuzers* Admiral Hipper (Stuttgart: Koehler's Verlagsgesellschaft, 1963), pp. 32 and 333.

5. Hadeler, "The Ships of the Soviet Navy," Saunders, ed., *The Soviet Navy* (New York: Frederick A. Praeger, 1958), p. 144.

6. *Ibid.,* p. 152, and Hadeler, "Die sowjetische Kriegsmarine," *Nauticus,* 29, p. 55.

7. Evers, *Kriegsschiffbau* (2d ed.; Berlin: Springer-Verlag, 1943), pp. 128ff.

8. Rohwer, "Die sowjetische U-Bootwaffe in der Ostsee 1939–45," *Wehrwissenschaftliche Rundschau,* 6, 1956, pp. 547ff.

9. *Ibid.,* Footnote 14, p. 548, and Hadeler, "The Ships of the Soviet Navy," Saunders, *op. cit.,* p. 157.

10. Tschernousko, *Der Eisbrecher* Lenin, *Kernenergie und Flotte* (German translation from Russian; Berlin [East]: Deutscher Militärverlag, 1961), p. 216.

11. Breyer, "Die Kreuzer der *Sverdlov*-Klasse," *Soldat und Technik,* 3, 1960, pp. 632ff.

12. Schreier, "Die Entwicklung der Motortorpedoboote," *Die Kriegsmarine,* 5, 1938, pp. 6ff.

13. von Senger and Etterlin, *Die deutschen Geschütze 1939–1945* (Munich: J. F. Lehmanns Verlag, 1959), p. 194;—*Taschenbuch der Panzer* (3rd ed.; Munich: J. F. Lehmanns Verlag, 1960), p. 192; Lusar, *Die deutschen Waffen und Geheimwaffen des Zweiten Weltkrieges und ihre Weiterentwicklung* (4th ed.; Munich: J. F. Lehmanns Verlag, 1962), p. 178; and

"Neuzeitliche Maschinenkanonen," *Soldat und Technik,* 4, 1961, pp. 8ff.

14. "Die militärische Stärke der Sowjetunion," Central Committee of the East German Communist Party, Agitation and Propaganda Section, Ag. 220/57 DDR, November 1957, 3, 18/97, p. 16.

15. Lusar, *op. cit.,* p. 257, sets out in detail German torpedo development up to 1945.

16. Krause-Larisch, *Von der U-Bootfalle zum Jagdhubschrauber* (Berlin [East]: Deutscher Militärverlag, 1961), p. 185, makes this inference.

17. Küster, *Das U-Boot als Kriegs- und Handelschiff* (Berlin: 1917), pp. 50–51, has a drawing, which was reproduced in *Soldat und Technik,* 2, 545, 1959.

18. Monasterev, *Vom Untergang der Zarenflotte* (Berlin: Mittler-Verlag, 1930) contains an instructive account of the building and wartime employment of the *Krab. See also,* H. Graf, *The Russian Navy in War and Revolution* (Munich: Verlag R. Oldenbourg, 1923).

19. *See also,* Rohwer and Huan, "Die Kriegsschiffe der sowjetischen Flotten im 2. Weltkrieg—Teil 2: U-Boote," *Marinerundschau,* 58, 1961, pp. 359ff., and *Das deutsche Bild der russischen und sowjetischen Marine,* a supplement to the *Marinerundschau* published by the Arbeitskreis für Wehrforschung (Berlin/Frankfurt on Main: E. S. Mittler Verlag GmbH., 1962).

20. The activities of Soviet submarines during the Second World War here recounted are based on Meister, *Der Seekrieg . . .* (Footnote No. 4) and Rohwer, "Die sowjetische U-Bootwaffe . . ." (Footnote No. 13).

21. *See also,* "Introduction," Saunders, ed., *op. cit.,* pp. 15–16.

22. Breyer, "Die U-Bootwaffe der Sowjetunion, Teil 2," *Soldat und Technik,* 2, 1959, pp. 598ff.

23. Breyer, "Zur Entwicklungsgeschichte atomkraftgetriebener U-Boote," *Wehr und Wirtschaft,* 3, 1959, pp. 38ff.

Bibliography

WORKS PUBLISHED IN THE EASTERN BLOC

Books

Bychnovski, *Atom-U-Boote* (translated from Russian), Berlin, 1959.

Central Committee of the German Socialist Party, *Die militärische Stärke der Sowjetunion,* Berlin, 1957.

Die jugoslawische Volksarmee.

Die Sowjetarmee—unser Waffenbruder, Berlin, 1957.

Die Streitkräfte der Sowjetunion, Berlin, 1961.

Israel-Kautz, *Seefliegerkräfte,* Berlin, 1961.

Krause-Larisch, *Von der U-Bootfalle zum Jagdhubschrauber,* Berlin, 1961.

Krysenko, *Rakete-Flugbahn-Lenksystem* (translated from Russian), Berlin, 1961.

Morosov, *Luftabwehr der Schiffe* (translated from Russian), Berlin, 1963.

Larisch, *Moderne Waffen im Seekrieg,* Berlin, 1963.

Peresda, *Fla-Raketen* (translated from Russian), Berlin, 1963.

Pöschel, *Froschmänner, Torpedoreiter, Zwerg-U-Boote,* Berlin, 1960.

Schiffe der Meerestiefen, Berlin, 1957.

Schatagin-Prussanov, *Die Sowjetarmee—Armee neuen Typus,* Berlin, 1959.

Solovjev, *Die Schiffsartillerie* (translated from Russian), Berlin, 1959.

Unsere Volksmarine, Berlin, 1961.

Various authors, *Kernenergie und Flotte* (translated from Russian), Berlin, 1961.

Periodicals

Armeerundschau (German).

Die Sowjetunion (German).

Die Volksarmee (German).

Flottenecho (German).

Krasnaia Szezda (Russian).

Kommunist Vooruzhennykh Sil (Russian).

Marinewesen (German).

Militärtechnik (German).

Morskoi Flot (Russian).

Morskoi Sbornik (Russian).

Morze (Polish).

Seesport (German).

Sovetski Flot (Russian).

Voennyie Znaniia (Russian).

Vestnik Vosdushnogo Flota (Russian).

Voennyie Vestnik (Russian).

Woisko Ludowe (Polish).

WORKS PUBLISHED IN THE WESTERN WORLD

Books

Defense Research Committee, *Das deutsche Bild der russischen und sowjetischen Marine,* Frankfurt on the Main, 1962.

Bidlingmaier, *Entstehung und Räumung der Ostseebrückenköpfe 1945,* Neckargemünd, 1962.

Bekker, *Ostsee—deutsches Schicksal 1944/45,* Oldenburg-Hamburg, 1959.

Brodie, *Naval Strategy,* 4th ed., Princeton, 1957.

Blackman, *The World's Warships,* London, 1957 and 1960.

Brennecke, *Eismeer, Atlantik, Ostsee, Die Einsätze des Schweren Kreuzers "Admiral Hipper,"* Stuttgart, 1963.

Calvert, *Aufgetaucht am Pol,* Oldenburg-Hamburg, 1961.

Couhat, *La Marine Sovietique,* Paris, 1956.

Dornberger, *V 2—Der Schuss ins Weltall,* Esslingen, 1952.

Evers, *Kriegsschiffbau,* Berlin, 1943.

Federal Department of Information, publisher, *SBZ—von A biz Z,* Bonn, 1959.

Feuchter, *Taschenbuch der Luftfahrt 1954* and Supplement *1955/57,* Munich, 1954 and 1957.

Fleming, *Warships of World War I,* combined volume, London, 1961.

Franke, *Handbuch der neuzeitlichen Wehrwissenschaften,* vol. 3 (Navy), Berlin and Leipzig, 1938.

Green, *Flugzeuge der Welt,* Zürich and Stuttgart, 1962.

Gröner, *Die Schiffe und Fahrzeuge der deutschen Kriegsmarine und Luftwaffe 1939–45 und ihr Verbleib,* Munich, 1954.

Graf, *The Russian Navy in War and Revolution 1914 up to 1918,* Munich, 1923.

Harbron, *Communist Ships and Shipping,* London, 1962.

Hart, *Die Rote Armee,* Bonn, 1957.

Höpker, *Die Ostsee—ein rotes Binnenmeer?,* Frankfurt on the Main, 1958.

————, *Das Mittelmeer—Meer der Entscheidungen,* Frankfurt on the Main, 1961.

Hümmelchen, *Handelsstörer,* Munich, 1960.

Internationaler Militärgerichtshof (IMT), *Der Prozess gegen die Hauptkriegsverbrecher vor dem Internationalen Militärgerichtshof,* Nuremberg, 1949.

Jost-Führing, *Wie stark ist die Sowjetunion?* Bonn, 1958.

Kafka-Pepperburg, *Warships of the World,* New York, 1946 and 1948.

Kens, *Flugzeugtypen,* Duisburg, 1958.

————, *Die Luftstreitkräfte der Sowjetunion,* Munich, 1962.

Küster, *Das U-Boot als Kriegs- und Handelsschiff*, Berlin, 1917.

Lusar, *Die deutschen Waffen und Geheimwaffen und ihre Weiterentwicklung*, 4th ed., Munich, 1961.

Meister, *Der Seekrieg in den osteuropäischen Gewässern 1941–45*, Munich, 1957.

Mitchell, *The Maritime History of Russia*, London, 1948.

Monasterev, *Vom Untergang der Zarenflotte*, Berlin, 1930.

Olbrich, *Die Schiffahrt in der sowjetischen Besatzungszone*, Bonn, 1958.

Paul, *Europa im Ostseeraum*, Göttingen, 1961.

Ploetz, *Geschichte des Zweiten Weltkrieges*, Würzburg, 1960.

Roskill, *Britische Seekriegsgeschichte 1939–45*, Oldenburg-Hamburg, 1961.

Rossi, *Zwei Jahre deutsch-sowjetisches Bündnis*, Cologne, 1954.

Rohwer, ed., *Seemacht heute*, Oldenburg-Hamburg, 1957.

Ruge, *Der Seekrieg 1939–45*, Stuttgart, 1954.

———, *Seemacht und Sicherheit*, Tübingen, 1955.

Saunders, ed., *Die Rote Flotte*, Oldenburg-Hamburg, 1959.

Steinweg, *Das Schicksal der deutschen Handelsflotte*, Göttingen, 1954.

von Senger and Etterlin, *Taschenbuch der Panzer 1960*, Munich, 1960.

——— and ———, *Die deutschen Geschütze 1939–45*, Munich, 1960.

Taylor, *Russian Aircraft*, London, 1960.

Troebst, *Der Griff nach dem Meer, Amerika und Russland im Kampf um die Ozeane*, Düsseldorf, 1960.

Wust, *Luftrüstung der Welt*, Bonn, 1958.

Zieb, *Logistik-Probleme der Marine*, Neckargemünd, 1962.

Annuals

Brassey's Annual, The Armed Forces Year-Book, London.
Almanacco Navale, Rome.
Jane's Fighting Ships, London.
Jane's All the World's Aircraft, London.
Le Marine Militare nel Mondo, Milan.
Les Flottes de Combat, Paris.
Marinkalender, Stockholm.
Naval Review, Annapolis.
Nauticus, Jahrbuch für Seefahrt und Weltwirtschaft, Frankfurt on the Main.
New Construction in Hand or on Order, London.
Taschenbuch für Wehrfragen, Frankfurt on the Main.
Weyers Taschenbuch der Kriegsflotten bzw. Flottentaschenbuch, Munich.

Periodicals

Atlantische Welt (German).
DATA (U.S.).
Daily Telegraph and Morning Post (British).
Der aktuelle Osten (German).
Der deutsche Soldat (German).
Die Bundeswehr (German).
Die Seekiste (German).
Europäische Wehrkorrespondenz (German).
Flottennachrichten—Ost (German).
Flugwehr und Technik (Swiss).
Hansa (German).
Herkenning (Dutch).
Interavia (Swiss).
Interconair (Italian).

La Revue Maritime (French).

Le Vie del Mare (Italian).

Marine News (British).

Marine Rundschau (German).

Military Review (U.S.).

Naval Aviation News (U.S.).

Notiziario Rassegna delle attivita della Marina (Italian).

Recognition Journal (British).

Rivista Marittima (Italian).

Schriftenreihe der Arbeitsgemeinschaft Demokratischer Kreise (German).

Ships of the World (Japanese).

Soldat und Technik (German).

Sveriges Flotta (Swedish).

The National Geographic Magazine (U.S.).

The Navy (British).

Tidskrift i Sjövärsendet (Swedish).

Truppenpraxis (German).

United States Naval Institute Proceedings (U.S.).

Wehrtechnische Hefte (German).

Wehr und Wirtschaft (German).

Wehrwissenschaftliche Rundschau (German).

Service and Related Publications

Chief of Air Operations, Intelligence, (German), *Die Kriegsschiffe und Häfen der Sowjetunion, Stand Juni 1942, Sonderbeilage des Frontnachrichtenblattes der Luftwaffe Nr. 41.*

Department of the Army, *Handbook on the Soviet Army,* Washington, 1958.

Department of the Navy, Office of Shipbuilding, (German), *Material für die Konstruktion von Kriegsschiffen.*

Department of the Navy, Office of Naval and Air Operations, (German), *Kriegsschiff-Erkennungstafeln Sowjetunion, Ausgabe Okt. 1943.*

Department of the Navy, Weapons Office, (German) *Waffentechnische Mitteilungen aus fremden Marinen, Tabellenheft (Stand 1.8.1943).*

Federal Defense Ministry (German)—Fü B VII–4, *Erkennungsblätter.*

Krupp Industries, Armament News Sheet.

Swedish Navy, *Fartygskort 1956.*

Index

Figures in *italic* indicate illustrations

Credits for Photographs

Special thanks are due to the following individuals for their assistance in providing photographs:

Mr. Harry Lowenkron, SOVFOTO Photo Agency, New York; Professor Claude P. Lemieux, U.S. Naval Academy; Ensign Rodney Moen, News Photo Branch, Office of Information, U.S. Navy; Mr. P. E. Neumann, Skyfotos Ltd, Lympne Airport, Kent, England; Mrs. Hazel Richardson, Office of Public Relations (Royal Navy), Ministry of Defence.

Numbers indicate the pages on which the photographs appear:

SOVFOTO: ii, x, xii, 2, 4, 5, 7, 9, 11, 14, 17, 18, 33, 34, 38, 43, 48, 49, 50, 51, 53, 55, 58, 59, 61, 72, 76, 79, 81, 102, 117, 118, 119, 121, 147, 148, 150, 154, 162, 169, 180, 183, 188, 192, 194, 198, 200, 203, 210, 216, 220, 222, 225, 229, 234, 236, 241, 253, 254.

Siegfried Breyer: 20, 56, 87, 88, 92, 104, 107, 109, 111, 116, 120, 122, 125, 126, 127, 130, 137, 138, 153, 158, 159, 173, 197, 242.

U.S. Navy: 77, 80, 82, 95, 97, 98, 105, 112, 136, 139, 151, 156, 161, 170, 177, 184, 186, 191, 326.

Claude P. Lemieux: 49, 115, 152, 164.

SKYFOTOS: 85, 91, 132, 134.

Aviation Week Magazine: 185, 187.

Erich Gröner: 83, 99.

Ministry of Defence, London: 74, 149.

Dieter Jung: 167.

R. Greger, *Warship International:* 129.

Edited by Mary Veronica Amoss.

Design and layout by Nick Kirilloff and Ed Holm.

Photographic Research by Ed Holm.

Composed, printed, and bound by Kingsport Press, Inc.

Composed in ten-point Garamond No. 3, with two points of leading.

Printed offset on fifty-pound Bookman Thin Publisher's White.

Bound in Columbia Tanotex.

The Soviet Union

Key to Maps Showing Major Naval Bases and Ports

Red outlines indicate areas covered by maps

Western Arctic Bases and Ports, page 2

Baltic Bases and Ports, page 204

Black Sea Bases and Ports, page 218

Key to Other Maps Appearing in this Book: